직독직해로 읽는

톨스토이 단편선
Tolstoy's Short Stories

직독직해로 읽는
톨스토이 단편선
Tolstoy's Short Stories

개정판 2쇄 발행 2020년 5월 20일
초판 1쇄 발행   2011년 1월 30일

원작	레오 N. 톨스토이
역주	이현구, 홍명표, 박기윤
디자인	IndigoBlue
일러스트	정은수
발행인	조경아
발행처	랭귀지북스
주소	서울시 마포구 포은로2나길 31 벨라비스타 208호
전화	02.406.0047
전화	02.406.0047 **팩스** 02.406.0042
이메일	languagebooks@hanmail.net
홈페이지	www.languagebooks.co.kr
등록번호	101-90-85278 **등록일자** 2008년 7월 10일
ISBN	979-11-5635-053-8 (13740)
가격	12,000원

ⓒ LanguageBooks 2011
잘못된 책은 구입한 서점에서 바꿔 드립니다.
blog.naver.com/languagebook에서 MP3 파일을 다운로드할 수 있습니다.

이 도서의 국립중앙도서관 출판예정도서목록(CIP)은 서지정보유통지원시스템 홈페이지(http://seoji.nl.go.kr)와
국가자료공동목록시스템(http://www.nl.go.kr/kolisnet)에서 이용하실 수 있습니다. (CIP제어번호 : CIP2016028787)

직독직해로 읽는
톨스토이 단편선
Tolstoy's Short Stories

레오 N. 톨스토이 원작
이현구 역주

Language Books

머리말

요즈음 영어 교육의 열기는 굳이 설명하지 않아도 누구나 알 것입니다. 수많은 학습자들은 자신에게 어울리는 공부법을 찾기 위해 학원을 다니고, 학습서로 공부해보지만, 좋은 공부법을 찾기란 쉽지 않은 일입니다.

이런 분들이 영어 실력을 효율적으로 기르는 방법으론 원서를 읽으며 공부하는 것이 있습니다. 원서로 읽기 능력을 키우고, 어휘력과 표현력을 신장하여 여러 시험에 필요한 영어 실력을 효과적으로 준비할 수 있습니다. 그러나 원어민들이 즐겨 읽는 원서나 고전 작품에는 어려운 어휘와 표현이 많다는 단점이 있습니다.

이렇게 자신에게 맞는 공부법을 찾는 데 어려움을 겪고 있는 분들과, 높은 수준의 원서를 혼자 공부하기 힘들어하는 분들을 위해 이 책을 쓰게 되었습니다. 다시 말하여 영어 학습에 도움이 될 만한 작품들을 여러분이 쉽게 이해할 수 있도록 직독직해로 설명해 놓았습니다. 게다가 원작의 내용을 이해하는데 아무런 문제가 없도록 글의 구성에 정성을 기울였습니다. 직독직해로 설명하는 목적은 직독직해로 읽는 습관을 익히면, 읽기 속도를 모국어 수준으로 높일 수 있기 때문입니다.

PREFACE

　또한 본 교재로 듣기와 말하기를 연습할 수 있도록, 원어민 성우가 녹음한 MP3 파일을 다운로드할 수 있게 구성하였습니다. 직독직해로 해설해 놓은 작품에는 대화체 표현이 많기 때문에, 회화에 필요한 수많은 표현을 익힐 수 있습니다.

　거기다 수능을 준비하는 학생들을 위하여 원서의 난이도를 조정했습니다. 실제로 본 책에서 설명된 대부분의 어휘들은 수능 수준의 어휘에 속합니다. 또한 문법, 숙어 표현, 회화 표현, 작가의 독특한 표현들을 설명하여 독자가 공부하는데 어려움이 없도록 하였습니다.

　분명 영어를 공부하는 것은 힘든 과정이지만, 유창하고 높은 수준의 영어를 자유자재로 사용할 수 있으려면, 영어를 장기간 공부해야 됩니다. 그 시간을 최대한 단축시키기 위해 저는 이 책을 쓰게 된 것입니다. 하지만 가장 중요한 것은 학습자의 마음가짐입니다. 부디 이 책과 여러분의 성실함을 무기로 큰 성과를 올리길 기대해 봅니다.

　본 책이 출판되도록 큰 도움을 주신 Language Books 사장님께 감사드립니다. 그리고 원고 준비에 도움을 준 제자 국주은 양과 물심양면으로 전폭적인 지지와 성원을 보내준 아내와 가족에게 감사의 뜻을 전합니다.

이현구

저자 소개

저자 톨스토이에 대해서

Leo Tolstoy (1828 - 1910)

톨스토이는 러시아의 대문호이며 세계적으로 널리 알려졌다. 특히 국내에서는 『전쟁과 평화』와 단편소설이 번역되었다. 그의 작품 및 모든 것에 대해 말한 다면, 도서관을 가득 채울 정도로 많다는 주장도 있다.

그는 러시아 야스나야 폴랴냐에서 귀족의 아들로 태어났고 어려서 부모를 잃었다. 카잔대하에 입학했으나 자유롭고 창의적이 생각을 억압하는 대학 교육방식에 실망을 느껴 중도에 자퇴하였다. 1847년에 낙향하여 농민 계몽운동을 하였으나 실패하였다. 이 시절엔 도박에 중독되고 빚을 지기도 했으며, 형과 주고받은 편지에는 작가의 실망감, 혼란, 열망이 표현되어있다. 그의 삶에 획기적인 변화는 형의 권유로 사관후보생으로 입대하여 글을 쓰면서 시작되었다.

INTRODUCTION

　처녀작 『유년 시대』와 『소년 시대』를 발표하면서 작가로서 명성을 얻기 시작했다. 1862년에 결혼한 소피아가 톨스토이의 노트와 초안을 정리해주었기 때문에 창작활동에 전념할 수 있었다. 이 시기에 『전쟁과 평화』, 『부활』과 같은 불후의 명작을 탄생시켰다. 또한 『사람은 무엇으로 사는가』, 『바보 이반』과 같은 많은 단편을 저술하였다.

　『직독직해로 읽는 톨스토이 단편선』에서는 『사람은 무엇으로 사는가』와 『바보 이반』을 소개하였다. 그의 단편에서는 감동적인 이야기로 어떻게 사는 것이 진정으로 행복한 삶인지 이야기해준다. 특히 이 책에 소개된 단편을 읽으면, 선과 악, 사랑, 죽음과 같은 보편적인 주제에 대해 진지하게 생각해 볼 수 있다.

직독직해 가이드

직독직해로 읽어야 영어소설을 감각적으로 즐길 수 있다.

직독직해로 영어를 빠르게 이해하려면, 영어 문장의 순서에 따라 앞에 있는 말과 다음에 나오는 말과 어떤 관계인지 자연스럽게 느낄 수 있어야 합니다. 즉 영어의 어순대로 문장의 의미를 파악하는 훈련을 해야 합니다. 게다가 직독직해로 영어를 이해하려면, 문장구조를 파악하면서 기본 문법 지식을 활용해야 합니다.

하지만 길고 복잡한 문장을 이해할 때, 더 많은 문법 지식이 필요한 것은 아닙니다. 이런 문장을 쉽게 이해하는 방법은 매우 간단합니다. 그것은 어려운 문법을 따져가며 문장을 분석하기보다 영어의 언어 논리를 익히는 것입니다.

아래에 있는 문장은 "마지막 잎새"에 나옵니다. 직독직해에 익숙하지 않은 사람이라면, 영어 문장을 앞뒤로 읽으며 해석합니다.

In one corner was a blank canvas on an easel
     1   2   3   4

that had been waiting there for twenty-five years to receive
                    5   6

the first line of the masterpiece.
          7

GUIDE

앞에 있는 문장을 우리말 어순에 따라 해석하면, 다음과 같습니다.

> 한쪽 구석에는(1) / 아무 그림도 없는 캔버스가(3) / 이젤 위에(4) / 있었는데(2) / 명작의 첫 번째 대열에 속한다는(7) / 대우를 받으려고(6) / 25년 동안 거기에 있었던 것이다.(5)

다시 말하여 영어 문장은 1-2-3-4-5-6-7 순서이지만, 우리말 어순에 맞게 해석해보면, 1-3-4-2-7-6-5 순으로 이해할 수 있습니다. 이런 순서로 이해하려면, 한 문장을 이해하는데 많은 시간이 걸립니다. 이런 방식으로 읽기를 지속하면, 긴 문장을 듣자마자 이해하는 것은 매우 어렵습니다. 또한 회화와 영작을 할 때, 영어로 유창하게 표현하는 능력이 개발되지 않습니다.

같은 문장을 영어 어순대로 이해하려면, 직독직해로 문장을 이해해야 합니다. 아래에 있는 설명처럼 이해할 수 있습니다.

> In one corner → 한쪽 구석에는
> was → 있었다.
> a blank canvas → (무엇이 있었는가?) 아무 그림도 없는 캔버스가
> on an easel → (캔버스는 어디에 있는가?) 이젤 위에
> that had been waiting there for twenty-five years →
> (그 그림 없는 캔버스는 어떤 것일까?) 25년 동안 거기에 있었던
> to receive → (왜 기다리고 있었을까?) 대우를 받으려고
> the first line of the masterpiece. → (어떤 대우를 받으려고 기다리는가?) 명작의 첫 번째 대열에 속한다는

앞의 설명에서 알 수 있듯이 영어는 우리말과 어순이 매우 다릅니다. 그래서 영어 어순대로 이해하는 연습을 해야 합니다. 이것이 직독직해를 익히는 첫 번째 단계일 뿐입니다. 그리고 앞에 나오는 단어나 표현을 보면, 다음에 어떤 내용이 올지 예측할 수 있는 힌트가 있습니다. 예를 들어 위의 문장을 보면, "was"라는 "be"동사가 "~이 있다, 존재하다"라는 의미로 쓰였습니다. "존재하다"라는 의미로 쓰인 "was"를 보자마자 "어떤 물건"이 "어디에" 있는지 예측할 수 있어야 합니다. 그래서 문장의 의미가 연결되는 힌트를 감각적으로 알아보려면, 영어의 언어논리를 익혀야 합니다.

영어의 논리를 쉽게 익히려면,

첫째, 주어, 동사, 목적어, 보어를 보고, 문장의 핵심 내용을 감각적으로 파악해야 합니다.

둘째, 동사의 종류에 따라 다음에 어떤 내용이 올지 예측할 수 있어야 합니다. 그래서 다양한 동사의 쓰임새에 익숙해져야 합니다.

셋째, 보통 관계 대명사나 부정사 앞에 나오는 내용을 보면, 다음에 어떤 내용이 올지 예측할 수 있어야 합니다. 즉 부정사와 관계대명사는 상황을 더 자세히 설명합니다.

넷째, 접속사를 보면서, 글에 나타나는 논리관계를 이해할 수 있어야 합니다.

다섯째, 대명사와 같은 기초 문법을 활용할 줄 알아야 합니다.

마지막으로 문법 학습에 지나치게 얽매이지 않도록 주의해야 합니다.

영어 문장을 읽자마자 이해하는 습관이 형성되면, 더 빠르게 읽고 이해할 수 있습니다. 이런 훈련을 하면, 스토리를 듣자마자 이해할 수 있습니다. 마지막 단계로 입으로 영작하는 연습을 게을리 하지 않습니다. 입으로 영어 문장을 유창하게 구사할 수 있다면, 회화와 영작이 즐거워집니다. 이런 입체적인 방법으로 공부하면, 원서를 읽고, 회화를 하는 것은 즐겁고 신나는 일이 됩니다.

읽기 가이드

『톨스토이 단편선』을 읽으면서 최대 효과를 낼 수 있는 공부방법이 있습니다.
그것은 읽기 능력을 토대로, 듣기 연습을 하고, 듣기 능력을 토대로,
말하기 연습까지 하는 것입니다.

첫째, 직독직해로 읽는 연습을 하여, 원어민 속도로 읽는 것입니다.
둘째, 듣기 연습을 하여, 원어민이 빠르게 말하는 것을 듣고 이해하는 것입니다.
셋째, 동시통역 연습을 하여, 유창하게 말하는 연습을 하는 것입니다.

이와 같은 능력을 개발하려면, 원어민과 비슷한 속도로 직독직해로 영어를 이해하고, 영어로 표현하는 훈련(동시통역 연습)을 해야 합니다. 다시 말하여 영어를 직독직해로 빠르게 읽는 연습을 하고, 직독직해로 해석한 내용을 보면서 영어로 말하는 연습(동시통역 연습)을 꾸준히 실천합니다. 이런 목적을 성취하도록 『톨스토이 단편선』을 직독직해로 읽고, 연습문제에서 동시통역 연습을 할 수 있도록 교재를 구성했습니다. 아래에 제시된 단계에 따라 공부하면, 영어 실력이 빠르게 향상됩니다.

READING GUIDE

Step 1 영어 어순대로 이해하기

원서를 직독직해로 읽는 능력을 키우려면, 영어 어순대로 읽는 능력과 풍부한 어휘력이 필요합니다. 먼저 『톨스토이 단편선』을 직독직해로 읽으면서 영어 어순대로 읽고 이해하는 연습을 합니다. 이야기를 읽는 동안 모르는 어휘나 이해하기 어려운 문장이 나오면, 중요한 의미만 파악하고, 빠르게 읽고 이해해야 합니다. 본 교재를 두 번째로 읽을 때는 모르는 어휘를 익히고, 어려운 문장을 좀 더 정확히 이해해야 합니다. 때로는 모르는 어휘와 문장을 단번에 모두 익히겠다고 지나치게 욕심을 부리면, 오히려 학습에 흥미가 떨어지고 지속적으로 공부할 수 없게 됩니다. 개인에 따라 차이가 있지만, 본 교재를 세 번 또는 네 번 읽으면서 모르는 어휘와 문장과 친숙해지면, 몰랐던 단어를 쉽게 익힐 수 있습니다. 또한 어렵게 느껴졌던 문장도 쉽게 이해됩니다.

Step 2 원어민 속도로 읽기

직독직해로 읽는 연습을 한 다음엔 원어민과 같은 속도로 읽는 연습을 해야 합니다. 이러한 속독 연습을 할 수 있도록 해설 없는 『톨스토이 단편선』을 후반부에 수록했습니다. 이 부분을 반복해서 읽으면, 빠르게 읽는 연습을 할 수 있기 때문입니다. 속독을 권장하는 이유는 두 가지가 있습니다. 첫째 영어 어순대로 이해하는 능력을 키워야 원어민과 비슷한 속도로 읽고 이해할 수 있기 때문입니다. 둘째 읽기 속도가 빨라져야 듣기가 즐겁고 편해지기 때문입니다.

Step 3 원어민 수준으로 듣고 이해하기

영어로 쓰인 이야기를 말하는 속도로 읽고 이해할 수 있으면, 원어민이 말하는 속도로 이해하는 연습에 들어갑니다. 그것은 MP3를 들으면서 원어민처럼 소설을 자연스럽게 이해하는 것입니다. 이런 연습을 반복 하면, 원어민이 빠르게 말하는 문장을 들으면서 이해할 수 있습니다. 이렇게 듣자마자 이해하는 능력을 키워야 유창하게 회화를 할 수 있는 기반이 마련됩니다.

Step 4 동시통역 연습

　　연습문제 중 동시통역을 연습할 수 있는 부분이 있습니다. 동시통역이란 입으로 영작하는 연습입니다. 즉 직독직해로 해석된 문장을 보자마자 영어로 유창하게 말하는 것입니다. 유창하게 영어로 말하려면, 읽고 이해하는 것보다 더 많은 노력과 연습이 필요합니다. 혼자서 영어 회화 연습을 할 때 활용하면, 매우 효과적인 영어 공부방법입니다.

　　하지만 동시통역 연습을 제대로 활용하려면, 세 가지 어려움을 극복해야 합니다. 첫째 영어 문장을 만들 때 필요한 단어를 뜸들이지 않고 생각해 내는 것입니다. 둘째 쉬운 문법을 제대로 활용하는 것입니다. 세 번째 자연스럽고 유창하게 발음하는 것입니다. 이런 연습을 꾸준히 하면, 읽기 속도가 빨라지고, 빠르게 듣고 이해할 수 있으며, 유창하게 말할 수 있습니다. 동시통역 연습을 실천하면, 원어민 수준으로 읽고 말할 수 있게 됩니다.

퀴즈 가이드

『톨스토이 단편선』을 읽으며 동시에 복습할 수 있도록
퀴즈를 만들어 놓았습니다. 모두 11개의 퀴즈로 구성되어 있습니다.
본문을 이해하고 본문에 나온 문장을 통해
영어 실력을 입체적으로 키우기 바랍니다.

* 퀴즈의 구성

각 퀴즈는 모두 4개의 파트(A. 내용 이해하기, B. 단어, C. 직독직해, D. 동시통역)로 구성되어 있습니다. 내용을 이해한 다음에 주요 단어를 복습하고 다시 직독직해 연습을 한 다음에 최종적으로 동시통역 연습을 통해서 입으로 영작하는 연습을 하기 바랍니다.

* 퀴즈의 사용방법

A. 내용 이해하기

본문의 내용을 잘 이해하셨는지 체크하기 위해 간단한 질문을 만들었습니다. 내용이 본문과 일치하면 T(True), 틀리면 F(False)를 표기하시면 됩니다.

B. 단어

　　영어로 설명된 정의에 어울리는 단어를 찾는 것입니다. 적당한 단어를 보기에서 선택하도록 했습니다. 단어 설명을 영문으로 한 까닭은 영어로 설명된 단어의 정의에 익숙해지면, 회화를 할 때 영어로 유창하게 설명할 수 있기 때문입니다.

C. 직독직해

　　본문에 나오는 문장 중에서 약간 까다롭거나 구조가 복잡한 문장을 4개씩 골랐습니다. 영어의 어순대로 읽고 이해하는 훈련을 한 번 더 해보기 바랍니다.

D. 동시통역

　　영어의 어순대로 한글로 제시하고, 한글 해석을 보면서 영어로 작문(동시통역)을 연습하는 파트입니다. 처음에는 힘이 들겠지만 문자로 영작하는 것보다 입으로 바로 말하는 것이 효과적입니다.

목차

What Men Live By (인간은 무엇으로 사는가)

Chapter **1**	track 02	20
Chapter **2**	track 02	23
Chapter **3**	track 02	27
Chapter **4**	track 02	32
Quiz 1		40
Chapter **5**	track 02	42
Chapter **6**	track 02	48
Chapter **7**	track 02	51
Quiz 2		58
Chapter **8**	track 03	60
Chapter **9**	track 03	65
Quiz 3		72
Chapter **10**	track 03	74
Chapter **11**	track 03	78
Chapter **12**	track 03	84
Chapter **13**	track 03	90
Quiz 4		94

CONTENTS

Ivan the Fool (바보 이반)

Chapter **1**	track 04	96
Chapter **2**	track 04	101
Quiz 5		108
Chapter **3**	track 04	110
Chapter **4**	track 04	114
Quiz 6		124
Chapter **5**	track 04	126
Chapter **6**	track 04	131
Quiz 7		136
Chapter **7**	track 05	138
Quiz 8		148
Chapter **8**	track 05	150
Chapter **9**	track 05	156
Quiz 9		160
Chapter **10**	track 05	162
Quiz 10		172
Chapter **11**	track 05	174
Chapter **12**	track 05	182
Quiz 11		198

Tolstoy's Short Stories를 다시 읽어 보세요.　200

What Men Live By

인간은 무엇으로 사는가

Chapter 1

A shoemaker named Simon, / who had neither house nor
시몬이라는 구두수선공은 / 집도 땅도 갖고 있지 않았던 /

land of his own, / lived / with his wife and children /
살았다 / 아내와 아이들과 함께 /

in a peasant's hut, / and earned his living / by his work.
소작농의 오두막에서 / 그리고 먹고 살았다 / 일해서

Work was cheap, but bread was expensive, /
임금은 적었지만 빵 값은 비쌌다 /

and what he earned / he spent / for food.
그래서 그가 번 것을 / 그는 사용하였다 / 식품을 사는 데

The man and his wife had but one sheepskin coat between
남편과 그의 아내는 양가죽 외투 한 벌밖에 없었다 /

them / for winter wear, /
겨울에 입을 것으론 /

and even that was torn to tatters, /
게다가 그것마저 갈기갈기 찢어진 상태였다 /

and this was the second year / he had been wanting to buy
그리고 올해는 2년째가 되는 해였다 / 그가 양가죽을 사고 싶어 하는 /

sheep-skins / for a new coat.
새 외투를 만들

Before winter Simon saved up / a little money: /
겨울이 오기 전에 시몬은 저축했다 / 적은 돈을 /

a three-rouble note lay hidden / in his wife's box, /
3루블 지폐가 숨겨져 있었다 / 아내의 상자에 /

and five roubles and twenty kopeks were owed to him /
그리고 5루블과 20코펙을 그에게 빚졌다 /

by customers in the village.
마을의 고객들은

So one morning / he prepared to go to the village /
어느 날 아침 / 그는 마을로 가려고 준비했다 /

to buy the sheep-skins / for his coat.
(왜?) 양가죽을 사러 / 외투를 만들

He put on / over his shirt / his wife's wadded jacket, /
그는 입었다 / 셔츠 위에 / 아내가 솜으로 기운 재킷을 /

and over that / he put his own cloth coat.
그리고 그 위에 / 그는 천으로 만든 외투를 입었다

He took the three-rouble note in his pocket, /
그는 3루블 지폐를 주머니에 넣었다 /

cut himself a stick / to serve as a staff, / and started off /
막대기를 잘랐다 / 지팡이로 쓰려고 / 그리고 출발했다 /

after breakfast.
아침을 먹고

"I'll collect the five roubles / that are owed to me," /
"나는 5루블을 받아낼 거야 / (마을 사람들이) 나에게 빚진 돈을" /

thought he, /
그는 생각했다 /

"add that / to the three I have got, / and that will be
"그 돈을 합치면 / 내가 가진 3루블에 / 그 돈은 충분할 거야 /

enough / to buy sheep-skins for the winter coat."
  겨울 외투를 살 수 있을 정도로"

He came to the village / and called at a peasant's hut, /
그는 마을로 가서 / 소작농의 오두막에 들렀다 /

but the man was not at home.
그러나 사람이 집에 없었다.

The peasant's wife promised / that the money should be
소작농의 아내는 약속했다 / (어떤 약속?) 다음 주에 돈을 갚겠다고

paid next week, / but she could not pay it herself.
  하지만 그녀는 갚을 수 없을 것이다

Then Simon called on / another peasant, /
그 다음에 시몬은 방문했다 / 다른 소작농을 /

but this one swore / he had no money, /
그러나 이 자는 말했다 / 그는 돈이 없다고 /

and would only pay twenty kopeks / which he owed /
그리고 20코펙만 주겠다고 (말했다) / (그 돈을) 그가 빚진 /

peasant 소작농 hut 오두막 wear 의류 to tatters 갈기갈기 note 지폐 Kopek 코펙(러시아의 화폐단위, 100분 1 루블)
customer 고객, 손님 wadded 솜으로 기운 serve ~에 도움이 되다, ~로 쓰이다 staff 지팡이
collect ~을 받다, 모으다 call at(on) 방문하다, 들르다 swear 맹세코 말하다, 맹세하다

for a pair of boots / Simon had mended.
장화 때문에 / 시몬이 고쳐준

Simon then tried to buy / the sheep-skins on credit, /
시몬은 그 후 사려고 시도했다 / 양가죽을 외상으로 /

but the fur dealer refused to sell / on credit.
그러나 가죽 장수는 팔려고 하지 않았다 / 외상으로

"Bring your money," said he, "then you may pick /
"돈을 가져오시오" 그가 말했다 "그러면 고를 수 있어요 /

the best skins / we have.
가장 좋은 가죽을 / 우리가 가지고 있는

We know / what debt-collecting is like."
우리는 안다 / 빚을 받는 게 어떤 것인지"

So all the business the shoemaker did / was to get the
그래서 구두수선공이 한 일이란 / 20코펙을 받는 것이었고 /

twenty kopeks / for boots he had mended, /
그가 수선한 장화 값으로

and to take a pair of felt boots / a peasant gave him /
그리고 펠트 부츠 한 켤레를 가져가는 것이었다 / 소작농이 그에게 준 /

to sole with leather. Simon felt downhearted.
가죽으로 (부츠의) 밑창을 대기 위해서. 시몬은 낙담했다

He spent the twenty kopeks / on vodka, /
그는 20코펙을 썼다 / 보드카를 마시기 위해 /

and started homewards / without having bought any skins.
그리고 집으로 향했다 / 가죽은 하나도 못산 채

In the morning he had felt the frost.
아침에 그는 추위를 느꼈다

But now, after drinking the vodka, / he felt warm, /
그러나 지금은 보드카를 마시고 나니 / 몸이 따뜻했다 /

even without a sheep-skin. He trudged along, /
양가죽을 사지 않았지만 그는 터벅터벅 걸었다 /

striking his stick on the frozen earth / with one hand, /
(그리고) 막대기로 얼어붙은 땅을 치면서 / 한손으로 /

swinging the felt boots / with the other, /
펠트 부츠를 흔들며 / 다른 한 손으로 /

and talking to himself.
혼잣말을 하면서

---

mend 수선하다, 고치다 on credit 외상으로 dealer 장수, 장사꾼 sole (신발의) 밑창 downhearted 낙담한 homewards 집으로 frost 추위, 서리 trudge 터벅터벅 걷다 swing 흔들다

Chapter 2

"I'm quite warm," said he, / "though I have no sheep-skin.
"아주 따뜻한데" 그가 말했다 / "그렇지만 양가죽이 없어

I've had a drop, / and it runs through all my veins.
한 잔 했더니 / (취기가) 온 혈관으로 흐르는군(온 몸에 퍼지는군)

I need no sheep-skins.
난 양가죽이 필요 없어

I walk along and all my vexation is forgotten.
걷다보니 모든 근심거리가 잊혀지는 군

That's the sort of man I am! What do I care?
나는 그런 사람이야!   걱정할 게 뭐야?

I can live without sheep-skins. I don't need them.
나는 양가죽이 없어도 살 수 있다고   나는 양가죽이 필요 없어

My wife will fret, / to be sure.
마누라가 애가 탈거야 / 확실해

And, true enough, it is a shame — /
그리고 정말로 유감스러운 일이야 /

one works all day long, / and then does not get paid.
(뭐가?) 하루 종일 일하고 /   결국 돈은 받지 못하다니

Hang on a minute!
잠깐만!

If you don't bring that money along, /
그 돈을 가져오지 않으면 /

sure enough I'll skin you, / not a sheep.
내가 꼭 당신의 가죽을 벗길 거야 /   양이 아니라

How's that? He pays twenty kopeks at a time!
그것이 어떠냐고?   그가 한번에 20코펙을 줬어

What can I do / with twenty kopeks?
뭘 하지 /   20코펙으로

Drink it-that's all one can do!
술 마시는 것-그것밖에 할 수 있는 것이 없어!

Hard up, / he says he is!
돈에 쪼들린다고, / 그가 말했지!

---

drop (소량의) 술 vein 혈관, 정맥 fret 애를 태우다, 안달하다 shame 유감스러운 일, 수치 skin 가죽을 벗기다
hard (생활이) 모진, 괴로운

So he may be, / but what about me?
그럴지도 모르지 / 그런데 나는 어떻게 하라고?

You have a house, and cattle, and everything.
(그렇게 말하는) 너는 집이 있고 소도 있고 다 있어

I've only got these clothes / I wear!
(하지만) 나는 이 옷밖에 없다고 / 내가 걸치고 있는!

You have corn / of your own growing.
너는 옥수수가 있어 / 직접 기른

I have to buy every grain. And I must spend three roubles /
나는 모든 곡물을 사야한다고 게다가 나는 3루블을 써야 해 /

every week for bread alone.
매주 빵 사는 데만

I come home and find / the bread all used up, /
나는 집에 돌아오면 발견하지 / 빵을 다 먹은 것을 /

and I have to fork out / another rouble and a half.
그러면 나는 마지못해 지불해야 한다고 / 1.5루블을 더

So just pay up what you owe, / and no nonsense about it!"
그러니까 네가 빌린 돈 전부 줘, / 그렇지 않으면 말이 안돼!"

By this time he had nearly reached /
이윽고 그는 거의 다 왔다 /

the chapel at the bend of the road.
도로의 모퉁이에 있는 교회에

Looking up, he saw something whitish / behind the chapel.
쳐다보니까 그는 뭔가 하얀 것을 봤다 / 교회 뒤에 있는

The daylight was fading, / and the shoemaker peered at the
날이 저물고 있었다 / 그리고 구두수선공은 그것을 주의해서 봤다 /

thing / without being able to make out / what it was.
알 수 없으면서도 / 그것이 뭔지

"There was no white stone / here before.
"하얀 돌이 없었는데 / 전에 이곳에는

Can it be an ox? It's not like an ox.
황소일까? 황소 같지는 않아

It has a head like a man, / but it's too white.
사람 같은 머리가 있는데 / 너무 하얗단 말이야

And what could a man be doing there?"
그리고 사람이 저기서 뭘 할 수 있는 거지?"

He came closer, / so that it was clearly visible.
그는 좀더 가까이 다가갔다 / 그러자 그것이 확실하게 보였다

To his surprise / it really was a man, / alive or dead,
놀랍게도 /   그것은 진짜 사람이었다 /   (어떤 사람?) 살았든 죽었든

sitting naked, / leaning motionless against the chapel.
발가벗고 앉아있었다 /   (그리고) 꼼짝 않고 교회에 기대어 있었다

Terror seized the shoemaker, / and he thought,
공포가 구두수선공을 사로잡았다 /   그리고 그는 생각했다 /

"Some one has killed him, stripped him, / and left him there.
"누군가가 죽여서 발가벗기고 /   그리고 저기에 놔뒀구나

If I meddle / I shall surely get into trouble."
내가 끼어든다면 /   무슨 봉변을 당할지도 몰라"

So the shoemaker went on.
그래서 구두장이는 그냥 갔다.

He passed in front of the chapel /
그가 교회 앞을 지나갔다 /

so that he could not see the man.
그래서 그가 그 남자를 볼 수 없었다

When he had gone some way, / he looked back, /
그가 어느 정도 갔을 때 /   그는 되돌아 봤다 /

and saw / that the man was no longer leaning against the
그리고 봤다 / (무엇을?) 그 남자가 더 이상 교회에 기대어 있지 않은 것을 /

chapel, / but was moving / as if looking towards him.
            그러나 그는 움직이고 있었다 / 마치 구두수선공을 쳐다보듯이

The shoemaker felt more frightened / than before, /
구두장수선공은 더 놀랐다 /   아까보다 /

and thought, / "Shall I go back to him, / or shall I go on?
그리고 생각했다 / "그 사람에게 돌아갈까 /   아니면 그냥 계속 갈까?

If I go near him / something dreadful may happen.
내가 가까이 가면 /   무서운 일이 일어날 지도 몰라

Who knows / who the fellow is? He has not come here /
누가 알까 /   저 친구가 어떤 사람인지 그는 여기에 온 것은 아니야 /

for any good. If I go near him / he may jump up /
좋은 일로   내가 가까이 가면 /   그가 덤벼들어서 /

and throttle me, / and there will be no getting away.
내 목을 조를지도 몰라 /   그러면 도망갈 수가 없을 거야

---

grain 곡물 use up ~을 다 사용하다 fork out ~을 지불하다, 건네주다 bend 모퉁이 fade (빛이) 희미해지다 peer 응시하다, 뚫어지게 보다 make out ~을 알다, 이해하다 visible 눈에 보이는, 현저한 to one's surprise 놀랍게도 lean 기대다 seize ~을 잡다 meddle 간섭하다, 끼어들다 dreadful 무서운 throttle 목을 조르다

25

Or if not, / he'd still be a burden / on one's hands.
또는 그렇지 않다면 / 그는 짐이 될 거야 / 다른 사람에게

What could I do / with a naked man?
어떻게 할 수 있어 / 발가벗은 사람을?

I couldn't give him / my last clothes.
그에게 줄 수는 없는데 / 내 마지막 옷을

That would be absurd."
그건 어리석은 짓이야."

So the shoemaker hurried on, /
그래서 구두수선공은 서둘렀다 /

leaving the chapel behind him, /
그를 뒤로 하고 교회를 떠날 때 /

when suddenly his conscience began to prick him, /
그때 갑자기 양심이 그에게 고통을 주기 시작했다 (양심의 가책을 받았다) /

and he stopped in the road.
그리고 길에서 멈췄다

"What are you doing, Simon?" said he to himself.
"뭘 하고 있지, 시몬?" 그가 혼잣말을 했다

"The man may be perishing of cold, /
"그 사람은 추위로 죽을 수도 있어 /

and you slip past afraid.
그런데 너는 두려워서 빠져나가려고 해

Have you grown so rich as / to be afraid of robbers?
네가 부자가 됐니 / 도둑맞을 것을 겁낼 정도로

Ah, Simon, shame on you!"
아, 시몬, 부끄러운 줄 알아!"

So he turned back / and went up to the man.
그래서 그는 되돌아갔다 / 그리고 그 남자에게 다가갔다

Key Expression

There is no 동사+ing; ~할 수 없다

이 표현을 사용할 때 동사를 반드시 동명사(동사+ing) 형태로 바꾸어야 한다. 그리고 이 표현은 It is impossible to +동사원형"과 같은 의미가 있다.

There will be no getting away. 도망갈 수 없다.
There is no telling what happened last weekend. 말할 수 없다 / 지난주 말에

---

absurd 어리석은, 터무니없는 conscience 양심 prick 고통을 주다 perish 죽다 slip 달아나다, 도망치다
shame on you 부끄러운 줄 알아

Chapter 3

Simon approached the stranger, / looked at him, /
시몬은 낯선 사람에게 다가갔다 / 그를 쳐다봤다 /

and saw / that he was a young man, / fit, with no bruises on
그리고 알게 되었다 / 그는 청년이라는 것을 / 건강하고, 몸에 타박상이 없는 /

his body, / only evidently freezing and frightened, /
단지 몸이 꽁꽁 얼어붙고 겁을 먹은 것 같았다 /

and he sat there leaning back /
그리고 거기서 기대어 앉았다 /

without looking up at Simon, / as if too faint to lift his eyes.
시몬을 쳐다보지 않고 / 마치 너무 힘이 없어 눈을 뜰 수 없는 것처럼

Simon went close to him, /
시몬은 그에게 가까이 갔다 /

and then the man seemed to wake up.
그러자 그 남자는 정신이 드는 것 같았다

Turning his head, / he opened his eyes /
그가 고개를 돌리면서 / 그는 눈을 뜨고 /

and looked into Simon's face.
시몬의 얼굴을 들여다보았다

That one look was enough / to make Simon fond of the man.
그런 모습은 충분했다 / 시몬이 그 남자를 좋아하게 만들 수 있기에

He threw the felt boots on the ground, / took off his belt, /
그는 펠트 부츠를 땅에 던지고 / 벨트를 풀고는 /

laid it on the boots, / and took off his cloth coat.
부츠 위에 놓았다 / 그리고 천으로 만든 외투를 벗었다

"It's not a time for talking," said he.
"얘기할 시간이 아니야" 그가 말했다

"Come, put this coat on / at once!"
"자, 이 외투를 입게 / 얼른!"

And Simon took the man / by the elbows /
그리고 시몬은 그 남자를 잡았다 / (어떤 부분을?) 팔꿈치를 /

and helped him to rise.
그가 일어나도록 부축했다

---

approach 다가가다 bruise 타박상 evidently (아무래도) ~인 것 같다 freezing 얼어붙듯이 추운
faint 힘이 없는, 희미한 look 모습, 표정 fond 좋아하는 at once 즉시

As he got up, / Simon saw / that his body was clean and
그가 일어섰을 때 / 시몬은 알아차렸다 / (무엇을?) 그의 몸이 깨끗하고 건강하다는 것을 /

in good condition, / his hands and feet shapely, /
그의 손과 발은 잘 생겼고 /

and his face good and kind.
그리고 얼굴은 잘 생겼고 인자해 (보였다.)

He threw his coat / over the man's shoulders, /
그는 외투를 걸쳤다 / 그 남자의 어깨에 /

but the latter could not find / the sleeves.
그러나 그 남자는 찾을 수 없었다 / 소매를

Simon guided / his arms into them, /
시몬은 도와주었다 / 그의 팔을 소매로 넣도록 /

and pull the coat up, / wrapped it closely about him, /
그리고 외투를 끌어 올렸고 / 그의 몸에 잘 맞게 감쌌다 /

and fastened the belt.
그리고 벨트를 조였다

Simon even took off / his tattered cap /
시몬은 심지어 벗었다 / 낡은 모자를

to put it on the man's head, /
(왜?) 그 남자의 머리에 씌우려고 /

but then his own head felt cold, / and he thought: /
그러나 그러자 자기 머리가 썰렁하다고 느꼈다 / 그리고 그는 생각했다 /

"I'm quite bald, / while he has long curly hair."
"나는 아주 대머리야 / 하지만 그는 길고 곱슬곱슬한 머리가 있어"

So he put his cap on his own head again.
그래서 그는 모자를 다시 자기 머리에 썼다

"It will be better / to give him something for his feet,"
"좋겠어 / 그에게 신을 것을 주는 것이"

thought he.
그는 생각했다

And he made the man sit down, / and helped /
그리고 그는 그 남자를 앉혔다 / 그리고 도와줬다 /

him to put on the felt boots, / saying, /
그가 펠트 부츠를 신도록 / 이렇게 말하면서 /

"There, friend, now move about /
"여보게, 친구, 이제 움직여봐 /

and will get warmed up.
그러면 몸이 따뜻해질 거야

28 Tolstoy's Short Stories

Other matters can be settled / later on. Can you walk?"
다른 문제들은 해결될 거야 / 나중에 걸을 수 있소?"

The man stood up and looked kindly / at Simon, /
그 남자는 일어서서 친절하게 바라봤다 / 시몬을 /

but could not say a word.
그러나 한마디도 말할 수 없었다

"Why don't you speak?" said Simon.
"왜 말을 하지 않는 거요?" 시몬이 말했다

"It's too cold / to stay here, / we must get to shelter.
"너무나 추워 / 여기에 있기에는 / 우리는 추위를 피할 곳으로 가야 해

There now, take my stick, /
이제, 내 지팡이를 집어봐 /

and if you're feeling weak, / lean on that. Now step out!"
그리고 힘이 없으면 / 지팡이에 의지하시오. 자 걸어보쇼!"

The man started walking, / and moved easily, /
그 남자는 걷기 시작했다 / 그리고 쉽게 움직였다 /

not lagging behind.
뒤처지지 않으면서

As they went along, / Simon asked him, /
그들이 걸어 갈 때 / 시몬은 그 남자에게 물었다 /

"And where do you belong to?"
"그리고 당신은 어디 사람이요?"

"I'm not from these parts."
"저는 이 부근에서 오지는 않았어요."

"I thought / as much. I know the folks hereabouts."
"난 생각했었지 / 그럴 거라고. 나는 이 동네 사람들을 알지."

Key Expression

make; ~을 ~한 상태로 하게다

"make" 동사 다음에 목적어가 오고, 그 다음에 형용사, 과거분사가 보어로 올 수 있다.

That one look was enough to make Simon fond of the man.
그런 모습은 (~하게 하기에) 충분했다 / 시몬이 그 남자를 좋아하게

This movie made her sad.
이 영화는 하게했다 / 그녀를 슬픈 상태로

---

in good condition 건강한 shapely (몸이) 균형이 잡힌, 잘 생긴 sleeve (옷의) 소매 wrap 감싸다, 포장하다 fasten 조이다, 매다 tattered 너덜너덜한, 낡은 curly 곱슬곱슬한 settle (문제를) 해결하다 shelter 피난처, 은신처 lag 뒤처지다, 느릿느릿 나아가다 belong (사람이 어떤 장소에) 속하다 hereabouts 이 부근의, 이근처의

"But, how did you come to be there / by the chapel?"
"그런데 당신은 어떻게 해서 있게 된 거요 / 교회 옆에"

"I cannot tell."
"저는 말할 수 없습니다."

"Has some one been ill-treating you?"
"누가 당신에게 몹쓸 짓을 했어요?"

"No one has ill-treated me. God has punished me."
"아무도 저에게 나쁜 짓을 하지는 않았어요. 신이 저를 벌하셨어요."

"Of course God rules all.
"물론 신이 모든 것을 조정하시지.

Still, you'll have to find / food and shelter / somewhere.
여전히 당신은 마련해야 할 거예요 / 음식과 거처를 / 어딘가에서

Where do you want to go to?"
어디로 가고 싶어요?"

"It is all the same to me."
"어디든지 상관없습니다."

Simon was amazed.
시몬은 놀랐다.

The man did not look / like a rogue, /
그 남자는 보이지는 않았다 / 악당같이 /

and he spoke gently, / but yet he gave no account /
게다가 점잖게 말했다 / 그러나 여전히 이야기를 하지 않았다 /

of himself. Still Simon thought, /
자신에 대한   여전히 시몬은 생각했다 /

"Who knows / what may have happened?"
"누군들 알겠나? / 무슨 일이 일어날지(말 못할 사정이 있을 수도 있다)"

And he said to the stranger: /
그리고 그는 낯선 사람에게 말했다 /

"Well then, come to my house, /
"그러면, 우리 집으로 가세 /

and at least warm yourself / for a while."
그리고 최소한 몸을 따뜻하게 합시다 / 잠시나마"

So Simon walked towards / his home, /
그래서 시몬은 걸어갔다 / 집을 향해 /

and the stranger kept up with him, / walking at his side.
그리고 낯선 사람은 그를 따라갔다 / 그의 옆에서 걸으면서

The wind had risen / and Simon felt it cold / under his shirt.
바람이 불었고 / 시몬은 춥다고 느꼈다 / 셔츠를 입어도

The effect of the wine had now passed away, /
술기운은 이제 사라졌고 /

and he began to feel the frost. He went along sniffling /
그는 추위를 느끼기 시작했다.　　　　　　　그는 코를 훌쩍이면서 갔다 /

and wrapping his wife's coat round him, /
그리고 그의 아내의 외투로 그를 감싸면서 /

and he thought to himself: /
그리고 혼자서 생각했다 /

"There now — talk about sheep-skins!
"자 이제,　　　　양가죽을 이야기해보자!

I went out for sheep-skins / and come home /
나는 양가죽을 사러 나갔는데 /　　집으로 가게 되다니 /

without even a coat to my back, /
외투도 걸치지 않고 /

and what is more, / I'm bringing /
그리고 게다가 /　　　나는 데리고 가고 있다 /

a naked man along with me. Matryona won't be pleased!"
발가벗은 남자를　　　　　마트료나가 좋아하지 않겠군!"

And when he thought of his wife / he felt depressed.
그리고 그가 아내 생각을 하자 /　　그는 우울해졌다

But when he looked at the stranger /
그러나 그가 낯선 사람을 쳐다보고 /

and remembered / how he had looked up at him
그리고 기억하자 /　　어떻게 그가 그를 쳐다봤는지 /

at the chapel, / his heart was glad.
교회에서 /　　그의 마음은 기뻤다

> ### Key Expression
>
> **What is more; 게다가, 더구나**
> 이 표현을 사용하여 자신이 말한 것을 강조하며 더 많은 정보를 제시한다.
> What is more, I'm bringing a naked man along with me.
> 게다가 / 나는 데리고 가고 있다 / 발가벗은 남자를
> She is beautiful and, What is more, very intelligent.
> 그녀는 아름답다 / 게다가 / 매우 총명하다

ill-treat ~을 학대하다 punish 벌하다, 처벌하다 shelter 피난처, 은신처 all the same 아무래도 상관없는, 똑같은
amazed 깜짝 놀란, 경탄한 rogue 악당, 불량배 account 설명, 이야기 keep up with 따라잡다 frost 추위, 서리
sniffle 코를 훌쩍이다 what is more 게다가 depressed 우울한

Chapter 4

Simon's wife had everything ready / early that day.
시몬의 아내는 모든 것을 준비했다 / 그날 일찌감치

She had chopped wood, / brought water, / fed the children, /
그녀는 장작을 패고 / 물을 길어오고 / 아이들을 먹이고 /

eaten her own meal, / and now she sat thinking.
식사를 하고 / 그리고 지금은 앉아서 생각하고 있었다

She wondered / when she ought to make bread: /
그녀는 궁금했다 / 언제 빵을 만들어야 할지 /

now or tomorrow? There was still a large piece left.
지금 아니면 내일? 아직 큰 빵조각이 남아있었다

"If Simon has had some dinner / in town," / thought she, /
"시몬이 저녁을 먹었으면 / 읍내에서" / 그녀는 생각했다 /

"and does not eat much / for supper, /
"그리고 많이 먹지 않으면 / 저녁을 /

the bread will last out / another day."
그 빵으로 견딜 수 있을 텐데 / 하루 더"

She weighed / the piece of bread / in her hand again and
그녀는 재봤다 / 빵조각의 무게를 / 손에 놓고 여러 번 /

again, / and thought: / "I won't make any more today.
그리고 생각했다 / "오늘은 더 이상 만들지 않을래

There's just enough flour / to make one more loaf.
충분한 밀가루가 있으니까 / 빵 한 덩어리를 만들 정도의

We can manage to get along / till Friday."
그럭저럭 지낼 수 있을 거야 / 금요일까지는"

So Matryona put away the bread, /
그래서 마트료나는 빵을 치웠다 /

and sat down at the table / to patch her husband's shirt.
그리고 테이블에 앉았다 / 남편의 셔츠를 수선하기 위해

While she worked / she thought /
그녀는 일하는 동안에 / 그녀는 생각해봤다 /

how her husband was buying skins / for a winter coat.
어떻게 남편이 가죽을 사올 것인지 / 겨울 외투를 만들

"If only / the fur dealer does not cheat him.
"좋을 텐데 (뭐가?) / 가죽 장수가 남편을 속이지 않는다면

My good man is much too simple.
내 남편은 너무 순진하단 말이야

He cheats nobody, / but any child can take him in.
그는 아무도 속이지 않아 / 그러나 어린 아이도 그를 속일 수 있지

Eight roubles is a lot of money.
8루블은 큰 돈이야.

He should get a fine sheepskin / at that price.
그는 좋은 양가죽을 사야 해 / 그 값으로

Not tanned skins, / but still a proper one.
무두질한 가죽은 안돼 / 여전히 적당한 가죽으로

How difficult it was / last winter to get on /
얼마나 힘들었는지 / 작년 겨울에 지내는 것이 /

without a warm coat.
따뜻한 외투 한 벌 없이

I could neither get down to the river, / nor go out anywhere.
나는 강에 갈 수도 없고 / 어디 나갈 수도 없었지

Whenever he went outdoors, / he put on all the clothes /
그가 외출할 때마다 / 모든 옷을 입었지 /

we had, / and there was nothing left for me.
우리가 가지고 있던 / 그러면 내가 입을 것은 없었지

He did not start / very early today, / but still it's time /
그는 떠나지는 않았지 / 오늘 아주 일찍 / 그러나 이제는 시간이야 /

he was back. I only hope / he has not gone on the spree!"
그가 돌아올. 나는 바랄 뿐이야 / 그가 실컷 술을 마시지 않았기를"

Just as Matryona had thought this, / steps were heard /
마트료나가 이런 생각하고 있었을 때 / 발자국 소리가 들렸다 /

on the threshold, / and some one entered.
문간에서 / 그리고 누군가가 들어왔다

Matryona stuck her needle / into her work /
마트료나는 바늘을 꽂아두고 / 수선하던 옷에 /

and went out into the entry.
그리고 입구로 나갔다

---

chop ~을 자르다 wonder ~을 알고 싶다고 생각하다, 궁금해 하다 last(식품이) 견디다, 지속되다 weigh 무게를 재다 loaf (빵의) 덩어리 get along 살아가다, 그럭저럭 해내다 patch ~에 덧대어 수선하다 simple 순진한 take in 속이다 tanned 무두질한 get on 살다, 지내다 spree 흥청대기, 흥청망청 마시기 threshold 문간, 문지방

There she saw two men: / Simon, and with him a man /
거기서 그녀는 두 남자를 봤다 /   시몬과 그와 함께 남자를 /

without a hat and in felt boots.
모자를 쓰지 않고   그리고 펠트 부츠를 신고 있던 (남자를)

Matryona noticed at once /
마트료나는 즉시 알아차렸다 /

that her husband smelt of spirits.
(무엇을?) 남편에게서 술 냄새가 나는 것을

"There now, he has been drinking," thought she.
"이제, 한잔 하셨구먼,"   그녀는 생각했다

And when she saw / that he had not his coat on, /
그리고 그녀가 봤을 때 /   그가 외투를 입지 않았고 /

had only her jacket on, / brought no parcel, /
그녀의 재킷만 입고 있었고 /   꾸러미가 없었고 /

stood there silent, / but only simpered, /
조용히 서있었고 /   바보 같은 웃음만 짓고 있는 것을(봤을 때) /

her heart was ready to break / with disappointment.
그녀의 가슴은 금방이라도 터질 것 같았다 /   실망해서

Key Expression

if only; ~만 할 수 있다면, ~이면 좋은 텐데

실제로 어떤 일이 일어날 가능성은 없지만, 그런 일이 일어나길 바라는 소망을 표현한다.

If only the fur dealer does not cheat him.
좋을 텐데 (뭐가?) / 가죽 장수가 남편을 속이지 않는다면.
If only I could sing like you.
좋을 텐데 (뭐가?) / 내가 너처럼 노래할 수 있다면

notice 알아차리다 spirits 알코올, 술 simper (바보같이) 웃다 ready to ~할 것 같은

"He has drunk the money," thought she, /
"그는 돈으로 술을 퍼마셨어" 그녀는 생각했다 /

"and has been on the spree / with some good-for-nothing
"그리고 진탕 퍼마셨군" / 아무짝에도 쓸데없는 인간과 /

fellow / whom / he has brought home with him."
게다가 그를 / 그는 집으로 데려왔구먼."

Matryona let / them pass into the hut, / followed them in, /
마트료나는 내버려 두었다 / 그들이 오두막으로 들어오도록 / 따라 들어왔다 /

and saw / that the stranger was a young, slight man, /
그리고 알았다 (무엇을?) / 낯선 사람은 젊고, 시시한 남자라는 것을 /

wearing her husband's coat.
(게다가) 그녀의 남편의 외투를 입고 있다는 것을(알았다)

There was no shirt / to be seen under it, /
셔츠를 입지 않았다 / 외투 안엔 /

and he had no hat.
그리고 그 남자는 모자가 없었다

Having entered, / he stood, neither moving, nor raising his
집에 들어선 후 / 그는 서서 움직이지도 않았고, 눈을 들지도 않았다 /

eyes, / and Matryona thought: /
그래서 마트료나는 생각했다 /

"He must be a bad man — he's afraid."
"그는 나쁜 사람임에 틀림없어 – 그는 두려워하고 있다고(생각했다)."

Matryona frowned, / and stood beside the oven looking to
마트료나는 눈살을 찌푸렸다 / 그리고 난로 옆에 서서 지켜보고 있었다 /

see / what they would do.
그들이 무엇을 하려는지

Simon took off his cap / and sat down on the bench /
시몬은 모자를 벗고 / 긴 의자에 앉았다 /

as if things were all right.
마치 이런 상황이 괜찮다는 듯이

"Come, Matryona. If supper is ready, / let us have some."
"자, 마트료나. 저녁이 준비됐으면 / 우리가 좀 먹게 해줘."

Matryona muttered something to herself /
마트료나는 혼잣말로 뭔가 중얼거렸고 /

and did not move, / but stayed / where she was, by the oven.
움직이지 않았다 / 그러나 있었다 / 그녀가 있던 곳인, 난로 옆에

good-for-nothing 쓸모없는, 도움이 되지 않는 frown 눈살을 찌푸리다 mutter 중얼거리다

She looked first at the one / and then at the other of them, /
그녀는 먼저 한 남자를 보고 / 다음에는 다른 한 남자를 봤다 /

and only shook her head.
그리고는 고개를 저을 뿐이었다

Simon saw / that his wife was out of temper, /
시몬은 알았다 / 자기 아내가 화가 났다는 것을 /

but tried to pass it off.
그러나 가볍게 받아 넘기려고 했다

Pretending not to notice anything, /
아무것도 눈치 채지 못한 척하면서 /

he took the stranger by the arm.
그는 낯선 사람의 팔을 잡았다

"Sit down, friend," said he, / "and let us have some supper."
"친구, 앉아," 그가 말했다 / "그리고 저녁을 먹읍시다." 라고

The stranger sat down on the bench.
그 낯선 사람은 긴 의자에 앉았다

"Haven't you cooked anything?" said Simon.
"요리하지 않았소?" 시몬이 말했다

Matryona's anger boiled over.
마트료나가 화가 치밀어 올랐다

"I've cooked, but not for you.
"요리는 했지만 당신들 것은 없어

It seems to me / you have drunk your wits away.
보아하니 / 당신들 정신이 나가도록 술을 마신 것 같군

You went to buy / a sheep-skin, /
당신은 사러 간다더니 / 양가죽을 /

but come home / without the coat you had on, /
그런데 집에 돌아왔어 / 외투도 없이 /

and bring / a naked vagabond home with you.
걸쳤던 / 그리고 데려왔어 / 발가벗은 부랑자를 집에

I have no supper / for drunkards / like you."
저녁은 없어 / 주정뱅이한테 줄 / 당신 같은"

"That's enough, Matryona.
"그만해, 마트료나.

What is the use / of waging your tongue / without reason?
무슨 소용이 있어 / 쉴 새 없이 지껄여봐야 / 근거 없이

You had better ask / what sort of man —
물어보는 것이 좋을 걸 / 어떤 사람인지"

And you tell me / what you've done / with the money?"
"그러면 나에게 말 해봐요 / 뭘 했는지 / 그 돈으로"

Simon found the pocket of the jacket, /
시몬은 재킷의 주머니를 찾았고 /

drew out the three-rouble note, / and unfolded it.
3루블 지폐를 꺼냈다 / 그리고 그 지폐를 폈다

"Here is the money. Trifonov did not pay me, /
"여기 그 돈이 있어. 트리포노프가 갚지 않았지 /

but promises to pay soon."
하지만 곧 준다고 약속했어."

Matryona grew still more angry.
마트료나는 여전히 더욱더 화가 났다

He had bought no sheep-skins, /
그는 양가죽을 사오지 않았다 /

but had put his only coat / on some naked fellow /
그러나 하나뿐인 외투를 입혔다 / 어떤 벌거벗은 친구에게 /

and had even brought him / to their house.
그리고 그를 데려오기까지 했다 / 집으로

She snatched up / the note from the table, / took it /
그녀는 낚아채서 / 그 지폐를 테이블에서 / 가져갔다 /

to put away in safety, /
안전하게 보관하려고 /

and said: / "I have no supper for you.
그리고 말했다 / "당신들을 위한 저녁 식사는 없어

We can't feed / all the naked drunkards in the world."
우리는 먹일 수는 없어 / 이 세상의 모든 벌거벗은 주정뱅이들을"

Key Expression

It sees to me ; 보아하니, ~처럼 보이다, ~인 것 같다

확신할 수 없는 상황을 공손하게 표현할때 "It seems to me"를 사용한다. 이 표현을 직역하면 "나에게 ~처럼 보인다, ~인 것 같다"이지만, "보아하니, 아마 ~인 것 같다"라고 해석할 수 있다.

It seems to me you have drunk your wits away.
보아하니 / 당신들 정신이 나가도록 술을 마신 것 (같군)

It seems to me he likes you.
보아하니 / 그는 너를 좋아하는 것 (같아)

---

out of temper 화가 난 pass off 가볍게 받아넘기다, 관심을 돌리다 pretend ~인척하다 boil over 몹시 화가 나다, 억제할 수 없게 되다 wits 이성, 정신 vagabond 부랑자 drunkard 술주정뱅이 wag one's tongue 쉴 새 없이 지껄이다 reason 근거, 이유 unfold 펼치다, 펴다 snatch 잡아채다, 낚아채다 put away (돈을) 저금하다

"There now, Matryona, hold your tongue a bit.
"자 이제, 마트료나, 좀 그만해봐

First hear / what a man has to say……"
먼저 들어 봐 / 사람이 말하는 것을"

"Much wisdom I shall hear / from a drunken fool.
"대단한 지혜라도 듣겠군 / 술 취한 멍청이한테서

Good reason I had / for not wanting to marry /
내가 옳았지 / 결혼하지 않으려 했던 것이 /

you-a drunkard. My mother gave me linen /
당신 같은 주정뱅이와 엄마가 나한테 옷감을 주었는데 /

and you have wasted it / in drink.
당신은 날려버렸지 / 술값으로

And now you've been to / buy a sheepskin, /
그리고 이제 당신은 갔었지 / 양가죽을 사러 /

and have drunk it, too!"
그런데 그것도 술값으로 날려버렸지!"

Simon tried to explain / to his wife /
시몬은 설명하려고 했다 / 아내에게 /

that he had only spent twenty kopeks.
(무엇을) 그가 겨우 20코펙만 썼다는 것을

He tried to tell / how he had found the man, /
그는 말하려고 했다 / 어떻게 그 남자를 발견했는지 /

but Matryona would not give him a chance /
그러나 마트료나는 그에게 기회를 주려하지 않았다 /

to speak a word.
(어떤 기회?) 한마디라고 말할 수 있는

She managed to speak two words at once, /
그녀는 한번에 두 마디씩 내뱉었다(끊임없이 말했다) /

and brought up / things / that had happened ten years before.
그리고 들추어냈다 / 일을 / (어떤 일?) 십 년 전에 일어났던

Matryona talked and talked, /
마트료나는 말하고 또 말했다 /

and at last she flew at Simon / and seized him by the sleeve.
그리고 마침내 그녀는 덤벼들었고 / 시몬에게 / 소매를 붙잡았다

"Give me my jacket. It is the only one / I have, /
"내 재킷 돌려줘. 그것은 하나밖에 없는 거야 / 내가 가진 /

and you took it from me / and put it on yourself.
그리고 당신은 나에게서 가져갔으면 / 당신이 입었어야지

Give it here, you mangy dog, and may the devil take you."
이리 줘, 못된 개 같으니, 악마가 데려가 버려라"

Simon began to pull off / the jacket, /
시몬은 급히 벗기 시작했다 / 재킷을 /

and turned a sleeve of it / inside out.
그리고 소매를 뒤집었다 / 안이 밖에 나오도록

Matryona seized the jacket / and it burst its seams, /
마트료나는 재킷을 잡아당기자 / 꿰맨 자리가 터졌다 /

She snatched it up, /
그녀는 재킷을 낚아채고 /

threw it over her head / and started for the door.
그녀의 머리 위로 뒤집어썼다 / 그리고 문 쪽으로 갔다

She intended to go out, / but stopped undecided.
그녀는 나가려고 했지만 / 멈춰서 결정하지 않았다

She wanted to work off / her anger, /
그녀는 해소하고 싶었다 / 울분을 /

but she also wanted to learn / what sort of a man /
그러나 그녀 역시 알고 싶었다 / (무엇을?) 어떤 사람인지 /

the stranger was.
낯선 사람이

Key Expression

have been to 장소 vs. have been to 동사원형

"have been to 장소"는 어떤 곳에 가보았다는 경험을 표현한다. 그리고 "have been to 동사원형"은 "~하러 갔다"는 의미다.

I have been to New York. 나는 뉴욕에 가보았다
You've been to buy a sheepskin, and have drunk it.
당신은 갔었지 / 양가죽을 사러 / 그런데 술값으로 날려버렸지

---

hold your tongue 잠자코 있어, 입 닥치고 있어 bring up 문제를 제기하다 fly at ~에 대들다
mangy 지저분한, 초라한 pull off (옷을) 벗다 seam (천의) 솔기, 꿰맨 자리 work off (분노를) 발산하다, 해소하다

Quiz 1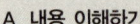

A. 내용 이해하기

다음 문장을 읽고 본문의 내용과 맞으면 T(True), 틀리면 F(False)를 쓰세요.

1. Simon went out to buy sheep-skins in order to sew a winter coat for his children.
2. Simon could save what he earned for a rainy day.
3. Simon already had enough money to buy sheep-skins for the winter coat.
4. Simon couldn't collect all the money owed to him by customers in the village.

B. 단어

다음 제시된 단어의 설명을 읽고, 어떤 단어의 정의를 설명하는지 아래의 박스에서 찾아 써 보세요.

1. a poor farmer who rents or owns a small amount of land
2. a torn piece of cloth
3. one who buys goods from a store
4. to gather or pick up
5. to say that what you are telling is true
6. low in spirits or depressed
7. to walk with slow heavy steps because you are tired
8. a small quantity of alcohol
9. to intrude into other people's business or affairs
10. to kill someone by pressing their throat; to choke

---

downhearted tatter throttle drop collect peasant

meddle swear trudge customer

Answer

A. 1. F 2. F 3. F 4. T

B. 1. peasant 2. tatter 3. customer 4. collect 5. swear 6. downhearted 7. trudge 8. drop 9. meddle 10. throttle

C. 직독직해

아래에 제시된 문장을 직독직해로 해석해보세요.

1. She wanted to work off / her anger, / but she also wanted to learn / what sort of a man / the stranger was.

   →

2. You went to buy / a sheep-skin, / but come home / without the coat / you had on, / and bring / a naked vagabond home with you.

   →

3. Simon saw / that his wife was out of temper, / but tried to pass it off.

   →

4. When she saw / that he had not his coat on, / had only her jacket on, / brought no parcel, / stood there silent, / but only simpered, / her heart was ready to break / with disappointment.

   →

D. 동시통역

아래에 제시된 직독직해를 보고, 영어로 말해보세요.

1. 그녀는 재봤다 / 빵조각의 무게를 / 손에 놓고 여러 번

   →

2. 게다가 / 나는 데리고 가고 있다 / 발가벗은 남자를

   →

3. 당신은 어떻게 해서 있게 된 거요 / 교회 옆에

   →

4. 소작농의 아내는 약속했다 / (어떤 약속?) 다음주에 돈을 갚겠다고 / 하지만 그녀는 갚을 수 없을 것이다.

   →

Answer

C. 1. 그녀는 해소하고 싶었다 / 그녀의 울분을 / 그러나 그녀 역시 알고 싶었다 / (무엇을?) 어떤 사람인지 / 낯선 사람이. 2. 당신은 사러 간다더니 / 양가죽을 / 그런데 집에 돌아왔어 / 외투도 없이 / 걸쳤던 / 그리고 데려고 왔어 / 발가벗은 부랑자를 집에. 3. 시몬은 알았다 / 자기 아내가 화가 났다는 것을 / 그러나 가볍게 받아 넘기려고 했다. 4. 그리고 그녀가 봤을 때 (무엇을?) 그가 외투를 입지 않았고 / 그녀의 재킷만 입고 있었고 / 꾸러미가 없었고 / 조용히 서있었고 / 바보 같은 웃음만 짓고 있는 것을(봤을 때) / 그녀의 가슴은 금방이라도 터질 것 같았다 / 실망해서

D. 1. She weighed / the piece of bread / in her hand again and again. 2. What is more, / I'm bringing / a naked man along with me. 3. How did you come to be there / by the chapel? 4. The peasant's wife promised / that the money should be paid next week, / but she could not pay it herself.

Chapter 5

Matryona paused and said: /
마트료나는 멈추고 말했다 /

"If he were a good man / he would not be naked.
"그가 좋은 사람이라면 / 발가벗지는 않았을 거야

Why, he hasn't even a shirt on him.
아니, 그는 셔츠도 입지 않았어

If he were all right, / you would say /
그가 좋은 사람이라면 / 당신은 말할 수 있겠네요 /

where you came across / the fellow."
어디서 만났는지 / 저 친구를"

"That's just / what I am trying to tell you," / said Simon.
"바로 그게 / 내가 말하려고 하던 거야" / 시몬이 말했다

"As I came to the chapel / I saw /
"내가 교회로 걸어갔을 때 / 나는 봤어 /

him sitting / all naked and frozen.
그가 앉아 있는 것을 / 발가벗고 거의 얼어 죽을 정도가 되어서

It isn't quite the weather / to sit about naked!
날씨가 아니잖아! / 발가벗고 앉아있을 만한

God sent me to him, / or he would have perished.
신이 나를 그에게 보냈어 / 그렇지 않으면 그는 죽어버렸을 거야

What should I do?
뭘 어떻게 해야 했지?

How do we know / what may have happened to him?
어떻게 우리가 알겠어 / 그에게 무슨 일이 있었는지

So I clothed him, / and brought him along.
그래서 나는 옷을 입히고 / 그리고 그를 데려온 거야

Don't be so angry, Matryona. It is a sin.
그렇게 화내지마, 마트료나. 그러는 것은 죄악이야

Remember, we all must die one day."
명심하라고, 우리는 모두 인젠가는 죽는다는 것을"

Angry words rose / to Matryona's lips, /
화가 나서 험한 소리가 올라왔다 / 마트료나의 입술까지(말할 뻔했다) /

but she looked at the stranger / and was silent.
그러나 그녀는 낯선 사람을 보고서 / 침묵했다

He sat / on the edge of the bench, / motionless.
그는 앉았다 / 긴 의자의 끄트머리에 / 움직이지 않고

His hands were folded on his knees, /
그의 손은 무릎 위에 포개었고 /

his head was drooping on his chest, /
머리는 가슴으로 수그리고 /

his eyes were closed, / and his brows were knit as if in pain.
눈은 감고 / 그리고 고통스러운 듯이 눈썹을 찌푸렸다

Matryona was silent. And Simon said: /
마트료나는 침묵했다 그리고 시몬이 말했다 /

"Matryona, have you no love / of God?"
"마트료나, 당신은 사랑하지 않아 / 신을?"

Matryona heard these words, /
마트료나는 이런 말을 들었다 /

and as she looked at the stranger, /
그리고 그녀가 낯선 사람을 바라봤을 때 /

suddenly her heart softened / towards him.
갑자기 그녀의 마음은 수그러들었다 / 그에 대한

She came back from the door, /
그녀는 문에서 다시 왔다 /

went to the oven / and she got out the supper.
그리고 난로 쪽으로 가서 / 저녁 식사를 가져왔다

Setting a cup on the table, / she poured out / some kvass.
컵을 테이블에 놓으면서 / 그녀는 따라주었다 / 호밀로 양조한 맥주를

Then she brought out / the last piece of bread, /
그런 다음 그녀는 가져왔다 / 마지막 남은 빵조각을 /

and set out / a knife and spoons.
그리고 놓았다 / 칼과 스푼을

"Have some food," said she.
"식사하세요," 그녀가 말했다

Simon drew / the stranger / to the table.
시몬은 끌어당겼다 / 낯선 사람을 / 테이블로

"Take your place, young man," said he.
"앉아요, 젊은이," 그가 말했다

come across 우연히 만나다 perish 죽다 clothe (옷을) 입히다, 주다 edge 끄트머리, 가장자리 droop 아래로 처지다, 수그리다 brows 눈썹 soften 부드러워지다 pour (액체를) 따르다 kvass (호밀로 만든) 러시아의 알코올음료

Simon cut the bread, / crumbled it into the broth, /
시몬은 빵을 잘랐다 / 빵을 부셔서 스프에 넣었다 /

and they began to eat.
그리고 그들은 먹기 시작했다

Matryona sat at the corner of the table /
마트료나는 식탁 모퉁이에 앉아있었다 /

resting her head on her hand / and looking at the stranger.
턱을 손에 괴고 / 그리고 낯선 사람을 쳐다보면서

And Matryona was touched / with pity for the stranger, /
그리고 마트료나는 마음이 뭉클해졌다 / 낯선 사람에 대한 동정심으로 /

and began to feel fond of him.
그러자 그가 마음에 들기 시작했다

And at once the stranger's face lit up.
그리고 즉시 낯선 사람의 얼굴이 밝아졌다

He ceased to frown, / raised his eyes, /
더 이상 인상을 찌푸리지 않았다 / 그는 눈을 들어서 /

and smiled at Matryona.
마트료나에게 미소 지었다

Key Expression

주어 + 동사 + 동사ing; 주어는 ~한다, ~하면서

한 문장에 주어 동사가 나온 다음에 "동사+ing"형태가 오면, "~하면서"라는 의미로 앞에 나온 동사와 동시에 일어나는 사건을 표현한다.

Matryona sat at the corner of the table resting her head on her hand and looking at the stranger.
마트료나는 테이블 코너에 앉아있었다 / 턱을 손에 괴고 / 그리고 낯선 사람을 쳐다보면서

crumple 일그러뜨리다, 구기다 broth 스프, 죽 touch (마음을) 뭉클하게 하다 cease 멈추다, 그만두다

When they had finished supper, /
그들이 저녁 식사를 끝냈을 때 /

the woman cleared away the things /
여인은 상을 치우고 /

and began questioning / the stranger.
질문하기 시작했다 / 낯선 사람에게

"Where are you from?" said she.
"어디서 왔어요?" 그녀가 말했다

"I am not from these parts."
"저는 이 부근 사람은 아닙니다."

"But how did you come to be on the road?"
"그러면 어떻게 길거리에 있었어요?"

"I may not tell."
"말씀드릴 수가 없습니다."

"Did some one rob you?"
"누가 당신을 도둑질했나요?"

"God punished me."
"신이 저에게 벌을 주셨습니다."

"And you were lying there naked?"
"그리고 발가벗고 거기에 누워있었어요?"

"Yes, naked and freezing."
"예, 발가벗고 얼어붙을 듯이 추웠습니다."

Simon saw me / and had pity on me.
시몬이 저를 봤고 / 저를 불쌍하게 생각했죠

He took off his coat, / put it on me / and brought me here.
그가 외투를 벗어서 / 저에게 입히고 / 저를 여기로 데려왔습니다

"And you have fed me, / given me drink, /
"그리고 당신이 저를 먹이고 / 마시게 하고 /

and shown pity on me. God will reward you!"
불쌍히 여겼죠. 신께서 보답하실 것입니다!"

Matryona rose, took / from the window /
마트료나는 일어난 후, 가져왔다 / 창가에서 /

Simon's old shirt / which she had been patching, /
시몬의 낡은 셔츠를 / (그 셔츠를) 그녀가 수선 하고있었던 /

and gave it / to the stranger.
그리고 그것을 줬다 / 낯선 사람에게

---

reward ~에게 보답하다

She also brought out / a pair of trousers / for him.
그녀는 또한 가져왔다 / 한 벌의 바지를 / 그에게

"There," said she, "I see you have no shirt.
"자" 그녀가 말했다. "당신은 셔츠가 없네요.

Put this on, / and lie down / where you please, /
이것을 입어요, / 그리고 누워요 / 눕고 싶은 곳에, /

in the loft or by the oven."
다락방이나 난로 옆에."

The stranger took off the coat, / put on the shirt, /
낯선 사람은 외투를 벗고 / 셔츠를 입었다 /

and lay down in the loft.
그리고 다락방에 누웠다

Matryona put out the candle, / took the coat, /
마트료나는 초를 끄고 / 외투를 가져갔다 /

and lay down / beside her husband.
그리고 누웠다 / 남편 옆에

Matryona drew the skirts of the coat over her /
마트료나는 외투자락을 끌어 당겨서 덮었다 /

and lay down, / but could not sleep.
그리고 누웠다 / 그러나 잘 수가 없었다

She could not get the stranger out of her mind.
그녀는 낯선 청년에 대한 생각을 떨쳐버릴 수 없었다

When she remembered /
그녀는 생각했을 때 /

that he had eaten their last piece of bread /
(무엇을?) 그가 마지막 빵조각을 먹어버린 것을 /

and that there was none for tomorrow, / and thought /
그리고 내일 먹을 빵이 없다는 것을 (생각했을 때) / 그리고 생각했을 때 /

of the shirt and trousers / she had given away, /
셔츠와 바지를 / 그녀가 줘버린 /

she felt grieved. But when she remembered /
그녀는 마음이 아팠다 그러나 그녀가 생각하자 /

how he had smiled, / her heart was glad.
어떻게 그가 미소 지었는지 / 그녀의 마음은 기뻤다

Long did Matryona lie awake, / and she noticed /
오랫동안 마트료나는 깨어 누워있었다 / 그리고 그녀는 눈치 챘다 /

that Simon also was awake. /
시몬도 깨어있다는 것을 /

"Simon!", said she.
"시몬!" 그녀는 말했다

"Well?"
"왜?"

"You have had the last of the bread, /
"너는 마지막 빵조각을 먹어버렸어 /

and there is no flour left / to make bread.
그리고 밀가루가 없어요 / 빵을 만들

I don't know / what we shall do tomorrow.
모르겠어 / 내일 뭘 해야 할지

Perhaps I can borrow / some of neighbor Martha."
아마 빌릴 수 있을 거야 / 이웃에 사는 마사에게"

"If we're alive / we shall find / something to eat."
"우리가 살아남는다면 / 찾을 거야 / 뭔가 먹을 것을"

The woman lay still awhile, / and then said, /
여인은 한동안 계속 누워있었다 / 그리고 나서 말했다 /

"He seems a good man, /
"그는 좋은 사람 같아 /

but why does he not tell us / who he is?"
그런데 왜 말하지 않지 / 자기가 누군지"

"I suppose / he has his reasons."
"내 생각엔 / 그럴 만한 이유가 있는 것 같아"

"Simon!"
"시몬!"

"Well?"
"왜?"

"We give. But why does nobody give us anything?"
"우리는 베풀어. 그런데 왜 아무도 우리에게 베풀지 않지?"

Simon did not know / what to say.
시몬은 할지 몰랐다 / 뭐라 말해야

So he only said, / "Let us stop talking," /
그래서 그저 이렇게 말했다 / "그만 말하고 자요" /

and he turned over and went to sleep.
그리고 그는 등을 돌리고는 잠들었다

---

put out (불을) 끄다 grieved 슬픈, 비탄에 잠긴 borrow ~을 빌리다 neighbor 이웃

Chapter 6

In the morning Simon awoke.
아침에 시몬은 일어났다

The children were still asleep.
아이들은 아직도 자고 있었다

His wife had gone to the neighbor's / to borrow some bread.
그의 아내는 이웃에 갔다 /   빵을 빌리러

The stranger alone was sitting / on the bench, /
낯선 사람은 홀로 앉아있었다 /   긴 의자에 /

dressed in the old shirt and trousers, / and looking upwards.
낡은 셔츠와 바지를 입고 /   그리고 위쪽을 바라보면서

His face was brighter / than it had been the day before.
그의 얼굴은 더 밝았다 /   전날보다

Simon said to him, /
시몬이 그에게 말했다 /

"Well, friend, / the belly wants bread, /
"자, 친구 /   배는 빵을 원해 /

and the naked body clothes. One has to work / for a living.
그리고 벌거벗은 몸은 옷이 필요하지   일해야 해 먹고 /   살려면

What work do you know?"
자네는 무슨 일을 할 줄 알지?"

"I do not know any."
"저는 아무것도 할 줄 몰라요."

Simon was amazed, but he said, /
시몬은 놀랐지만,   그는 말했다 /

"Men who want to learn / can learn anything."
"사람이라면 (어떤 사람?) 배우고 싶은 / 뭐든지 배울 수 있지."

"Men work, and I will work also."
"인간이 일한다면 저도 일할게요."

"What is your name?"
"자네 이름은 뭔가?"

"Michael."
"마이클" ("미하일"로 번역하기도 하지만, 영어 발음에 가까운 마이클로 표기)

"Well, Michael, / if you don't wish to talk /
"좋아, 마이클 /   말하고 싶지 않다면 /

about yourself, / that is your own affair.
자신에 대해 / 그건 자네 마음대로 해(아무래도 좋아)

But you'll have to earn a living for yourself.
그러나 자네는 밥벌이를 해야 해

If you will work as I tell you, /
일한다면 / 내가 말하는 대로 /

I will give you food and shelter."
내가 자네에게 음식과 잘 곳을 주겠네."

"May God reward you!
"신께서 당신에게 보답하시기를!

I will learn. Show me / what to do."
배우겠습니다 저를 가르쳐 주세요 / 어떻게 해야 할지"

Simon took yarn, / put it round his thumb /
시몬은 실을 집었고 / 실을 엄지손가락에 감고 /

and began to twist it.
실을 꼬기 시작했다

"It is easy enough — see!"
"아주 쉬워 − 보라고!"

Michael watched him, /
마이클은 그를 지켜봤다 /

put some yarn round his own thumb / in the same way, /
실을 엄지에 감았다 / 똑같이 /

got the knack, / and twisted the yarn also.
요령을 터득했다 / 그리고 실도 또한 꼬았다

Then Simon showed him / how to wax the thread.
그 다음에 시몬은 그에게 가르쳐줬다 / 실에 왁스칠하는 방법을

This also Michael immediately learned to do.
이것 역시 마이클은 즉시 배웠다

Next Simon showed him / how to twist the bristle in, /
다음에 시몬은 그에게 가르쳐줬다 / 억센 털을 꼬는 법을 /

and how to sew, / and this, too, / Michael learned at once.
그리고 꿰매는 방법을 / 그리고 이것 역시 / 마이클은 금방 배웠다

belly 배 amazed 매우 놀란 Michael 대천사 미가엘(영어 발음에 가깝도록 마이클로 표기)
affair 관심사, 일 shelter 피난처, 은신처 yarn 실 twist (실을) 꼬다 knack 요령, 솜씨 immediately 즉시, 곧
bristle 강모, 억센 털

Whatever Simon showed him / he understood at once, /
시몬이 뭘 가르치든지 /   그는 즉시 이해했다 /

and after three days / he worked /
그리고 3일 뒤에 /   그는 일했다 (어떻게?) /

as if he had sewn boots all his life.
마치 평생 부츠를 꿰매어 온 듯이

He worked without stopping, / and ate little.
그는 쉬지 않고 일했다 /   그리고 조금 먹었다

When work was over / he sat silently, / looking upwards.
일이 끝났을 때 /   그는 조용히 앉아서 /   위쪽을 바라봤다

He hardly went into the street, / spoke /
그는 밖으로 잘 나가지 않았고 /   말했고 /

only when necessary, / and neither joked nor laughed.
필요할 때만 /   그리고 농담하지도 웃지도 않았다

They never saw him smile, / except that first evening /
그들은 보지 못했다 / 그가 웃는 것을 /   첫 번째 저녁을 제외하고는 /

when Matryona gave them supper.
마트료나가 저녁을 주었던

Key Expression !

except; ~을 제외하고

"except"는 전치사로 "but"과 같은 의미로 사용된다.

They never saw him smile, except that first evening when Matryona gave them supper.
그들은 보지 못했다 / 그가 웃는 것을 / 첫 번째 저녁을 제외하고는 / (첫 번째 저녁이란?) 마트료나가 저녁을 주었던

The library is open everyday except Sunday.
도서관은 매일 열려 있다 일요일을 제외하고

sew 꿰매다

Chapter 7

Day by day and week by week / the year went round.
날이 가고 주가 가서 / 해가 바뀌었다

Michael lived and worked / with Simon.
마이클은 살면서 일했다 / 시몬과 같이

His fame spread / till people said /
그의 명성은 퍼져갔다 / 사람들이 말할 정도로 /

that no one sewed boots so neatly and strongly /
(뭐라고?) 어떤 사람도 장화를 깔끔하고 튼튼하게 꿰맬 수 없다고 /

as Simon's apprentice, Michael.
시몬의 견습공인 마이클만큼

And people from all around the area came / to Simon /
그리고 사방에서 사람들이 찾아 왔다 / 시몬을 /

for their boots, / and he began to be well off.
부츠를 고치러 / 그래서 그의 형편은 나아지기 시작했다

One winter day, / as Simon and Michael sat working, /
어느 겨울날 / 시몬과 마이클이 앉아서 일하고 있었을 때 /

a carriage / with three horses and with bells /
마차가 / 세 마리의 말과 종을 단 /

drove up to the hut. They looked out of the window.
오두막으로 왔다. 그들은 창밖을 봤다

The carriage stopped at their door, /
마차는 문 앞에서 멈췄고 /

a fine servant jumped down / from the box /
근사한 하인이 내려온 후 / 마차의 운전석에서 /

and opened the door.
문을 열었다

A gentleman in a fur coat got out / and walked up /
모피 코트를 입은 신사가 나와서 / 걸어왔다 /

to Simon's hut.
시몬의 오두막으로

Matryona hurried to the door, / and opened it wide.
마트료나는 급히 문 쪽으로 가서 / 문을 활짝 열었다

---

fame 명성 apprentice 견습공, 도제 be well off 살기 좋다 carriage 마차 box (마차의) 운전석

The gentleman stooped / to enter the hut, /
그 신사는 몸을 꾸부렸다 / 오두막에 들어가기 위해 /

and when he drew himself up again /
그리고 몸을 다시 폈을 때 /

his head nearly reached the ceiling, /
머리가 천장에 닿을 뻔했다 /

and he seemed quite to fill / his end of the room.
그리고 그는 꽉 채우는 것 같았다 / 방 한쪽을.(그의 몸집은 건장했다)

Simon rose, bowed, / and looked at the gentleman /
시몬은 일어서서 절했다 / 그리고 그 신사를 쳐다봤다 /

with astonishment. He had never seen / any one like him.
놀라서 그는 본 적이 없었다 / 그와 같은 사람을

Simon himself was lean, / Michael was thin, /
시몬은 말랐고 / 마이클은 야위었고 /

and Matryona was dry as a bone, /
그리고 마트료나는 거의 뼈밖에 없었다

but this man seemed to be from a different world.
하지만 이 남자는 다른 세상에서 온 사람 같았다 /

His face was red-faced and full, /
그의 얼굴은 혈색이 좋았고 살집이 있었고, /

and his neck was like a bull's.
목은 황소 같은 목덜미가 있고, /

It seemed as if he were cast in iron.
마치 온 몸이 철로 만든 것처럼 보였다

The gentleman puffed, / threw off his fur coat, /
그 신사는 숨을 헐떡이며 / 모피 코트를 벗고 /

sat down on the bench, / and said, /
긴 의자에 앉았다 / 그리고 말했다 /

"Which of you is the master bootmaker?"
"당신들 중 누가 구둣방 주인이야?"

"I am, your honor," said Simon, / coming forward.
"전데요, 나리," 시몬이 말했다 / 앞으로 나오면서

Then the gentleman shouted / to his lad,
그러자 그 신사는 소리쳤다 / 젊은이에게,

"Hey, Fedka, bring me the leather!"
"야, 페드카, 가죽을 가져와봐!"

The servant ran out / and brought back a parcel.
하인이 달려 나가서 / 꾸러미를 가지고 왔다

52 Tolstoy's Short Stories

The gentleman took the parcel / and put it on the table.
그 신사는 꾸러미를 받아서 / 테이블 위에 올려놨다

"Untie it," said he. The lad untied it.
"풀어 봐," 그가 말했다. 젊은이가 풀었다

The gentleman pointed / to the leather.
그 신사는 가리켰다 / 그 가죽을

"Look here, shoemaker," said he, "do you see this leather?"
"여기를 봐, 구두장이," 그가 말했다. "이 가죽이 보이지?"

"Yes, your honor."
"예, 나리."

"But do you know / what sort of leather it is?"
"그런데 당신은 알아 / 이것이 어떤 가죽인지?"

Simon felt the leather / and said, "It is good leather."
시몬이 가죽을 만져보더니 / 말했다. 좋은 가죽인데요.

"Good, indeed! Why, you fool, you never saw such leather /
"좋다고, 정말! 아, 이 바보야, 자네는 이런 가죽을 보지 못했을 거야 /

before in your life. It's German, and cost twenty roubles."
평생. 독일산이고 20루블짜리야"

Simon was startled, and said, /
시몬은 놀랐다. 그리고 말했다 /

"Where should I ever see / leather like that?"
"어디서 구경할 수 있죠 / 이런 가죽을"

"Well, that's all right. Can you make it into boots for me?"
"그야 당연하지. 이 가죽으로 장화를 만들 수 있어?"

"Yes, your honor, I can."
"예, 나리, 할 수 있습니다."

Then the gentleman shouted at him: / "You can, can you?
그러자 그 신사는 시몬에게 소리쳤다 / "당신이 할 수 있냐고, 할 수 있다는 거지?

Well, remember / whom you are to make them for, /
음, 명심해 / 누구를 위해서 장화를 만드는 것인지 /

and what the leather is.
그리고 어떤 가죽인지도 (명심해)

You must make me boots / that will wear for a year, /
나에게 장화를 만들어 주어야 해 / (그런데 그것은) 1년은 신을 수 있는 /

neither losing shape / nor coming unstitched."
모양이 변하지 않고 / 실밥이 터지지 않는"

stoop 몸을 꾸부리다 with astonishment 놀라서 lean 야윈, 깡마른 cast 틀에 넣어 만들다, 주조하다
puff 숨을 헐떡이다 your honor(지위가 자신보다 높은 사람을 부를 때) 나리 feel 만져보다 startled 깜짝 놀란
wear (신을) 신다 unstitched 실밥이 터지지 않는

"If you can do it, / take the leather / and cut it up.
"당신이 할 수 있다면 / 가죽을 가져다가 / 가죽을 재단해 봐

But if you can't, / say so. I warn you now /
그러나 할 수 없으면 / 그렇다고 말해. 당신한테 경고하는데 /

if your boots become unsewn or lose shape / within a year, /
만약 장화가 실밥이 터지거나 변형되면 / 1년 안에

I will have / you put in prison.
나는 할 거야 / 네가 감옥에 있게(감옥에 처넣을 거야)

If they don't burst or lose shape / for a year /
만일 장화가 터지거나 변형되지 않으면 / 1년 동안에 /

I will pay you ten roubles / for your work."
내가 10루블을 주지 / 품삯으로"

Simon was frightened, / and did not know what to say.
시몬은 놀랐다 / 그리고 몰랐다 / 뭐라고 말해야 할지

He glanced at Michael / and nudging him with his elbow, /
그는 마이클을 흘긋 보았고 / 그리고 팔꿈치로 슬쩍 찔렀다 /

whispered: / "Shall I take the work?"
속삭이면서 / "이 일을 맡을까?"

Michael nodded his head / as if to say, "Yes, take it."
마이클은 고개를 끄덕였다 / 말하듯이 / "예, 합시다." 라고

Simon did / as Michael advised, / and undertook to make
시몬은 했다 / 마이클이 조언한 대로 / 그리고 장화를 만들기로 약속했다 /

boots / that would not lose shape or split / for a whole year.
(어떤 장화?) / 변형되거나 망가지지 않는 / 1년 내내

Calling his servant, / the gentleman told him /
그의 하인을 부르면서 / 그 신사는 그에게 명령했다 /

to pull the boot off / his left leg, / which he stretched out.
장화를 벗기라고 / 왼발에서 / 그리고 나서 왼발을 그는 뻗었다

"Take the measure!" said he. Simon cut off a piece of paper /
"내 (발) 치수를 재시오!" 그는 말했다. 시몬은 종잇조각을 잘랐다 /

seventeen inches long, / smoothed it out, / knelt down, /
17인치 길이로 / (종이의) 주름을 폈고 / 무릎을 꿇고 /

wiped his hand well on his apron /
손을 앞치마에 잘 닦았다 /

so as not to soil the gentleman's sock, /
신사의 양말을 더럽히지 않도록 /

and began to measure.
그리고 치수를 재기 시작했다

He measured the sole, / and round the instep, /
그는 발바닥을 쟀다 /   그리고 발등 주위를 (쟀다) /

and began to measure / the calf of the leg, /
그리고 재기 시작했다 /   종아리치수를 /

but the paper was too short.
그러나 종이 자가 너무 짧았다

The calf of the leg was as thick / as a beam.
다리의 종아리는 굵었다 /   대들보처럼

"Take care. Don't make it too tight / round the calf."
"조심해.   너무 꽉 끼게 해서는 안돼 /   종아리 둘레를"

Simon was going to cut / another piece of paper.
시몬은 자르려던 중이었다 /   다른 종잇조각을

The gentleman sat there, rubbing / his toes together in his
신사는 그곳에 앉아있었다 /   비비면서 /   양말속의 발가락을 서로 /

stocking, / and looking at / the residents of the hut.
        그리고 둘러보았다 /   오두막 안의 사람들을

And he caught sight of Michael.
그리고 마이클이 있는 것을 알아보았다.

"Whom have you there?" asked he.
"거기 있는 사람은 누구요?"   그가 물었다

"That is my workman. He will sew the boots."
"저 사람은 제 직공입니다.   그가 부츠를 꿰맬 것입니다."

"Look here," said the gentleman to Michael, /
"이 봐,"   신사가 마이클에게 말했다 /

"remember / that they are to be made / so as to last a whole
"명심하게 /   장화를 만들어야 한다는 것을 /   내가 1년을 신을 수 있도록"

year." Simon also looked at Michael, / and saw /
    시몬도 마이클을 쳐다봤다 /   그리고 봤다 /

that Michael was not looking at the gentleman,
(무엇을?) 마이클이 신사를 바라보고 있지 않는 것을 /

but was gazing / into the corner behind the gentleman, /
그러나 쳐다보고 있었다 /   신사의 뒤에 있는 방구석을 /

as if he saw some one / there.
마치 누군가를 본 듯이 /   그곳에 있는

---

warn 경고하다 unsewn 실밥이 터지지 않는 glance 힐긋 쳐다보다 nudge 팔꿈치로 찌르다 whisper 속삭이다
advise 조언하다 undertake ~할 약속을 하다 soil 더럽히다 sole 발바닥 instep 발등 calf 종아리 beam 대들보
rub 비비다 resident 사는 사람, 거주자 catch sight of ~을 알아차리다

Michael looked and looked, / and suddenly he smiled, /
마이클은 보고 또 봤다 / 그리고 갑자기 미소 지었다 /

and his face became brighter. "What are you grinning at,
그리고 그의 얼굴은 더 밝아졌다 "뭘 보고 히죽 웃고 있는 거야,

you fool?" thundered the gentleman.
이 멍청아?" 신사가 고함쳤다

"You had better look to it / that the boots are ready / in time."
"신경을 쓰는 게 좋을 거야 / 부츠가 완성되도록 / 제 때"

"They shall be ready in good time," said Michael.
"시간에 맞춰 준비될 것입니다," 마이클이 말했다

"Mind it is so," said the gentleman, /
"그렇게 하도록 주의해," 신사가 말했다 /

and he put on his boots and his fur coat, /
그리고 그는 장화와 모피 코트를 입었다 /

wrapped the latter round him, / and went to the door.
모피로 몸을 감쌌다 / 그리고 문으로 갔다

But he forgot to stoop, / and struck his head against the door
그러나 그는 고개를 숙이는 것을 까먹고 / 머리를 문틀 위에 부딪혔다

frame. He swore / and rubbed his head.
그는 욕을 하고 / 머리를 문질렀다

Then he took his seat in the carriage / and drove away.
그 다음 그는 마차의 좌석에 앉았고 / 떠났다

When he had gone, Simon said, /
그가 갔을 때, 시몬이 말했다 /

"that's a man of high station! You could not kill him /
"그 사람은 지체가 높은 양반이군! 너는 그를 죽일 수는 없어 /

with a mallet. He almost knocked out / the door frame, /
망치로(때려도) 그는 거의 부서지게 할 정도였어 / 문틀을 /

but little harm it did him." And Matryona said:
별로 다치지 않았어." 그리고 마트료나가 말했다

"Living as he does, / it is natural that he should be strong.
"그 양반처럼 산다면 / 당연하지 / 강한 것이

Death itself can't touch / such a rock as that."
죽음조차도 건드릴 수 없어요 / 저렇게 바위처럼 튼튼한 사람은."

---

gaze 응시하다, 지켜보다 grin 히죽 웃다, 벙긋 웃다 thunder 고함치다 look to ~에 주의하다
mind ~에 주의하다, 조심하다 stoop (몸을) 숙이다, 상체를 굽히다 door frame 문틀 swear 욕을 하다
station 지위, 신분 mallet 나무망치 harm 해, 손상

Key Expression

so as not to; ~하지 않도록

"so as to"는 "in order to"와 같은 의미로 "~하기 위하여"라는 뜻이다. 부정의 의미를 표현할때 "not"은 "to" 앞에 온다. 그래서 "so as not to"가 된다.

Simon wiped his hand well on his apron so as not to soil the gentleman's sock, and began to measure.
시몬은 손을 잘 닦았다 / 앞치마에 / 신사의 양말을 더럽히지 않도록 / 그리고 치수를 재기 시작했다.

Quiz 2

A. 내용 이해하기
다음 문장을 읽고 본문의 내용과 맞으면 T(True), 틀리면 F(False)를 쓰세요.

1. Simon couldn't remember where he met the stranger.
2. Matryona pitied the stranger because he wore shabby clothes.
3. When the children was asleep, Matryona went to borrow some bread.
4. Michael's fame spread because no one sewed boots so neatly as he did.

B. 단어
다음 제시된 단어의 설명을 읽고, 어떤 단어의 정의를 설명하는지 아래의 박스에서 찾아 써 보세요.

1. to bend forward and down from the waist
2. to smile widely
3. to push somebody gently with your elbow
4. to make something dirty on the surface
5. to move your fingers over something in order to find out about it
6. to make a candle stop burning
7. a room under a roof; attic
8. to stop something from happening
9. to die
10. to make a liquid flow into a container

---

put out   cease   grin   soil   perish   loft

feel   nudge   stoop   pour

A. 1. F 2. F 3. T 4. T
B. 1. stoop 2. grin 3. nudge 4. soil 5. feel 6. put out 7. loft 8. cease 9. perish 10. pour

C. 직독직해

아래에 제시된 문장을 직독직해로 해석 해보세요.

1. "Look here," said the gentleman to Michael, / "remember / that they are to be made / so as to last a whole year."

   →

2. Calling his servant, / the gentleman told him / to pull the boot off / his left leg, / which he stretched out.

   →

3. His face was red-faced and full, / and his neck was like a bull's. It seemed as if he were cast in iron.

   →

4. When she remembered / that he had eaten their last piece of bread / and that there was none for tomorrow, / and thought / of the shirt and trousers / she had given away, / she felt grieved.

   →

D. 동시통역

아래에 제시된 직독직해를 보고, 영어로 말해보세요.

1. 그가 좋은 사람이라면 / 당신은 말할 수 있겠네요 / 어디서 만났는지 / 저 친구를

   →

2. 그리고 당신이 저를 먹이고 / 마시게 하고 / 불쌍히 여겼어요.

   →

3. 시몬은 일어서서 절했다 / 그리고 그 신사를 쳐다봤디 / 놀라서

   →

4. 그러나 그는 고개를 숙이는 것을 까먹고 / 머리를 문틀 위에 부딪혔다.

   →

Answer

C. 1. 이봐, 신사가 마이클에게 말했다 / 명심하게 / 장화를 만들어야 한다는 것을 / 내가 1년을 신을 수 있도록 2. 그의 하인을 부르면서 / 그 신사는 그에게 명령했다 / 장화를 벗기라고 / 왼발에서 / 그리고 나서 왼발을 그는 뻗었다. 3. 그의 얼굴은 혈색이 좋고 살집이 있었고, / 목은 황소 같은 목덜미가 있고, / 마치 온 몸이 철로 만든 것처럼 보였다. 4. 그녀는 생각했을 때 / (무엇을?) 그가 마지막 빵조각을 먹어버린 것을 / 그리고 내일 먹을 빵이 없다는 것을 (생각했을 때) / 그리고 생각했을 때 / 셔츠와 바지를 / 그녀가 줘버린 / 그녀는 마음이 아팠다

D. 1. If he were all right, / you would say / where you came across / the fellow. 2. And you have fed me, / given me drink, / and shown pity on me. 3. Simon rose, bowed, / and looked at the gentleman / with astonishment. 4. But he forgot to stoop, / and struck his head against the door frame.

Chapter 8

Then Simon said to Michael: /
그러고 나서 시몬은 마이클에게 말했다 /

"Well, we have taken the work, / but we must see /
"자, 우리는 일을 맡았다 / 그러나 조심해야 해 /

we don't get into trouble / over it.
곤경에 빠지지 않도록 / 이 일로

The leather is expensive, / and the gentleman is
가죽은 비싸다 / 그리고 그 신사는 화를 잘 낸다

hot-tempered. We must make no mistakes.
실수는 해서는 안돼

Come, your eye is truer / and your hands have become
자, 네 눈이 나보다 정확하고 / 너의 손이 민첩해졌어 /

nimbler / than mine.
내손보다

So you take this measure / and cut out the boots.
그러니까 이 치수 잰 것(치수본)을 가져가고 / 장화를 재단해

I will finish off / the sewing of the vamps."
나는 끝낼 테니까 / 장화의 윗거죽을 꿰매는 것을"

Michael did / as he was told.
마이클은 했다 / 그가 들은 대로

He took the leather, / spread it out on the table, /
그는 가죽을 가져다가 / 테이블 위에 가죽을 펼쳤고 /

folded it in two, / took a knife and began to cut out.
가죽을 둘로 접어서 / 칼을 쥐고 자르기 시작했다

Matryona came and watched / him cutting, /
마트료나는 와서 봤다 / 그가 자르는 것을 /

and was surprised to see / how he was doing it.
그리고 보고 놀랐다 / 그가 어떻게 하는지

Matryona was accustomed to / seeing boots made, /
마트료나는 익숙해졌다 / 장화를 만드는 일을 구경하는데 /

and she looked and saw /
그리고 그녀는 지켜봤다 /

that Michael was not cutting the leather / for boots, /
(무엇을?) 마이클이 가죽을 자르고 있지 않다는 것을 / 장화를 만들려고 /

but was cutting it round.
그러나 그는 둥그렇게 자르고 있는 것을 (지켜봤다)

She wished to say something, / but she thought to herself: /
그녀는 뭔가 말하고 싶었다 / 그러나 속으로만 생각했다 /

"Perhaps I do not understand /
"어쩌면 나는 이해하지 못하는지도 몰라 /

how gentleman's boots should be made.
어떻게 신사의 장화를 만드는지.

I suppose / Michael knows more about it /
내 생각엔 / 나는 마이클이 더 잘 아는 것 같아 /

—and I won't interfere."
그래서 참견하지 않을 거야"

When Michael had cut up the leather, /
마이클이 가죽을 잘랐을 때 /

he took a thread / and began to sew / not with two ends, /
그는 실을 갖고 / 꿰매기 시작했다 / 양쪽 끝을 함께 꿰매지 않고 /

as boots are sewn, / but with a single end, /
평소에 장화를 꿰매는 것처럼 (양쪽 끝을 꿰매는 방식) / 그러나 한쪽 끝만으로 (꿰맸다) /

as for soft slippers.
부드러운 슬리퍼를 만드는 방식으로

Again Matryona wondered, / but again she did not interrupt.
다시 마트료나는 궁금했지만 / 역시 참견하지는 않았다

Michael sewed on steadily / till noon.
마이클은 계속 꿰맸다 / 오전까지

Then Simon rose for dinner, / looked around, /
시몬이 저녁 먹으려고 자리에서 일어났고 / 주위를 둘러봤다 /

and saw / that Michael had made slippers /
그리고 봤다 / 마이클이 슬리퍼를 만든 것을 /

out of the gentleman's leather.
신사의 가죽으로

"Ah," groaned Simon, and he thought, /
"아" 시몬이 신음했다, 그리고 그는 생각했다 /

"How is it that Michael, / who has been with me /
"어떻게 된 일이지 마이클이 / (어떤 마이클?) 나하고 지냈고 /

a whole year / and never made a mistake / before, /
1년 내내 / 한번도 실수한 적이 없던 / 전에 (마이클이) /

see 조심하다 get into trouble 곤경에 빠지다 hot-tempered 화를 잘 내는 nimble 민첩한 vamp (구두의) 윗가죽 interfere 참견하다 interrupt 참견하다 groan 신음하다

should do such a dreadful thing?
이런 엄청난 일을 저지르다니?

The gentleman ordered / thick-soled boots, /
신사는 주문했다 / 두꺼운 밑창을 댄 장화를 /

but Michael has made / soft single-soled slippers, /
그리고 마이클은 만들었다 / 밑창이 하나밖에 없는 부드러운 슬리퍼를 /

and has wasted the leather.
그래서 가죽을 낭비했다

What am I to say / to the gentleman?
뭐라고 말할까 / 그 신사에게?

I can never replace / leather such as this."
다시 교체할 수가 없는데 / 이런 가죽을"

And he said to Michael, "What are you doing, friend?
그리고 그는 마이클에게 말했다, "뭐하는 거야, 이 사람아

You have ruined me!
자넨 날 망쳐놨어!

You know / the gentleman ordered boots, /
자넨 알잖아 / (무엇을?) 그 신사는 장화를 주문했는데 /

but see what you have made!"
네가 만든 것을 보라고!"

Key Expression

be accustomed to; ~하는데 익숙하다

"be accustomed to" 다음에는 동명사(동사ing)나 명사가 온다. "be used to"는 같은 의미로 사용되지만, 회화에 더 많이 사용한다.

Matryona was accustomed to seeing boots made.
마트료나는 익숙해졌다 / 장화를 만드는 일을 구경하는데

My eyes grew accustomed to the dark. 내 눈은 익숙해졌다 / 어둠에

---

replace 교체하다, 대체하다 ruin 못쓰게 하다, 망치다

He was right in the midst of his talk / with Michael /
그가 이야기하던 중이었다 /　　　　　　　　　　마이클과 /

when a knock came / at the door.
그때 노크소리가 들렸다 /　　문에서

Someone was at the entrance.
누군가 있었다 /　　　입구 쪽에

They looked out of the window.
그들은 창 밖을 봤다

A man had come / on horseback, /
한 남자가 왔다 /　　말을 타고 /

and was fastening his horse.
그리고 말을 묶고 있었다.

They opened the door, / and the servant /
그들은 문을 열었다 /　　　　그리고 하인이 /

who had been with the gentleman / came in.
(어떤 하인?) 그 신사와 함께 왔었던 /　　　들어왔다

"Good day," said he.
"안녕하십니까," 그가 말했다

Good day to you," replied Simon.
"안녕하세요," 　　시몬이 말했다

"What can we do for you?"
"뭘 도와드릴까요?"

"My mistress has sent me / about the boots."
"우리 마님이 저를 보내셨어요 /　장화 때문에"

"What about the boots?"
"장화 때문이라고요?"

"It is this. My master no longer needs them. He is dead."
"무슨 말이냐 하면요. 우리 주인님이 더 이상 장화가 필요없게 되었어요. 돌아가셨거든요."

"Is it possible?"
"그럴 리가?"

"He did not live to get home / after leaving you, /
"주인님은 살아서 집에 도착하지 못했어요 /　이곳을 떠나고 /

but died in the carriage.
마차 안에서 돌아가셨어요

When we reached home / and the servants came /
우리가 집에 도착했고 /　　　하인들이 왔을 때 /

---

in the midst of ~하는 도중에, ~이 한창 진행되는 가운데　entrance (건물의) 입구　fasten 묶다, 조이다　reply 대답하다　mistress 마님, 여주인

to help / him alight from the carriage, /
(왜?) 도와주려고 / (무엇을?) 주인님이 마차에서 내리는 것을 /

he rolled over / like a sack.
주인님은 굴러 떨어지셨어요 / 자루처럼

He was dead already, / and so stiff /
주인님은 이미 돌아가셨어요, /　　　게다가 몸이 너무 뻣뻣해져서 /

that they could hardly get him out of the carriage.
하인들은 마차에서 꺼내기 힘들 정도였어요

My mistress sent me here, / saying:
우리 마님이 저를 이리로 보냈어요, /　　　그리고 이렇게 말씀하셨어요 /

'Tell the bootmaker / that the gentleman /
　구두장이한테 말해라 /　　　신사는 /

who ordered boots of him and left the leather for them /
(어떤 신사?) 장화를 주문하고 가죽을 주었던(신사는) /

no longer needs the boots, /
더 이상 장화가 필요 없다고 /

but that he must quickly make soft slippers / for the corpse.
그러나 구두장이는 부드러운 슬리퍼를 빨리 만들어야 한다고(말해라) /　　시신에 신길 수 있는

Wait / till they are ready, / and bring them back with you.'
기다려라 / 슬리퍼가 완성될 때까지 /　　　가져와라

That is why I have come."
이래서 제가 온 거예요."

Michael gathered up / the remnants of the leather, /
마이클은 모았다 /　　　자투리 가죽 조각을 /

rolled them up, took the soft slippers / he had made, /
조각들을 말았고,　　부드러운 슬리퍼를 집어 들었다 /　　자기가 만든 /

slapped them together, / wiped them down with his apron, /
(그리고) 슬리퍼를 함께 탁탁 쳤고 /　　슬리퍼를 앞치마로 닦았다 /

and handed / them and the roll of leather / to the servant, /
그리고 건네주었다 / 슬리퍼와 가죽 말은 것을 /　　　하인에게 /

who took them and said: /
그러자 그 하인은 받으면서 말했다 /

"Good-bye, masters, / and good day to you!"
"안녕히 계세요, 주인장, /　　　그리고 이만 가보겠습니다!"

---

alight (마차에서) 내리다, 하차하다　sack 자루　stiff 뻣뻣한　corpse 시체　remnant 자투리, 나머지　slap 탁치다,
철썩 때리다　wipe 닦다, 훔치다　roll (종이, 돗자리) 둥글게 말아 놓은 것, 두루마리

Tolstoy's Short Stories

Chapter 9

Another year passed, / and another, /
또 한 해가 지났고 /   그리고 또 1년이(지나갔다) /

and Michael was now living his sixth year / with Simon.
그리고 마이클은 이제 함께 6년을 살고 있다 /   시몬과

He lived as before.
그는 예전처럼 살았다.

He went nowhere, / only spoke / when necessary, /
그는 다른 데는 가지 않았고 /   오직 말했다 /   필요할 때만 /

and had only smiled twice / in all those years /
그리고 딱 두 번 미소 지었다 /   그 동안에 (6년 내내) /

—once when Matryona gave him food,
한 번은 마트료나가 그에게 음식을 줬을 때 /

and a second time when the gentleman was in their hut.
그리고 두 번째는 신사가 오두막에 왔을 때

Simon was more than pleased / with his apprentice.
시몬은 대단히 대견스러웠다 /   자신의 제자가

He never now asked him / where he came from,
그는 이제 묻지 않았다 /   어디서 마이클이 왔는지 /

and only feared / lest Michael should go away.
두려워 할 뿐이었다 /   그저 떠나면 안 되니까

They were all at home / one day.
집에 모두 있었다 /   어느 날

Matryona was putting iron pots / on the oven.
마트료나는 쇠로 만든 냄비를 올려놓고 있었다 /   난로 위에

The children were running along the benches /
아이들은 긴 의자 주위를 뛰어다니면서 /

and looking out of the window.
창밖을 보고 있었다

Simon was sewing / at one window, /
시몬은 꿰매고 있었다 /   한쪽 창가에서 /

and Michael was fastening / on a heel / at the other.
그리고 마이클은 조이고 있었다 /   신발의 굽을 /   다른 쪽 창가에서

---

more than 대단히, 매우 apprentice 견습공, 도제 lest ~should ~하지 않도록, ~하면 안 되니까 heel 뒤꿈치

One of the boys ran / along the bench to Michael, /
한 소년이 뛰어 갔다 / 긴 의자를 따라 마이클에게 /

leaned on his shoulder, / and looked out of the window.
마이클의 어깨에 기대었다 / 그리고 창밖을 봤다

"Look, Uncle Michael! There is a lady / with little girls!
"마이클 삼촌, 봐! 아주머니가 있어요 / 어린 소녀들과 함께 오는!

She seems to be coming here. And one of the girls is lame."
이리로 오고 있는 것 같은데. 그리고 한 명은 절뚝거려."

When the boy said that, / Michael dropped his work, /
소년이 그렇게 말했을 때 / 마이클은 하던 일에서 손을 놓았고 /

turned to the window, / and looked out into the street.
창쪽으로 몸을 돌렸고 / 그리고 거리를 내다보았다.

Simon was surprised. Michael never used to look out /
시몬은 놀랐다. 마이클은 내다본 적이 없었다 /

into the street, / but now he pressed against the window, /
거리를 / 그러나 지금은 그는 창문을 밀쳤다 /

staring at something.
뭔가를 응시하면서

Simon also looked out, / and saw /
시몬도 밖을 봤다 / 그리고 봤다 /

that a well-dressed woman was really coming /
(무엇을?) 잘 차려입은 여인이 진짜로 오고 있는 것을 /

to his hut, / leading by the hand / two little girls /
그의 오두막으로 / (또한) 손잡고 데려오고 있었다 / 두 명의 어린 소녀를 /

in fur coats.
모피 외투를 입고 있는

The little girls looked so much alike / that it was hard /
두 여자아이는 너무 닮았다 / 그래서 어려웠다 /

to tell them apart, / except that one of them was crippled /
그들을 구별하는 것은 / (제외하고는) 한 소녀가 불구였고 /

in her left leg / and walked with a limp.
왼쪽 다리가 / 절뚝거리며 걷고 있는 것을 (제외하고는)

The woman stepped into the porch / and entered the entry.
여인은 현관에 들어왔다 / 그리고 입구로 들어왔다.

Feeling about for the entrance, / she found the latch, /
그녀는 입구를 더듬어서 / 그녀는 문고리를 발견했고 /

which she lifted, / and opened the door.
그리고 그 문고리를 들어올리고 / 문을 열었다

Tolstoy's Short Stories

She let the two girls go in / first, /
그녀는 두 소녀를 들어가게 했다 /　　　　먼저 /

and followed them into the hut.
그리고 그들을 따라 오두막으로 들어왔다

"How do you do, friends!"
"안녕하세요,　　　　여러분!"

"Please come in," said Simon.
"어서 들어오세요,"　　시몬이 말했다.

"What can we do for you?"
"뭘 도와드릴까요?"

Key Expression

more than; 매우, 대단히

"more than"은 비교하는 문장에 사용되면, "~보다 더"라는 의미이고, 부사나 형용사에 앞에서 그들을 수식하면, "매우, 대단히"라는 의미로 사용된다.

Simon was more than pleased with his apprentice.
시몬은 대단히 대견스러웠다 / 자신의 제자가
I was more than happy to hear the news.
나는 매우 기뻤다 / 그 소식을 들어서

---

lean 기대다　lame 절름발이의, 절뚝거리는　stare 응시하다　except ~을 제외하고　crippled 절름발이의, 다리를 저는　limp (다리를) 절름거림, 절뚝거림　porch 현관　entry 입구　feel 더듬다　latch 문고리

The woman sat down / by the table.
그 여인은 앉았다 / 테이블 곁에

The two little girls pressed close / to her knees, /
두 어린 소녀들은 바싹 붙었다 / 그 여인의 무릎에 /

afraid of the people / in the hut.
사람들을 두려워했기 때문에 / 오두막에 있던

"I want / leather shoes made / for these two little girls /
"나는 원해요 / 가죽신발을 만들길 / 이 어린 소녀들을 위해 /

for spring."
봄에 신을"

"We can do that. We don't generally make /
"만들어 드릴 수 있습니다. 저희는 보통 만들지 않아요 /

such small shoes, / but we can make them.
그렇게 작은 신발을 / 그렇지만 만들 수는 있지요

My man, Michael, is a master / at the work."
제 직공, 마이클은 대가입니다 / 그런 일에는"

Simon glanced at Michael / and saw /
시몬은 마이클을 흘긋 봤다 / 그리고 봤다 /

that he had left his work / and was sitting /
그는 하던 일은 내려놓고 / 그리고 앉아있는 것을 (봤다) /

with his eyes fixed / on the little girls.
그의 시선을 고정한 채로 / 어린 소녀에게(소녀를 쳐다보면서)

Simon was surprised.
시몬은 놀랐다

To be sure / they were pretty and plump girls.
분명히 / 그들은 예쁘고 토실토실한 소녀였다

They had dark eyes and rosy cheeks.
그들의 눈은 검고 뺨이 붉었다

And they wore nice kerchiefs and fur coats, /
그리고 질 좋은 스카프를 하고 모피 외투를 입고 있었다 /

but still Simon could not understand /
그러나 여전히 시몬은 이해할 수 없었다 /

why Michael should look at them / like that, /
왜 마이클이 아이들을 쳐다보는지 / 그런 식으로 /

just as if he had known them before.
마치 그가 전부터 아이들을 알고 있었다는 듯이

He was puzzled, / but went on talkintg with the woman, /
그는 혼란스러웠다 / 그러나 여인과 계속 이야기했다 /

and arranging the price.
그리고 가격을 조정했다

Having fixed it, / he began to take the measures.
가격을 정한 다음에 / 그는 치수를 재기 시작했다

The woman lifted / the lame girl on to her lap / and said: /
여인은 들어올렸다 / 절름발이 소녀를 무릎 위에 / 그리고 말했다 /

"Take two measures from this little girl.
"두 아이의 치수를 재 주세요 / 이 아이로

Make one shoe / for the lame foot /
신발을 한 개 만들고 / 절름발에는 /

and three / for the sound one.
신발을 세 개 만들어주세요 / 정상인 발에 맞는

They both have the same size feet. They are twins."
이 아이들은 신발 사이즈가 똑같아요. 쌍둥이니까요"

Simon took the measure / and, speaking of the lame girl, /
시몬은 치수를 쟀고 / 절름발이 소녀에 대해 말하면서 /

said: / "How did it happen to her?
다음과 같이 말했다 / "어쩌다가 이렇게 되었어요?

She is such a pretty girl. Was she born so?"
애는 참 예쁜 아이네요. 태어날 때부터 장애였나요?"

"No, her mother crushed her leg."
"아니요, 저 애의 엄마가 다리를 눌러 부러뜨렸어요."

Then Matryona joined in.
그러자 마트료나가 끼어들었다.

She wondered / who this woman was, /
그녀는 궁금했다 / 이 여인이 누군지 /

and whose the children were, / so she said: /
그리고 누구의 아이들인지 / 그래서 그녀가 말했다 /

"Are not you their mother then?"
"그러면 당신은 애들 엄마가 아닌가요?"

"No, my good woman.
"아니요, 아주머니

I am neither their mother / nor related to them.
저는 애들 엄마도 아니고 / 친척도 아니에요

They were quite strangers to me, / but I adopted them."
애들은 완전히 남이었는데 / 제가 입양했어요."

master 대가, 명인 glance 힐끗 보다 plump 토실토실한 kerchief 스카프 puzzled 혼란스런, 당황한 arrange ~
을 조정하다 crush 눌러 부러뜨리다 join in 끼어들다, 참여하다 related 친척의, 혈연의 adopt 입양하다

"Even if they are not your children, /
"비록 애들이 당신 아이들이 아니지만 /

you take good care of them."
당신은 그 애들을 돌보네요."

"Why shouldn't I take good care of them?
"어떻게 돌보지 않을 수가 있나요?

I fed them both / at my own breasts.
제가 둘 다 제 젖을 먹였지요 / 제 젖으로

I had a child of my own, / but God took him.
저는 제 자식이 하나 있었지요, / 하지만 신께서 데려가셨어요

I was not so fond of him / as I now am of them."
제 아이를 사랑하진 못 했어요 / 지금 이 아이들을 사랑하는 만큼"

"Then whose children / are they?"
"그러면 누구 아이예요 / 이 아이들은?"

Key Expression

연속되는 사건을 표현하는 분사 구문

가격을 정한 사건이 일어난 다음에 그가 치수를 재는 사건이 발생한다. 두 사건이 연속적으로 일어나는 경우엔, "가격을 정한 후에, 그는 ~했다"라고 해석한다.

Having fixed the price, he began to take the measures.
가격을 정했고, (누구일까?) 그가 치수를 재기 시작했다

take good care of ~를 잘 보살피다

Quiz 3

A. 내용 이해하기

다음 문장을 읽고 본문의 내용과 맞으면 T(True), 틀리면 F(False)를 쓰세요.

1. Michael made soft leather slippers rather than thick leather boots.
2. It was too late for Simon to ask why Michael would do such a foolish things.
3. A messenger changed the order to slippers because his mistress wanted to wear them.
4. Simon was grateful for Michael's faithful assistance.

B. 단어

다음 제시된 단어의 설명을 읽고, 어떤 단어의 정의를 설명하는지 아래의 박스에서 찾아 써 보세요.

1. able to move quickly with light neat movements; deft
2. to voice a deep inarticulate sound because you are in pain or disappointed
3. to make someone lose all their money; to destroy totally
4. to attach something firmly to something else
5. to set down from a carriage; dismount
6. a dead body of a human
7. one who works for an employer in order to learn the skills needed in their trade or occupation
8. unable to walk properly because someone's legs are injured
9. to look at something for a long time
10. to take somebody else's child in your family and legally become its parent

---

adopt fasten crippled apprentice alight groan
stare ruin corpse nimble

Answer
A. 1. T 2. T 3. F 4. T
B. 1. nimble 2. groan 3. ruin 4. fasten 5. alight 6. corpse 7. apprentice 8. crippled 9. stare 10. adopt

C. 직독직해

아래에 제시된 문장을 직독직해로 해석해보세요.

1. Matryona came and watched / him cutting, / and was surprised to see / how he was doing it.

   →

2. How is it that Michael, / who has been with me / a whole year / and never made a mistake / before, / should do such a dreadful thing?

   →

3. Tell the bootmaker / that the gentleman / who ordered boots of him and left the leather for them / no longer needs the boots.

   →

4. Simon glanced at Michael and saw that he had left his work and was sitting with his eyes fixed on the little girls.

   →

D. 동시통역

아래에 제시된 직독직해를 보고, 영어로 말해보세요.

1. 우리는 일을 맡았다 / 그러나 조심해야 해 / 곤경에 빠지지 않도록 / 이 일로

   →

2. 주인님은 살아서 집에 도착하지 못했어요 / 이곳을 떠나고 / 마차 안에서 돌아가셨어요.

   →

3. 나는 원해요 / 가죽신발을 만들길 / 이 어린 소녀들을 위해 / 봄에 신을.

   →

4. 그들은 문을 열었다 / 그리고 하인이 / (어떤 하인?) 그 신사와 함께 왔었던 / 들어왔다.

   →

Answer

C. 1. 마트로나는 와서 봤다 / 그가 자르는 것을 / 그리고 보고 놀랐다 / 그가 어떻게 하는지
2. 어떻게 된 일이지 마이클이 / (어떤 마이클?)나하고 지냈고 / 1년 내내 / 한번도 실수한 적이 없던 / 전에 (마이클이) / 이런 엄청난 일을 저지르다니? 3. 구두장이한테 말해라 / 신사는 / (어떤 신사?) 장화를 주문하고 가죽을 주었던(신사는) / 더 이상 장화가 필요 없다고 4. 시몬은 마이클을 흘긋 봤다 / 그리고 봤다 / 그는 하던 일은 내려놓고 / 그리고 앉아있는 것을 (봤다) / 그의 시선을 고정한 채로 / 어린 소녀에게(소녀를 쳐다보면서)
D. 1. We have taken the work, / but we must see / we don't get into trouble / over it.
2. He did not live to get home / after leaving you, / but died in the carriage.
3. I want / leather shoes made / for these two little girls / for spring.
4. They opened the door, / and the servant / who had been with the gentleman / came in.

Chapter 10

The woman became confidential /
그 여인은 마음을 터놓게 되었다 /

and told them the whole story.
그래서 모든 이야기를 했다

"It is about six years / since their parents died, /
"약 6년이 되었어요 /   아이들 부모가 죽은 지 /

both in one week. Their father was buried on the Tuesday, /
둘 다 일주일 만에   애들 아빠는 화요일에 묻혔고 /

and their mother died on the Friday.
그리고 애들 엄마는 금요일에 죽었어요

These orphans were born / three days after their father's
이 고아들은 태어났어요 /   아빠가 죽고 나서 3일 후에 /

death, / and their mother did not live / another day.
   그리고 애들 엄마는 (애 낳고) 살지 못했어요 /   하루도 더

My husband and I were then living /
제 남편과 저는 그 당시 살고 있었어요 /

as peasants in the village.
소작농으로 마을에서

We were neighbors of theirs, / our yard being next to theirs.
저희는 그 사람들의 이웃이었지요, /   저희 땅이 애들 부모 땅 옆에 있었지요

Their father was a lonely man, / a wood-cutter in the forest.
애들 아빠는 고독한 사람이었어요 /   숲에서 나무를 베는 사람이었지요

One day a tree fell on him.
어느 날 나무가 그를 덮쳤어요

It fell across his body / and crushed his bowels out.
나무가 그의 몸에 걸쳐서 쓰러졌고 /   나무에 눌려 내장이 튀어나왔어요

As soon as they got him home, / his soul went to God.
사람들이 그를 집으로 데려가자마자 /   그의 영혼은 신에게 가버렸어요

And that same week / his wife gave birth / to twins
그리고 같은 주에 /   그의 아내가 낳았어요 /   쌍둥이를,

—these little girls. They were poor and alone, /
여기 있는 소녀들.   그들은 가난했고 외로웠어요 /

no one to take care of them, / either grandmother or sister.
그들을 보살펴줄 사람이 아무도 없이 /   할머니나 누이도 없이

Alone she gave them birth, / and alone she met her death."
혼자서 그녀는 애들을 낳고 / 홀로 죽음을 맞이했어요."

"The next morning I went to see her, /
"다음날 아침 저는 그녀를 보러 갔었어요 /

but when I entered the hut, / she, poor thing, was already
그런데 오두막에 들어갔을 때 / 그녀는 가엽게도 이미 죽었고 차가웠어요

dead and cold. In dying she had rolled on /
죽으면서 그녀는 굴렀고 /

to this child / and crushed her leg.
이 아이 쪽으로 / 위로 한쪽 다리를 뭉갰어요

The village folk came to the hut, / washed the body, /
마을 사람들이 오두막으로 와서 / 시체를 닦고 /

laid her out, / made a coffin, / and buried her.
입관 준비를 하고 / 관을 짜고 / 그리고 그녀를 매장했어요

They were good folk. The babies were left alone.
마을 사람들이 좋은 사람들이었어요. 애기들이 홀로 남았지요

What was to be done with them?
아이들을 어떻게 해야 했을까요?

I was the only woman / there / who had a baby at the time.
제가 유일한 여자였어요 / 그 마을에서 / 그 당시 아기가 있던

I was nursing my first-born, eight weeks old.
저는 8주된 첫 아이에게 젖을 먹이고 있었어요

So I took them / for a time.
그래서 제가 이 아이들을 맡았어요 / 당분간

The peasants came together, / and thought and thought /
소작농들이 함께 왔어요 / 그리고 궁리하고 궁리했어요 /

what to do with them. And at last they said to me: /
아이들을 어떻게 할지 / 그리고 마침내 저에게 이렇게 말했어요 /

'For the present, Mary, / you had better keep the girls, /
'당분간, 마리 / 당신이 아이들을 맡는 게 좋겠소 /

and later on we will arrange / what to do for them.'
그리고 나중에 우리들이 준비하겠소 / 애들을 어떻게 할지'

So I nursed the sound one at my breast, /
그래서 저는 정상인 아이에게 젖을 먹였어요 /

but at first I did not feed / this crippled one.
그러나 처음에는 젖을 주지 않았어요 / 절름발이 아이에게는

confidential 마음을 털어놓는, 비밀을 털어놓는 bury (시체를) 매장하다 orphan 고아 peasant 소작농 lonely 고독한, 외로운 bowel 내장 coffin 관 nurse (아이에게) 젖을 먹이다, 돌보다 take 받아들이다, 맡다 for the present 현재로서는, 당분간 arrange 마련하다, 준비하다 sound 정상인 crippled 절름발이의

75

I did not suppose / she would live.
생각하지 않았어요 / 그 아이가 살 것이라고는.

But then I thought to myself, /
그러나 그때 저는 혼자 생각했어요 /

why should the poor innocent suffer?
왜 불쌍하고 순진한 사람이 고통 받아야지?

I pitied her, / and began to feed her.
저는 그 아이를 동정했고 / 젖을 주기 시작했어요

And so I fed / my own boy and these two /
그리고 젖을 주었어요 / 제 아들과 이 두 아이들에게 /

— the three of them — at my own breast.
모두 셋에게   내 젖으로 (키웠어요)

I was young and strong, / and had good food, /
저는 젊었고 건강했었어요 / 그리고 좋은 음식을 먹었어요 /

and God gave me so much milk /
그리고 신은 저에게 너무나 많은 모유를 주셔서 /

that at times it even overflowed.
때때로 젖이 넘쳐 흐르기까지 했어요

I used sometimes to feed / two at a time, /
저는 어떤 때는 먹이곤 했지요 / 두 아이를 동시에 /

while the third was waiting.
셋째가 기다리는 동안.

When one had enough / I nursed the third.
하나가 충분히 먹었을 때 / 저는 셋째에게 젖을 먹였어요

And God so ordered it that /
그리고 신은 이렇게 명령했어요 /

these grew up, / while my own was buried /
이 아이들이 성장하라고 / 제가 낳은 아들은 (죽어서) 매장되었지만 /

before he was two years old.
두 살이 되기도 전에

And I had no more children, / though we prospered.
그리고 저는 더 이상 아이가 없었어요 / 저희는 잘 살았지만

Now my husband is working / for the corn merchant /
현재 제 남편은 일하고 있어요 / 옥수수 장사꾼으로 /

at the mill. The pay is good, / and we are well off.
방앗간에서   월급도 많고 /   저희는 잘 살아요

But I have no children of my own, /
그러나 저는 제 아이가 없어요 /

76 Tolstoy's Short Stories

and how lonely I should be / without these little girls!
그래서 얼마나 외롭겠어요 / 이 아이들이 없다면

I can't help loving them! They are the joy of my life!"
이 아이들을 예뻐할 수밖에 없지요! 애들은 제 인생의 기쁨이에요!"

She pressed the lame little girl to her / with one hand, /
그녀는 절름발이 소녀를 끌어안았다 / 한 손으로 /

while with the other she wiped / the tears from her cheeks.
다른 한 손으로는 닦으면서 / 뺨에서 흐르는 눈물을

And Matryona sighed, and said: /
그리고 마트료나가 한숨을 쉬고 말했다 /

"The proverb is true that says, /
"속담이 맞네요(다음과 같이 말하는) /

'One may live / without father or mother, /
'인간은 살 수 있다 / 아버지나 어머니가 없어도 /

but one cannot live without God.'"
그러나 신 없이는 살 수 없다.'"

So they talked together, /
그래서 그들은 함께 얘기했다 /

when suddenly the whole hut was lighted up /
그때 갑자기 오두막 전체가 밝아졌다 /

as though by summer lightning /
마치 여름날의 번개가 비추는 것처럼 /

from the corner where Michael sat.
마이클이 앉은 방구석에서.

They all looked towards him / and saw him sitting, /
그들 모두는 쳐다보았고 / 마이클이 있는 쪽을 / 그가 앉아있는 것을 봤다 /

his hands folded on his knees, /
그의 손은 무릎 위에 포개어져 있었다 /

gazing upwards and smiling.
위쪽을 응시하면서 미소를 짓고 있을 때

---

suppose ~라고 믿다, 생각하다 innocent 순진한 pity ~을 동정하다, 불쌍히 여기다 overflow 넘쳐흐르다 used to (과거 습관) ~하곤 했다 have enough 충분히(배불리) 먹다 prosper 잘살다, 번영하다 merchant 상인, 장사꾼 mill 방앗간 joy 기쁨 sigh 한숨을 쉬다 proverb 속담, 격언 light up 밝게 빛나다 fold 접다, 접어 포개다 gaze 응시하다 바라보다

77

Chapter 11

The woman went away / with the girls.
그 여인은 떠났다 / 소녀들을 데리고

Michael rose from the bench, / put down his work, /
마이클은 긴 의자에서 일어나 / 일감을 내려놓고 /

and took off his apron.
그리고 앞치마를 벗었다

Then, bowing low to Simon and his wife, he said: /
그 다음에 시몬과 아내에게 낮게 절하면서, 그는 말했다 /

"Farewell, masters. God has forgiven me.
"주인님, 안녕히 계세요. 신께서 저를 용서하셨습니다

I ask your forgiveness, too, / for anything done wrong."
저를 용서해주세요, 또한 / 잘못한 것에 대해서도"

And they saw / that a light shone / from Michael.
그리고 그들은 봤다 / 한 줄기 빛이 빛나는 것을 / 마이클로부터.

And Simon rose, bowed down to Michael, and said, /
그리고 시몬은 일어서고, 마이클에게 절을 했다, 그리고 말했다 /

"I see, Michael, / that you are no common man.
"나는 알아, 마이클, / 네가 보통 사람이 아니라는 것을

And I can neither keep you nor question you.
그리고 나는 너를 붙잡을 수도 질문할 수도 없어

Only tell me this: / how is it that /
이것만은 말해줘 / 어째서 /

when I found you and brought you home, /
내가 자네를 발견하고 집으로 데려왔을 때, /

you were gloomy, / and when my wife gave you food /
너는 우울했었지 / 그리고 내 아내가 너에게 음식을 줬을 때 /

you smiled at her and became brighter?
너는 미소를 지었고 밝아졌지?

Then when the gentleman came / to order the boots, /
그런 다음에 신사가 왔을 때 / 장화를 주문하려고 /

you smiled again / and became brighter still?
너는 다시 미소 지었고 / 또 밝아졌는지

And now, when this woman brought the little girls, /
그리고 지금 이 여인이 어린 소녀들을 데려왔을 때 /

you smiled a third time, /
너는 세 번째로 미소 지었어 /

and have become as bright as day?
그리고 대낮처럼 밝아졌어?

Tell me, Michael, / why does your face shine so, /
마이클, 말해 줘 / 왜 네 얼굴이 그렇게 밝은지 /

and why did you smile those three times?"
그리고 왜 이렇게 세 번 미소 지었는지"

And Michael answered, /
그리고 마이클은 대답했다 /

"Light shines from me / because I have been punished, /
"저에게서 빛나는 것입니다 / 제가 벌을 받았기 때문에 /

but now God has pardoned me.
그러나 이제는 신께서 저를 용서하셨어요

And I smiled three times, / because God sent me /
그리고 제가 세 번 미소 지었습니다 / 왜냐하면 신께서 저를 보내셨기 때문입니다 /

to learn three truths, / and I have learned them.
세 가지 진리를 배우라고 / 그리고 제가 그것을 배웠어요

One I learned / when your wife pitied me, /
한 가지 진리를 배웠습니다 / 아주머니가 저를 동정했을 때 /

and that is why I smiled / the first time.
그래서 제가 미소 지은 것입니다 / 첫 번째로

The second I learned / when the rich man ordered the boots, /
두 번째 진리를 제가 배웠습니다 / 부자가 부츠를 주문했을 때 /

and then I smiled again.
그래서 다시 저는 미소 지었습니다.

And now, when I saw / those little girls, /
그리고 지금은 제가 봤을 때 / 그 어린 소녀들을 /

I learn the third and last truth, /
끝으로 세 번째 마지막 진리를 배웠습니다 /

and I smiled the third time."
그래서 세 번째로 미소 지었습니다."

And Simon said, /
그리고 시몬이 말했다 /

"Tell me, Michael, what did God punish you for?
"마이클 말해줘, 왜 신께서 너를 벌하셨는지?

forgive ~을 용서하다 forgiveness 용서 gloomy 우울한 order 주문하다 pardon ~을 용서하다, 사면하다 pity 동정하다, 불쌍히 여기다

and what were the three truths?"
그리고 세 개의 진리가 뭐였지?"

And Michael answered, /
그러자 마이클이 대답했다 /

"God punished me / for disobeying Him.
"신께서는 저를 벌하셨어요 / 신에게 불복종했기 때문에

I was an angel in heaven / and disobeyed God.
저는 천국에서 천사였고 / 신을 불복종했어요.

God sent me / to fetch a woman's soul."
신께서 저를 보내셨지요 / 한 여인의 영혼을 데리고 오라고"

Key Expression

How is it that; 어째서(왜) ~한 거야?

"how is it that"라는 표현 중에 "how"가 핵심단어이며, "is it that"은 "how"를 강조할 뿐이다. 즉 어째서(how) "that" 이하의 사건이 발생했는지 물어볼 때, 그 사건이 발생한 원인이나 이유를 강조하기 위하여 "is it that"을 사용한 것이다.

how is it that when I found you and brought you home, you were gloomy?
어째서 / 내가 자네를 발견하고 집으로 데려왔을 때 / 너는 우울해 했는지

truth 진리, 진실 disobey 불복종하다 fetch 데리고 오다

"I flew to earth, and saw / a sick woman lying alone, /
"저는 지구로 날아가서 보았어요 / 혼자 누워있는 병든 여인을 /

who had just given birth to twin girls.
(그 여인은) 쌍둥이 여자 아이들을 방금 낳았어요

They moved feebly / at their mother's side, /
아이들은 힘없이 움직였어요 / 엄마 옆에서 /

but she could not lift them / to her breast.
그러나 그녀는 아기들을 들어올릴 수 없었어요 / 가슴으로

When she saw me, / she understood /
그녀가 저를 봤을 때 / 그녀는 알았어요 /

that God had sent me / for her soul, /
신이 절 보내신 것을 / 그녀의 영혼을 데리고 오라고 /

and she wept and said, /
그리고 그녀는 울면서 말했어요 /

'Angel of God! My husband has just been buried, /
'신의 천사이시여! 제 남편은 막 매장됐어요, /

killed by a falling tree.
쓰러지는 나무에 깔려죽어서

I have neither sister, nor aunt, nor mother: /
저는 여동생도 숙모도 엄마도 없어요 /

no one to care / for my orphans.
돌볼 사람이 없어요 / 제 고아를

Do not take my soul!
제 영혼을 가져가지 마세요!

Let me / nurse my babes, feed them, /
저를 허락해주세요 / 내 아기들을 젖을 먹여 키우고 먹이도록 /

and set them on their feet / before I die,
그래서 아기들이 걸을 수 있게 (해주세요.) / 제가 죽기 전에

Children cannot live / without father or mother.'
아이들은 살 수 없어요 / 엄마나 아빠 없이'

And I listened to / the mother's request.
그리고 저는 귀를 기울였어요 / 그 어머니의 요청에

I placed / one child at her breast / and laid /
저는 놓았어요 / 한 아이를 그녀의 가슴에 / 그리고 놓았어요 /

the other in her arms, / and returned to the Lord in heaven.
또 한 아이는 팔에 / 그리고 돌아갔지요 / 천국에 계신 주님에게로

feebly 힘없이, 약하게 lift 들어올리다 orphan 고아 nurse 젖을 먹이다, 키우다 request 요청, 요구
place ~을 놓다

I flew to the Lord, and said, /
저는 주님에게 날아가서 말씀 드렸어요 /

'I could not take / the soul of the mother.
'저는 가져올 수 없었습니다 / 그 엄마의 영혼을

Her husband was killed by a tree.
그녀의 남편은 나무에 깔려 죽었습니다

The woman has twins, / and prays /
그 여인은 쌍둥이가 있어요 / 그리고 기도했습니다 /

that her soul may not be taken.
영혼을 데려가지 말라고

She says to me: / 'Let me / nurse and feed my children, /
그녀가 나에게 말했어요 / '허락해주세요 / 아이들을 키우고 먹이도록 /

and set them on their feet.
그리고 아이들이 걸을 수 있도록 (허락 해주세요.)

Children cannot live / without father or mother.'
아이들은 살 수 없어요 / 아빠나 엄마 없이'

I have not taken her soul.
저는 그녀의 영혼을 가져올 수 없었습니다

And God said: / 'Go and take the mother's soul, /
그러자 신께서 말씀하시길 / '가서 그 엄마의 영혼을 데려와라 /

and learn three truths. Learn / What dwells in man, /
그리고 세 가지 진리를 배워라   배워라 / (무엇을) / 인간에게는 무엇이 살고 있는지 /

What is not given to man, / and What men live by.
인간에게는 무엇이 주어지지 않은지 / 그리고 인간은 무엇으로 사는지

When you has learned these things, /
네가 이 세 개를 배웠을 때 /

you shall return to heaven.'
천국으로 돌아올 수 있을 것이다'

So I flew again to earth / and took the mother's soul.
그래서 저는 다시 지상으로 날아가 / 그 엄마의 영혼을 데려갔습니다

The babes dropped from her breasts.
아기들은 엄마의 젖에서 떨어졌지요

Her body rolled over on the bed / and crushed one babe, /
그녀의 시신이 침대 위에서 굴렀고 / 한 아기를 짓눌러서 /

twisting its leg.
아기 다리를 뒤틀어버렸어요

I rose above the village, /
저는 마을 위로 솟아올랐어요, /

wishing / to take her soul to God.
바라면서 / 그녀의 영혼을 신에게 데려가기를

But a wind seized me, / and my wings drooped and dropped off.
그러나 바람이 저를 붙잡았어요 / 그리고 제 날개가 축 늘어졌고 떨어졌어요

Her soul rose alone to God, / while I fell back to earth."
그녀의 영혼 혼자 신에게 갔어요 / 한편 저는 지상으로 떨어졌어요."

Key Expression

관계대명사의 계속 용법

연속적으로 발생하는 사건을 표현할 수 있다. 이 때 관계대명사 앞에는 코마(,)를 사용한다. 이 패턴을 관계대명사의 계속 용법이라고 부른다. 또한 과거완료(had given)를 보면, 쌍둥이가 태어난 사건은 앞에 사건(날아가서 보기)보다 먼저 발생한 것임을 알 수 있다. 그래서 이 문장은 "내가 날아가서 병든 여인을 보았더니 그녀는 이미 쌍둥이를 출산했다"라는 의미다.

I flew to earth, and saw a sick woman lying alone, who had just given birth to twin girls.
저는 지구로 날아가서 보았어요 / (누구를?) 혼자 누워있는 병든 여인을 / (그런데 그 여인은) 쌍둥이 여자 아이를 방금 낳았어요.

the Lord 주님, 하나님 dwell ~에 살다, 거주하다 twist 일그러뜨리다, 뒤틀리게 하다 seize ~을 붙잡다 drop 아래로 쳐지다, 늘어지다

Chapter 12

And Simon and Matryona understood / who it was that /
그리고 시몬과 마트료나는 이해했다 (무엇을?) / 누구였는지 /

had lived with them, / and whom / they had clothed and fed.
자신들과 함께 살았던 사람이 / 그리고 누구를 / 그들이 입히고 먹였는지

And they wept / with awe and with joy.
그리고 그들은 눈물을 흘렸다 / 경외와 기쁨으로

And the angel said: / "I was alone in the field, / naked.
그리고 그 천사가 말했다 / "저는 들판에서 홀로 있었어요 / 발가벗고

I had never known / human poverty, cold and hunger, /
저는 몰랐었어요 / 인간세상의 가난, 추위와 배고픔을 /

till I became a man.
인간이 되기 전에는

I was famished, frozen, / and did not know / what to do.
저는 배고팠고 추워서 얼 것 같았어요 / 그리고 몰랐어요 / 어떻게 해야 할지

I saw, / near the field I was in, / a chapel built for God, /
저는 봤어요, / 제가 있는 밭 근처에서 / 신을 위해서 지은 교회를 /

and I went to it / hoping to find shelter.
그리고 저는 교회로 갔어요 / 거처를 찾기를 바라면서

But the chapel was locked, / and I could not enter.
그러나 그 교회는 잠겨있었어요 / 그래서 저는 들어갈 수 없었지요

So I sat down behind the chapel / to shelter myself /
그래서 저는 교회 뒤에 앉아 있었어요 / 피하려고 /

at least from the wind.
최소한 바람이라도

Evening drew on. I was hungry, frozen, and in pain.
저녁이 되었어요. 저는 배고팠고 추위로 얼었고 고통 받았어요

Suddenly I heard / a man coming along the road.
갑자기 저는 들었어요 / 한 남자가 길을 따라 걸어오는 소리를

He carried a pair of boots, / and was talking to himself.
그는 한 켤레의 장화를 들고 있었어요 / 그리고 혼잣말을 하고 있었어요

For the first time / since I became a man / I saw /
처음으로 / 제가 인간이 된 후 / 저는 봤어요 /

the mortal face of a man, /
인간의 얼굴을 /

and his face seemed terrible to me / and I turned from it.
그리고 그의 얼굴은 저에게는 무서워 보였고 / 저는 고개를 돌렸지요

And I heard / the man talking to himself /
그리고 저는 들었어요 / 그 남자가 혼잣말을 하는 것을 /

of how to cover his body / from the cold in winter, /
어떻게 몸을 보호할지 / 겨울에 추위로부터 /

and how to feed wife and children.
그리고 어떻게 아내와 아이들을 먹일지

And I thought: / 'I am perishing / of cold and hunger, /
그리고 저는 생각했어요 / '나는 죽고 있다고 / 추위와 배고픔으로 /

and here is a man thinking only /
그리고 여기 있는 남자는 생각만하고 있다고 /

of how to clothe himself and his wife, /
자기와 아내를 어떻게 입힐지 /

and how to get bread for themselves. He cannot help me.'
그리고 어떻게 가족을 먹여 살릴지(만 생각하고 있어요) 그는 나를 도와줄 수가 없다.'

When the man saw me / he scowled /
그 남자가 나를 봤을 때 / 그는 노려보았으며 /

and became still more terrible, /
그래서 더 무서워졌다 /

and passed me by / on the other side.
그리고 나를 지나갔어요 / (길의) 다른 쪽으로

I despaired. Suddenly I heard / him coming back.
나는 절망했어요. 갑자기 나는 들었어요 / 그가 되돌아오는 것을

I looked up, / and did not recognize / the same man.
내가 쳐다봤어 / 알아차리지 못했어요 / 같은 사람이라는 것을

Before, I had seen death / in his face, /
좀 전에는 나는 죽음을 보았어요 / 그의 얼굴에서 /

but now he was alive, / and I recognized in him /
그러나 지금 그는 살아있었어요 / 그리고 나는 그에게서 알아봤다 /

the presence of God. He came up to me, / clothed me, /
신의 존재를(신이 있다는 것을 알았다). 그는 나에게 와서 / 나에게 옷을 입히고 /

and took me / to his home.
그리고 저를 데리고 갔어요 / 그의 집으로

---

clothe 옷을 입히다 awe 경외, 감탄 famished 배고픈, 배가 고파 죽을 지경인 shelter 피난처, 은신처 draw on 다가오다, 접근하다 mortal 인간의 perish 죽다, 소멸하다 scowl 노려보다, 쏘아보다 despair 절망하다 recognize 알아차리다 presence 존재, 있음

I entered the house.
저는 그 집에 들어갔어요

A woman came to meet us / and began to speak.
한 여인이 우리를 마중 나왔고 / 말하기 시작했어요

The woman was still more terrible /
그 여인은 더 무서웠어요 /

than the man had been.
그 남자가 무서웠던 것보다

The spirit of death came / from her mouth.
죽음의 영혼이 나왔어요 / 그녀의 입에서

I could not breathe / for the stench of death /
저는 숨을 쉴 수가 없었어요 / 불쾌한 죽음의 냄새 때문에 /

that spread around her.
(그 냄새는) 그녀의 주위에 퍼져있던

She wished to drive me out / into the cold, /
그녀는 저를 내쫓고 싶어 했어요 / 추위 속으로 /

and I knew / that if she did so / she would die.
그리고 저는 알았어요 / 그녀가 그렇게 하면(내쫓았다면) / 그녀가 죽을 것이라는 것을.

Suddenly her husband spoke to her / of God,
갑자기 그녀의 남편이 그녀에게 이야기했어요 / 신에 대하여 /

and the woman changed at once."
그리고 그 여인은 즉시 변했어요."

Key Expression

문장을 복잡하게 만드는 동사

문장이 아무리 복잡하고 어려워 보여도 문장을 길게 만들 수 있는 것은 관계대명사, 분사, 접속사, 부정사, 동사 등이다. 아래 예문의 경우 복잡한 문장을 쉽게 이해할 수 있는 방법은 동사와 분사에서 찾을 수 있다. 동사를 보면, 그 다음에 어떤 내용이 올지 예측할 수 있기 때문이다. 동사 "see"를 보자마자 주어가 어디에서 무엇을 보았는지 체크한다. 그리고 "went ~ hoping"이라는 표현을 보고, 주어가 교회로 갈 때 뭔가를 바라면서 갔는지 예측한다. 즉 교회로 가는 사건(went)과 거처를 찾기를 바라는 상황(hoping)이 동시에 일어난 것이다.

I saw, near the field I was in, a chapel built for God, and I went to it hoping to find shelter.
저는 봤어요 / (어디에서?) 제가 있는 밭 근처에서 / (무엇을?) 신을 위해서 지은 교회를 /
그리고 저는 교회로 (뭔가를) 바라면서 갔어요 / 거처를 찾기를

stench (불쾌한) 냄새 drive out 쫓아내다 at once 즉시, 곧

"And when she brought me food / and looked at me, /
그리고 그녀가 저에게 음식을 가져와서 / 저를 쳐다봤을 때 /

I glanced at her and saw / that death no longer dwelt in her.
저는 그녀를 응시했고 그리고 봤어요 / 죽음이 더 이상 그녀에게 있지 않다는 것을

She had become alive, / and in her, too, I saw God.
그녀는 살게 되었고 / 그녀에게서도 저는 신을 봤어요

Then I remembered / God's first lesson: /
그때 저는 기억했어요 / 하나님의 첫 번째 가르침을 /

'Learn / what dwells in man.'
'배워라 / 인간에게 무엇이 있는지를'

And I understood / that in man dwells Love!
그리고 저는 알았어요 / 인간에게는 사랑이 있다는 것을!

I was glad / that God had already begun to show me /
저는 기뻤어요 / 신께서 벌써 보여주기 시작하셨다는 것이 /

what He had promised, / and I smiled / for the first time.
신께서 저에게 약속하셨던 것을. 그래서 저는 미소 지었던 것이에요. / 처음으로

But I had not yet learned all. I did not yet know /
그러나 제가 아직 전부 배운 것이 아니었어요. 저는 아직 몰랐어요 /

What is not given to man, / and What men live by."
무엇이 인간에게 주어지지 않은지 / 그리고 인간은 무엇으로 사는지를"

"I lived with you, / and a year passed.
"저는 당신들과 함께 살았고 / 1년이 흘렀어요

A man came to order / boots / that should wear for a year /
한 남자가 주문하러 왔어요 / 장화를 / (어떤 장화?) 1년 동안 신을 수 있는 /

without losing shape or cracking.
변형되거나 금이 가지 않고

I looked at him, / and suddenly, behind his shoulder, /
저는 그를 쳐다봤고 / 그리고 갑자기 그의 어깨 뒤에서 /

I saw my comrade / —the angel of death.
저는 저의 동료를 봤어요 / 죽음의 천사인

None but me saw / that angel. But I knew him, /
저 이외에는 아무도 보지 못했어요 / 그 천사를. 그러나 저는 그 천사를 알았어요 /

and knew / that before the sun set /
그리고 알았어요 / 해가 지기 전에 /

he would take that rich man's soul.
그가 그 부자의 영혼을 데려갈 것이라는 것을

---

glance 응시하다, 쳐다보다 dwell 살다, 거주하다 crack 금이 가다, 갈라지다 comrade 동료, 동무

And I thought to myself, /
그리고 저는 혼자 생각했어요 /

'The man is making preparations / for a year, /
'그 남자는 대비하고 있다고 /   1년을 /

not knowing / that he will die / before evening.'
모르면서도 /   그가 죽을 것이라는 것을 / 저녁이 오기 전에'

And I remembered God's second saying, /
그리고 저는 신의 두 번째 말씀을 기억했어요 /

'Learn / what is not given to man.'
'배워라 /   인간에게 무엇이 주어지지 않은지.'

What dwells in man / I already knew.
인간에게 무엇이 있는지를 /   저는 이미 알았어요

Now I learned / what is not given him.
이제 저는 배웠어요 /   무엇이 인간에게 주어지지 않은지

It is not given to man / to know / what is needed for their
인간에게는 주어지지 않았어요 /   아는 능력이 /   자신의 육체에 무엇이 필요한지

bodies. And I smiled / for the second time.
           그래서 저는 미소 지었어요 / 두 번째로

I was glad / to have seen my comrade angel /
저는 기뻤어요 /   제 동료 천사를 보아서 /

—glad also / that God had revealed to me /
  또한 기뻤어요 /   신께서 저에게 드러내셔서 /

the second saying. But I still did not know all.
두 번째 말씀을.   그러나 여전히 저는 모두 알지 못했어요

I did not know / What men live by.
저는 몰랐어요 /   인간이 무엇으로 사는지

And I lived on, / waiting / till God should reveal to me /
그래서 저는 계속 살았어요 / 기다리면서 / 신께서 저에게 드러내시길 /

the last lesson.
마지막 가르침을

In the sixth year came / the girl-twins / with the woman.
6년째가 되자 왔어요 /   쌍둥이 자매가 /   여인과 함께

And I recognized the girls, / and heard /
그리고 저는 그 소녀들을 알아봤어요 /   그리고 들었어요 /

how they had been kept alive.
어떻게 그 아이들이 살아남았는지를

Having heard the story, /
그 이야기를 듣고 난 후에 /

I thought: / 'Their mother begged me / for the children's
저는 다음과 같이 생각했어요 / '애들 엄마가 나에게 간청했어요 / 아이들을 위해서 /

sake, / because she thought / that it would be impossible /
그녀는 생각했기 때문에 / 불가능하다고 /

for children to live / without father or mother, /
(뭐가?) 아이들이 사는 것이 / 아빠나 엄마 없이 /

but a stranger has nursed them, / and has brought them up.
하지만 어느 낯선 사람이 그 아이들에게 젖을 먹였고 / 그리고 그 아이들을 잘 키웠어요

And when the woman showed her love / for the children /
그리고 그 여인이 사랑을 보여줬을 때 / 아이들에게 /

that were not her own, / and wept over them, /
자기 아이가 아닌 / 그리고 그들을 위해 울었을 때 /

I saw in her / the living God / and understood /
저는 그녀에게서 봤고 / 살아있는 신을 / 알았어요 /

What men live by. And I knew / that God had revealed to
인간은 무엇으로 사는지. 그리고 저는 알았어요 / 신께서 저에게 드러내신 것을 /

me / the last lesson, / and had forgiven / my sin.
마지막 가르침을 / 그리고 용서하신 것도 (알았어요) / 제가 지은 죄를

And then I smiled / for the third time."
그리고 나서 저는 미소 지었어요 / 세 번째로"

Key Expression

but; ~이외는(전치사), 그러나(접속사)

한 문장에 "but"이 두 번 등장하지만, 그 쓰임새가 다르다. 첫 번째 "but"은 전치사고, 두 번째 나온 "but"은 접속사로 쓰였다.

None but me saw / that angel; / but I knew him.
저 이외에는 아무도 보지 못했어요 / 저 천사를 / 그러나 저는 그 천사를 알았어요.

---

preparation 준비, 대비 reveal 드러내다, 계시하다 beg 간청하다 for one's sake ~을 위하여 nurse 젖을 먹이다
bring up 키우다, 기르다

Chapter 13

And the angel's body became manifest, /
그리고 그 천사의 몸은 분명하게 나타났다, /

and he was clothed in light / so bright /
그리고 그는 빛으로 싸여 있어서 / 너무나 밝게 /

that the eyes could not look on him.
눈으로 그를 쳐다볼 수가 없을 정도였다

And his voice grew louder, / as though it came not from
그리고 그의 목소리는 점점 커졌다, / 마치 목소리가 그에게서 나는 것이 아니라 /

him / but from heaven above.
하늘 위에서 나는 것처럼

And the angel said: / "I have learned / that all men live /
그리고 그 천사는 말했다 / "저는 배웠어요 / 모든 인간이 산다는 것을 /

not by care for themselves but / by love.
자신에 대한 보살핌(애착)이 아니라 / 사랑으로

It was not given to the mother / to know /
그 어머니에게는 주어지지 않았어요 / (뭐가?) 알 수 있는 능력이 /

what her children needed for their life.
자기 아이들이 살아가는데 뭐가 필요한지

Nor was it given to the rich man / to know /
또한 그 부자에게는 주어지지 않았어요 / (뭐가?) 알 수 있는 능력이 /

what he himself needed.
그 자신이 뭐가 필요한지

Nor is it given to any man / to know whether, /
어떤 인간에게도 주어지지 않았지 / (뭐가?) 알 수 있는 능력이 /

when evening comes, /
(무엇을 알까?) 저녁이 올 때 /

he will need boots for his body / or slippers for his corpse.
몸을 위해서 장화가 필요할지 / 아니면 시신에 슬리퍼가 필요할지

I remained alive / when I was a man, / not by care of
제가 살아남게 되었어요 / 인간이었을 때 / 저 자신에 대한 보살핌(애착)이

myself, / but because love was present / in a passer-by, /
아니라 / 사랑이 있었기 때문에 / 지나가는 사람의 /

and because he and his wife pitied and loved me.
그리고 그와 그의 아내가 저를 동정하고 사랑했기 때문에

The orphans remained alive /
그 고아들은 살아남았어요 /

not because their mother cared for them, /
그 아이들 엄마가 그들을 보살폈기 때문이 아니라 /

but because there was love / in the heart of a woman, /
사랑이 있었기 때문에 (살아남았어요) / 한 여인의 마음속에 /

a stranger to them, / who pitied and loved them.
(그 여인은) 그들에게는 타인이었지만 / 그들을 동정했고 사랑했던

And all men live / not by the thought /
그리고 모든 인간은 살지요 / 생각에 의해서가 아니라 /

they spend on their own welfare, /
(어떤 생각?) 자신들의 복지에 쏟는 /

but because love exists in man.
인간에 대한 사랑이 존재하기 때문에 (살지요)

I knew before / that God gave life to men /
저는 예전에 알았어요 / 신께서 인간에게 생명을 주셨다는 것을 /

and desires that they should live.
그리고 그들이 살아야하는 욕망들을 (주셨다는 것을)

Now I understood more than that.
이제 저는 그 보다 더 많이 이해했어요

I understood / that God does not wish / men to live apart, /
저는 알았어요 / 신께서 바라지 않는다는 것을 / (무엇을?) 인간들이 따로 떨어져 살길 /

and therefore He does not reveal to them /
그러므로 신께서 인간들에게 알려주지 않는다는 것을 /

what each one needs for himself. /
무엇이 자신에게 필요한지 /

But He wishes / them to live united, /
하지만 신께서는 바라신다는 것을 / 사람들이 화합하며 살길 /

and therefore reveals to each of them /
그래서 인간 각자에게 드러내십니다 /

what is necessary for all.
모두에게 뭐가 필요한 지를

I have now understood /
이제 저는 이해했어요 (무엇을?) /

---

manifest (보거나 이해하기에) 분명한 clothe 옷을 입히다 remain 계속(여전히) ~ 다 passer-by 행인, 지나가는 사람 welfare 복지 therefore 그러므로 reveal 드러내다, 계시하다 united 화합하며, 뭉쳐서

that though it seems to men / that they live by care for
비록 인간은 생각하지만 / 자신에 대한 보살핌(애착)으로 산다고 /

themselves, / in truth it is love alone / by which they live.
사실은 오직 사랑만으로 / 인간이 산다는 것을(이해했어요)

He who has love, / is in God, and God is in him, /
사랑을 하는 사람은 / 신 안에 존재하고 / 신은 그 사람 안에 있습니다 /

for God is love."
왜냐하면 신이란 사랑이기 때문입니다"

And the angel sang a hymn of praise / to God, /
그리고 그 천사는 찬송가를 불렀다 / 신에게 /

so that the hut trembled / at his voice.
그래서 오두막이 흔들렸다 / 그의 목소리 때문에

The roof opened, / and a column of fire rose /
지붕이 열렸다 / 그리고 불기둥이 솟아올랐다 /

from earth to heaven. Simon and his wife and children
지상에서 하늘로. 시몬과 그의 아내와 아이들은

lay prostrate to the ground.
땅에 엎드렸다

Wings appeared / upon the angel's shoulders, /
날개가 생겼다 / 천사의 어깨에 /

and he rose into the heavens.
그리고 그는 하늘로 올라갔다

And when Simon came to himself / the hut stood /
그리고 시몬이 정신을 차렸을 때 / 오두막은 서있었다 /

as before, / and there was no one in it / but his own family.
예전처럼 / 그리고 오두막 안에는 아무도 없었다 / 자신의 가족 이외에

Key Expression

not A but B; A가 아니라 B다

이런 종류의 접속사에 사용되는 A와 B는 동일해야 한다. 예를 들어 A가 명사면, B도 명사가 되어야 하고, A가 부사구면, B도 부사구가 되어야 한다.

I have learned that all men live not by care for themselves but by love.
저는 배웠어요 / 모든 인간이 산다는 것을 / 자신에 대한 보살핌(애착)때문이 아니라 / 사랑으로.

The orphans remained alive not because their mother cared for them, but because there was love in the heart of a woman.
그 고아들은 살아남게 되었어요 / 그 아이들 엄마가 보살폈기 때문이 아니라 / 그들을 / 사랑이 있었기 때문에 (살아남았어요) / 한 여인의 마음속에

---

hymn of praise 찬송가 **tremble** 떨다 **column** 기둥 **prostrate** 엎드린, 엎어져 있는 **come to oneself** 제정신을 차리다

Quiz 4

A. 내용 이해하기

다음 문장을 읽고 본문의 내용과 맞으면 T(True), 틀리면 F(False)를 쓰세요.

1. God punished Michael for disobedience and he must find the answers to the three questions.

2. Michael learned the answer to the first question when Simon's wife felt pity for him.

3. The answer to the second question came to Michael when he saw that the angel of death was looming over the gentleman.

4. Michael found the answer to the last question when he learned "What is not given to man."

B. 단어

다음 제시된 단어의 설명을 읽고, 어떤 단어의 정의를 설명하는지 아래의 박스에서 찾아 써 보세요.

1. a child whose parents are dead
2. a box in which a corpse is buried or cremated
3. to be successful in making a lot of money
4. to feed a baby with milk from its mother's breast
5. one who runs a business by buying and selling goods for profit
6. a short saying that expresses a basic truth or gives advice
7. to live somewhere; to be in a place
8. to bend or hang downward because of being weak
9. depressed or sad
10. greatly hungry or starving

---

nurse orphan gloomy proverb prosper droop coffin

dwell famished merchant

Answer

A. 1. T 2. T 3. T 4. F

B. 1. orphan 2. coffin 3. prosper 4. nurse 5. merchant 6. proverb 7. dwell 8. droop 9. gloomy 10. famished

C. 직독직해

아래에 제시된 문장을 직독직해로 해석해보세요.

1. None but me saw / that angel. But I knew him, and knew / that before the sun set / he would take that rich man's soul.

   →

2. Their mother begged me / for the children's sake, / because she thought / that it would be impossible / for children to live / without father or mother.

   →

3. The orphans remained alive / not because their mother cared for them, / but because there was love / in the heart of a woman.

   →

4. The angel sang a hymn of praise / to God, / so that the hut trembled / at his voice.

   →

D. 동시통역

아래에 제시된 직독직해를 보고, 영어로 말해보세요.

1. 갑자기 그녀의 남편이 그녀에게 이야기했어요 / 신에 대하여 / 그리고 그 여인은 즉시 변했어요.

   →

2. 한 남자가 주문하러 왔어요 / 장화를 / (어떤 장화?) 1년 동안 신을 수 있는 / 변형되거나 금이 가지 않고

   →

3. 그녀의 시신이 침대 위에서 굴렀고 / 한 아기를 짓눌러서 / 아기의 다리를 뒤틀어버렸어요

   →

4. 그들은 가난했고 외로웠어요 / 그들을 보살펴줄 사람이 아무도 없이 / 할머니나 누이도 없이

   →

Answer   C. 1. 저 이외에는 아무도 보지 못했어요 / 그 천사를. 그러나 저는 그 천사를 알았어요 / 그리고 알았어요 / 해가 지기 전에 / 그가 그 부자의 영혼을 데려갈 것이라는 것을.   2. 얘들 엄마가 나에게 간청했어요 / 아이들을 위해서 / 그녀는 생각했기 때문에 / 불가능하다고 / (뭐가?) 아이들이 사는 것이 / 아빠나 엄마 없이   3. 그 고아들은 살아남았어요 / 그 아이들 엄마가 보살폈기 때문이 아니라 / 그들을 / 사랑이 있었기 때문에 (살아남았어요) / 한 여인의 마음속에   4. 그 천사는 찬송가를 불렀다 / 신에게 / 그래서 오두막이 흔들렸다 / 그의 목소리 때문에

D. 1. Suddenly her husband spoke to her, / of God, / and the woman changed at once.
2. A man came to order / boots / that should wear for a year / without losing shape or cracking.
3. Her body rolled over on the bed / and crushed one babe, / twisting its leg.
4. They were poor and alone, / no one to take care of them, / either grandmother or sister.

Ivan the Fool
바보 이반

Chapter 1

In a certain kingdom there lived / a rich peasant, /
어느 왕국에 살았다 / 한 부자 소작농이 /

who had three sons / -Simeon (a soldier), Tarras (fat man), /
(그는) 세 아들이 있었다 / 세몬(군인), 타라스 (뚱보) /

and Ivan (a fool). He also had one daughter, Milania, /
그리고 이반(바보). 그는 또한 밀라니아라는 딸이 있었다 /

born dumb. Simeon went to war / to serve the Czar.
벙어리로 태어난. 세몬은 전쟁터로 나갔다 / 러시아 황제를 섬기려고

Tarras went to a city / and became a merchant.
타라스는 도시로 가서 / 상인이 되었다

And Ivan, with his sister, / remained at home /
그리고 이반은 여동생과 함께 / 집에 남았다 /

to work on the farm. For his valiant service /
농장에서 일하기 위해서. 용맹하게 복무했기 때문에 /

in the army, / Simeon received an estate with high rank, /
군대에서 / 세몬은 높은 계급과 땅을 받았다 /

and married a noble's daughter.
그리고 귀족의 딸과 결혼했다

Besides his large pay, / he was in receipt of a handsome
많은 급여 이외에도 / 그는 상당한 수입을 얻고 있었다 /

income / from his estate, /
자기 땅에서 /

but he was unable to make ends meet.
그렇지만 그는 여전히 수입 내에서 생활할 수 없었다(돈이 모자랐다)

What the husband saved, / the wife wasted /
남편이 저축한 것을 / 아내는 낭비했다 /

in extravagance.
사치하느라고

One day Simeon went to the estate / to collect his money, /
어느날 세몬은 자기 땅에 갔다 / 돈(도지세)을 받으러 /

when the steward informed him /
그때 재산관리인이 그에게 알렸다 /

that there was no income, / saying: / "We have neither /
수입이 없다고 / (이렇게) 말하면서 / "저희는 없어요 /

horses, cows, fishing-nets, nor implements.
말도, 소도, 어망도 농기구도

It is necessary to buy everything first, /
먼저 모든 것을 살 필요가 있어요 /

and then to look for profits."
그런 다음 수입을 바래야죠."

So Simeon went to his father and said: /
그래서 세몬은 자기 아버지한테 가서 말했다 /

"You are rich, father, / but you have given nothing / to me.
"아버지는 부자예요 / 그런데 아무것도 주시지 않았어요 / 저한테

Give me one-third / of what you possess / as my share, /
3분의 1을 주세요 / 아버지가 소유한 재산의 / 제 몫으로 /

and I will transfer it / to my estate."
그러면 그것을 이전하겠어요 / 제 재산으로"

The old man replied: / "You did not help /
노인(아버지가)이 대답했다 / "너는 돕지 않았다 /

to bring prosperity to our household.
우리 집안에 부를 가져오는 일을 (살림을 불리는 일을)

For what reason, then, / should you now demand /
그러면서 무슨 이유로 / 너는 지금 달라고 하니 /

a third of everything?
모든 재산의 3분의 1을

It would be unjust / to Ivan and his sister."
그러면(재산을 주면) 불공평해 / 이반과 네 여동생에게"

"Yes," said Simeon, "but he is a fool, /
"그렇지요" 세몬이 말했다 "하지만 그는 바보고 /

and she was born dumb.
그녀는 벙어리로 태어났어요

certain 어느, 어떤 valiant 용맹한, 용감한 service 군 목부 estate 땅, 사유지 noble 귀족 in receipt of ~을 받는 handsome 상당한 make ends meet 수입 내에서 꾸려나가다, extravagance 사치 steward 재산 관리인, 집사 inform 알리다 implement 기구, 연장 possess 소유하다 transfer 이전하다 prosperity 번영 household 세대, 가구, 온 집안사람들 demand 요구하다, 요청하다 unjust 불공정한

They don't need much."
재들은 필요한 게 뭐 없어요."

"See / what Ivan will say."
"알아보자 / 이반이 뭐라고 말할 지"

Ivan's reply was: / "Well, let him take his share."
이반의 대답은 다음과 같았다 / "아, 형 몫을 가져가라고 하세요."

Simeon took / the portion allotted to him, /
세몬은 가져갔다 / 자신에게 할당된 몫을 /

and went again / to serve in the army.
그리고 다시 갔다 / 군복무를 하러

Key Expression

inform; (사람들에게) ~을 알리다

"누군가에게 어떤 사실을 알리다"라고 말할 때, "tell" 동사처럼 "동사+목적어+that절"을 사용한다.

The steward informed him that there was no income.
재산관리인은 그에게 알렸다 / 수입이 없다고
Nobody informed me that they would marry within the year.
아무도 나에게 알려주지 않았다 / 그들이 올해 결혼할 것이라는 것을

portion (전체의) 일부, 부분   allot ~을 할당하다, 주다

Tarras the Fat also became successful.
뚱보 타라스 역시 성공했다

He became rich / and married a merchant's daughter, /
그는 부자가 되었고 / 어느 상인의 딸과 결혼했다 /

but even this failed to satisfy / his desires, /
그러나 이것도 만족시킬 수 없었다 / 그의 욕망을 /

and he also went to his father and said, /
그래서 그도 아버지한테 가서 말했다 /

"Give me my share."
"제 몫을 주세요."

The old man, however, refused /
그러나 노인은 거절했다 /

to comply with his request, / saying: /
그의 요구를 들어주기를 / 이렇게 말하면서 /

"You didn't give me a hand / accumulating our property, /
"너는 전혀 돕지 않았지 / 우리 재산을 모으는데 /

and everything our household contains /
그리고 우리 집안에 있는 모든 것(재산)은 /

is the result of Ivan's hard work. It would be unjust,"
이반이 열심히 일한 결과다. 그러면 불공평해"

he repeated, "to Ivan and his sister."
그가 반복하여 말했다, "이반과 그의 여동생에게"

Tarras replied: "But he does not need it.
타라스는 대답했다 "그러나 이반은 재산이 필요 없어요

He is a fool, and cannot marry, / for no one will have him.
그는 바보라서 결혼할 수 없어요 / 아무도 시집오려고 하지 않기 때문에

And sister does not require anything, /
그리고 여동생은 아무것도 필요 없어요 /

for she was born dumb."
벙어리로 태어났기 때문에."

Tarras Turned to Ivan and continued: /
타라스는 이반 쪽으로 향하면서 계속 말했다 /

"Give me half the grain / you have, /
"나에게 곡식의 절반을 줘 / 네가 가진 /

and I will not touch / the implements or fishing-nets. /
그러면 나는 건드리지 않을 게(필요 없어) / 농기구나 어망을 /

desire 욕망, 욕구 refuse 거절하다 comply 따르다, 응하다 request 요구 accumulate 모으다, 축적하다
property 재산, 자산 repeat 반복하여 말하다 require 필요하다

And from the cattle / I will take / only the dark mare, /
그리고 가축 중에서는 / 가져갈게 / 까만 암말만 /

as she is not fit / to plow." /
그 말은 적합하지 않으니까 / 밭을 갈기에"

Ivan laughed and said: /
이반은 웃으면서 말했다 /

"Well, I will go and arrange everything /
"응, 내가 가서 모든 일을 준비할 거야 /

so that Tarras may have his share," /
그러면 타라스 형이 자기 몫을 가져갈 수 있도록 /

whereupon Tarras took / the brown mare with the grain /
그리고 그 후에 타라스가 데리고 갔다 / 곡식을 실은 갈색 암말을 /

to town, / leaving Ivan / with one old horse /
읍내로 / 이반에게는 남겨두고 / 늙은 말 한필을 /

to work on as before /
예전처럼 일할 /

and support his father, mother, and sister.
그리고 그의 아버지, 어머니, 그리고 여동생을 부양할 (말 한필을)

Key Expression

so that ~(in order that); ~하기위해

보통 "so that"절 안에 조동사로 "can, will, could, would"를 사용한다. "may, might"를 사용하면, 더 격식을 차린 표현이 된다.

I will arrange everything so that Tarras may have his share.
내가 모든 일을 준비할 거야 / 그러면 타라스 형이 자기 몫을 가져갈 수 있도록

mare 암말 plow (밭이랑을) 갈다 arrange 준비를 하다, 조정하다 whereupon 그리고 그 후에
support 부양하다, 양육하다

Chapter 2

It was disappointing / to the Old Devil /
실망스러운 일이었다 / 늙은 악마에게는 (무엇이?) /

that the brothers did not quarrel /
그 형제들이 싸우지 않는 것이 /

over the division of the property, /
재산을 분배하는 문제로 /

and that they separated / peacefully.
그리고 그들이 헤어진 것이 / 평화롭게

And he cried out, / calling his three small devils.
그래서 그는 외쳤다 / 3명의 작은 악마들을 부를 때

"See here," said he, / "there are three brothers /
"이봐" 그가 말했다 / "세 명의 형제가 있다 /

-Simeon the soldier, Tarras the merchant, and Ivan the Fool.
군인인 세몬, 상인인 타라스, 그리고 바보 이반

It is necessary / that they should quarrel.
필요가 있어 / 그들이 싸워야할

Now they live peacefully, / and enjoy /
지금은 그들이 평화롭게 살아 / 게다가 즐기고 있지 /

each other's hospitality. The Fool spoiled all my plans.
서로 친절하게 대하는 삶을. 바보가 나의 모든 계획을 망쳤어

Now you three go / and work with one brother each /
이제 너희 셋은 가서 / 각자가 형제에게 맡는 일을 해봐라 /

until they will be ready / to tear each other's eyes out.
그들이 준비가 될 때까지 / 서로 잡아 뜯으며 싸울

Can you do this?" "We can," they replied.
너희들 할 수 있냐?" "네, 할 수 있어요." 그들이 대답했다

"How will you accomplish it?"
"어떻게 해서 할래?"

"In this way: / We will first ruin them /
"이런 식으로요. / 우리는 먼저 그들을 파멸시킬 것입니다 /

to such an extent that they will have nothing to eat, /
그들이 먹을 것이 없을 정도로 /

---

quarrel 싸우다 division 분배 hospitality 친절한 접대, 환대 spoil 망치다 tear out ~을 잡아 뜯다
accomplish (업무를) 완성하다, 이루다

and we will then gather them together / in one place /
그러면 우리는 그들 모두를 모이게 할 것입니다 / 한 곳에 /

and they will fight."
그렇게 되면 그들은 싸울 것입니다."

"Very well. I see you understand your business.
"아주 좋아. 내 생각엔 너희들이 할일을 알고 있군

Go, and do not return to me /
가서 내게로 돌아오지 말라 /

until you have created / a feud between the three brothers /
너희가 만들(일으킬) 때까지 / 세 형제 사이에 불화를 /

or I will skin you alive."
그렇게 못하면 내가 너희를 산 채로 가죽을 벗기겠다."

The three small devils went to a swamp / to consult /
세 명의 작은 악마들은 늪으로 갔다 / 상의하러 /

as to the best means of accomplishing their mission.
자신들의 임무를 이룰 수 있는 가장 적합한 방법에 대해

They disputed for a long time /
그들은 오랫동안 다투었다 /

each one wanting the easiest part of the work /
각자가 가장 쉬운 부분을 하고 싶어 했고 /

and not being able to agree, / concluded to draw lots.
그래서 합의할 수가 없었기 때문에 / 제비뽑기를 하기로 결정했다

And it was decided / that the one who was first finished /
그리고 결정되었다 (어떻게?) / 먼저 끝내는 사람이 /

had to come and help the others.
와서 다른 악마들을 돕기로

This agreement being entered into, / they appointed a time /
이와 같은 합의에 이르자 / 그들은 시각을 정했다 /

when they were again to meet in the swamp / to find out /
늪에서 다시 만나는 / (왜?) 알아내려고 /

who was through / and who needed assistance.
누가 일을 끝냈고 / 누가 지원이 필요한지(알기 위해서)

feud (가족간의) 불화, 반목 swamp 늪 as to ~대하여 dispute 다투다, 논쟁하다 conclude 결정하다
lot 제비뽑기, 추첨 agreement 합의, 동의 assistance 지원, 도움

The time having arrived, / the young devils met in the swamp / as agreed, / when each related his experience.

The first, / who went to Simeon, / said: / "I have succeeded in my undertaking, / and tomorrow Simeon returns to his father."

His comrades, / eager for particulars, / inquired / how he had done it.

"Well," he began, "the first thing I did / was to blow some courage / into his veins, / and, on the strength of it, / Simeon went to the Czar / and offered / to conquer the whole world for him.

The Emperor made him / commander-in-chief of the forces, / and sent him with an army / to fight the Viceroy of India.

Having started on their mission of conquest, / they were unaware / that I, / following in their wake, / had wet all their powder.

I also went to the Indian ruler / and showed him / how I could create numberless soldiers / from straw.

---

relate 이야기하다 undertaking 일, 사업 particulars 상세, 전말 vein 혈관 commander-in-chief (군대의) 사령관 Viceroy 총독, 부왕 conquest 정복 unaware 모르는 in one's wake ~의 뒤에

103

Simeon's army, / seeing / that they were surrounded /
세몬의 군대는 / 알고서 / (무엇을?) 그들이 포위된 것을 /

by such a vast number of Indian warriors / of my creation, /
엄청난 숫자의 인도 용사들로 / 내가 만든 /

became frightened, / and Simeon commanded to fire /
(세몬의 군대는) 놀랬지 / 그러자 세몬은 발사하도록 명령했어 /

from cannons and rifles, / which of course /
대포와 총을 / 그런 일을 물론 /

they were unable to do.
그들은 할 수가 없었지

The soldiers, / discouraged, / retreated / in great disorder.
병사들은 / 사기가 꺾였던 / 후퇴했어 / 혼란에 빠져

Thus Simeon brought upon himself /
그래서 세몬은 자초했지 /

the terrible disgrace of defeat. His estate was confiscated, /
패배의 엄청난 모욕을 / 그의 재산은 몰수되었고 /

and tomorrow he is to be executed. All that I have to do," /
내일 그는 처형될 거야 / 내가 해야 될 모든 일은 /

concluded the young devil, /
젊은 악마가 결론을 내렸다 /

"is to release him / tomorrow morning.
그를 놔주는 것이야 / 내일 아침에

Now, then, who wants my assistance?"
그러면, 이제 누가 내 지원이 필요하지?"

Key Expression

원인/이유를 나타내는 분사 구문

아래에 있는 예문처럼 현재분사가 있는 부사구가 나온 다음에 새로운 문장이 다시 나오면, 분사구문이라고 말한다. 분사가 있는 부분과 새로운 문장이 모두가 사건을 묘사한다. 그리고 첫 번째 사건 때문에 또 다른 사건이 발생한다. 이런 패턴의 문장을 원인이나 이유를 나타내는 분사 구문 이라고 부른다. "having arrived"의 의미상 주어는 "the time"이며, 주절의 주어는 "the young devils"이다.

The time having arrived, the young devils met in the swamp as agreed.
(정한) 시간이 되었기 때문에 / (그래서) 젊은 악마들은 늪에서 만났다 / 약속한대로

---

vast 엄청난, 대단히 큰 warrior 전사 retreat 후퇴하다, 퇴각하다 disgrace 모욕, 치욕
confiscate (재산을) 몰수하다 release 풀어주다, (속박에서) 해방하다

The second small devil (from Tarras) then / related his story.
두 번째 작은 악마(타라스에게 갔다 온)가 그 다음에 / 자기 이야기를 했다

"I do not need any help," he began.
"나는 도움이 필요 없어" 그는 시작했다

"My business is also all right.
"내 일도 잘 되었어

My work with Tarras will be finished / in one week.
타라스에게 할 일은 끝날 거야 / 일주일 안에

In the first place I made / him grow greedy and fat.
첫 번째로 나는 만들었어 / 그를 탐욕스럽고 뚱뚱하게

He afterward became so covetous /
결국 그는 너무나 탐욕스럽게 되어서 /

that he wanted to possess / everything he saw, /
그는 갖고 싶어졌어 / 눈에 보이는 모든 것을 /

and he spent all the money / he had /
그리고 그는 모든 돈을 써버렸어 / 그가 가진 /

in the purchase of immense quantities of goods.
엄청난 양의 물건을 사는데.

When his capital was gone / he still continued to buy /
그의 자본이 바닥났을 때에도 / 그는 여전히 계속 사들였지 /

with borrowed money, /
빌린 돈으로 /

and has become involved in such difficulties /
그래서 곤경에 빠지게 되었어 /

that he cannot free himself.
그가 벗어날 수 없는

At the end of one week / the date for the payment of his
일주일만 있으면 / 어음을 지불해야 되는 날짜가 /

notes / will have expired, /
다될 거야(어음의 만기가 돌아온다) /

and, his goods being seized upon, /
그리고 그의 물건들은 저당 잡혔기 때문에 /

he will become a bankrupt.
그는 파산자가 될 거야

and he also will return to his father."
그래서 그도 자기 아버지한테 돌아갈 거야"

---

greedy 탐욕스러운 covetous 욕심이 많은, 탐내는 purchase 구매, 구입 immense 엄청난, 거대한
goods 물건, 상품 note 어음 expire 만기가 되다 bankrupt 파산자

At the conclusion of this narrative / they inquired of the
이 이야기가 끝났을 때 / 그들은 세 번째 악마에게 물었다 /

third devil / how things had fared / between him and Ivan.
어떻게 일이 진행되었는지 / 그와 이반과는

"Well," said he, "my report is not so encouraging.
"응" 그가 말했다 "내 보고는 그렇게 희망적이진 않아

The first thing I did / was to spit into his jug of quass
내가 첫 번째로 한 것은 / 그의 콰스(호밀로 만든 시큼한 음료) 주전자에 침을 뱉는 것

[a sour drink made from rye], /
이었어 /

which / made / him sick at his stomach.
그 일(침을 뱉은 일은) / 만들었지 / 그의 배가 탈나도록

He afterward went to plow / his summer-fallow, /
그 후에 그는 갈러 갔지 / 여름 휴경지를 /

but I made the soil so hard / that the plow could scarcely
그러나 나는 땅을 매우 단단하게 만들어서 / 쟁기가 거의 들어갈 수 없을 정도였지

penetrate it. I thought / the Fool would not succeed, /
나는 알았는데 / 바보가 성공하지 못할 줄로 /

but he started to work nevertheless.
그래도 그는 일하기 시작했어

Moaning with pain, / he still continued to labor.
고통으로 신음하면서 / 그는 여전히 열심히 일을 계속했지

I broke one plow, / but he replaced it with another, /
내가 쟁기를 하나 망가뜨렸지 / 그래도 그는 다른 것으로 바꾸고 /

fixing it securely, / and resumed work.
확실하게 고치고 / 일을 다시 했어

Going under the ground / I took hold of the plowshares, /
땅의 밑으로 들어가서 / 나는 쟁깃날을 잡았지 /

but did not succeed / in stopping Ivan.
그래도 성공하지 못했지 / 이반의 일을 방해하는 일에

He pressed so hard, / and the plow was so sharp, /
그가 (쟁기를) 꽉 눌렀고 / 쟁기는 아주 날카로웠지 /

that my hands were cut.
그래서 내 손이 베었어

And despite my utmost efforts, / he went over all /
그리고 나의 최대한 노력에도 불구하고 / 그는 모든 밭을 갈았지 /

but a small portion of the field."
밭의 작은 부분만 제외하고"

He concluded with: / "Come, brothers, and help me, /
그는 (다음과 같이) 이야기를 끝냈다 / "자 형제들이여 나를 도와줘 /

for if we do not conquer him /
왜냐하면 만일 우리가 그를 정복하지 못하면 /

our whole enterprise will be a failure.
우리의 모든 사업은 실패할 거야

If the Fool is permitted /
바보가 내버려둔다면 /

successfully to conduct his farming, /
성공적으로 자기 농사를 지을 수 있도록 /

his brothers will not be hungry, / for he will support them."
그의 형제들은 배고프지 않을 거야 / 그들을 도울 것이기 때문에"

Key Expression

permit; ~하도록 내버려 두다

누군가 어떤 사건이 일어나도록 방치했다면, 그 사건이 발생하도록 내버려 두는 것이다.
이런 상황에 "permit"라는 동사를 사용할 수 있다.

If the Fool is permitted successfully to conduct his farming, his brothers will not be hungry, for he will support them.
바보가 내버려둔다면 / 성공적으로 자기 농사를 지을 수 있도록 /
그의 형제들은 배고프지 않을 거야 / 그가 그들을 도울 것이기 때문에

---

narrative 이야기 inquire ~을 묻다 fare (일이) 되어가다, 진행되다
encouraging 희망을 가지게 하는, 격려가 되는 jug 주전자 rye 호밀 fallow 휴경지 scarcely 거의 ~않다
penetrate ~의 내부에 들어가다, 침투하다 labor 열심히 일하다 resume ~을 다시 시작하다
plowshares 쟁기 날 utmost 최대한의, 최고의 enterprise 사업

Quiz 5

A. 내용 이해하기

다음 문장을 읽고 본문의 내용과 맞으면 T(True), 틀리면 F(False)를 쓰세요.

1. Ivan went to a city and became a merchant.
2. Simeon received an estate with high rank because of his valiant service in the army.
3. Ivan's father gave one-third of his property to Ivan as his share.
4. The Old Devil was happy because the brothers did not quarrel over the division of the property.

B. 단어

다음 제시된 단어의 설명을 읽고, 어떤 단어의 정의를 설명하는지 아래의 박스에서 찾아 써 보세요.

1. very brave; possessing valor; courageous
2. the act of spending a lot of money more than you can afford
3. the condition of being successful in terms of one's finances
4. to obey another's request, command or wish
5. generous and friendly behavior towards visitors or guests
6. to have a bad effect on something; to change something good into something useless; ruin
7. a bitter quarrel or a state of hostilities between two people
8. to move away from an enemy after being defeated in battle
9. to take private property away from someone
10. a description of an event in a story

---

retreat prosperity narrative feud valiant

spoil hospitality confiscate extravagance comply

Answer A. 1. F 2. T 3. F 4. F
B. 1. valiant 2. extravagance 3. prosperity 4. comply 5. hospitality 6. spoil 7. feud 8. retreat 9. confiscate 10. narrative

C. 직독직해

아래에 제시된 문장을 직독직해로 해석해보세요.

1. One day Simeon went to the estate / to collect his money, / when the steward informed him / that there was no income.

   →

2. He became rich / and married a merchant's daughter, / but even this failed to satisfy / his desires.

   →

3. Thus Simeon brought upon himself / the terrible disgrace of defeat. His estate was confiscated, and tomorrow he is to be executed.

   →

4. He afterward became so covetous / that he wanted to possess / everything he saw.

   →

D. 동시통역

아래에 제시된 직독직해를 보고, 영어로 말해보세요.

1. 3분의 1을 주세요 / 아버지가 소유한 재산의 / 제 몫으로 / 그러면 그것을 이전할게요 / 제 재산으로

   →

2. 내가 가서 모든 일을 준비할 거야 / 그러면 타라스 형이 자기 몫을 가져갈 수 있도록

   →

3. "나는 도움이 필요 없어" 그는 시작했나. "내 일도 잘 되었이."

   →

4. 나는 알았는데 / 바보가 성공하지 못할 줄로 / 그래도 그는 일하기 시작했어.

   →

Answer

C. 1. 어느날 세몬은 자기 땅에 갔다 / 돈(도지세)을 받으러 / 그때 재산관리인이 그에게 알렸다 / 수입이 없다고. 2. 그는 부자가 되었고 / 어느 상인의 딸과 결혼했다 / 그러나 이것도 만족시킬 수 없었다 / 그의 욕망을. 3. 그래서 세몬은 자초했지 / 패배의 엄청난 모욕을. 그의 재산은 몰수되었고 내일 그는 처형될 거야. 4. 결국 그는 너무나 탐욕스럽게 되어서 / 그는 갖고 싶어졌다 / 눈에 보이는 모든 것을.

D. 1. Give me one-third / of what you possess / as my share, / and I will transfer it / to my estate.

2. I will go and arrange everything / so that Tarras may have his share.

3. "I do not need any help," he began, "My business is also all right."

4. I thought / the Fool would not succeed, / but he started to work nevertheless.

Chapter 3

Ivan having succeeded / in plowing all / but a small portion
이반은 성공했다 / 모든 밭을 가는 일에 / 자기 땅의 작은 부분을 제외하고 /

of his land, / he returned the next day / to finish it.
그는 다음날 돌아왔다 / 그 일을 끝내려고.

The pain in his stomach continued, / but he felt /
배에 통증은 계속되었다 / 그러나 그는 생각했다 /

that he must go on / with his work.
그는 일을 계속 해야만 한다고 / 자기 일을

He tried to start his plow, / but it would not move.
그는 쟁기를 움직이려 했지만 / 쟁기가 움직이지 않았다

But it seemed to have struck a hard root.
하지만 쟁기가 딱딱한 뿌리에 부딪힌 것 같았다

It was the small devil / in the ground /
바로 작은 악마가 / 땅속에 있던 /

who had wound his feet around the plowshares /
쟁깃날 주위를 발로 감았고 /

and held them. "This is strange," thought Ivan.
붙잡고 있었다. "이상한데" 이반은 생각했다

"There were never any roots / here before, / and this is
"뿌리가 하나도 없었는데 / 이곳에 전에는 / 여기

surely one." Ivan put his hand in the ground, /
확실히 (뿌리)하나가 있네" 이반은 땅 속으로 손을 넣었다 /

and, feeling something soft, / grasped / and pulled it out.
그리고 부드러운 뭔가를 느끼자 / 잡아서 / 밖으로 끌어냈다

It was like a root / in appearance, / but seemed to possess
그것은 뿌리 같았다 / 외관상으론 / 그러나 생명이 있는(살아있는) 것 같았다

life. Holding it up / he saw / that it was a little devil.
그것을 들어 올렸을 때 / 그는 알았다 / 그것은 작은 악마였다는 것을

Disgusted, he exclaimed, / "See the nasty thing," /
혐오감을 느껴서 그가 소리쳤다 / "이 역겨운 놈을 봐" /

and he proceeded to strike it a blow, / intending to kill it, /
그리고 그는 그것을 때리기 시작했다 / 그것을 죽이려고 /

when the young devil cried out: /
그 때 어린 악마가 소리쳤다 /

"Do not kill me, / and I will give you anything / you wish."
"절 죽이지 마세요 / 그러면 제가 뭐든지 줄게요 / 당신이 원하는"

"What can you do / for me?"
"뭘 해줄 수 있는데 / 나에게"

"Tell me / what it is / you most wish for," /
"말해보세요 / 무엇인지 / 당신이 가장 원하는 것이"

the little devil replied.
어린 악마가 대답했다

Ivan scratched the back of his head / as he thought, /
이반은 머리를 긁적였다 / 생각하면서 /

and finally he said: /
그리고 마침내 말했다 /

"I am dreadfully sick at my stomach. Can you cure me?"
"나는 배가 굉장히 아파. 네가 치료해줄 수 있니?"

"I can," the little devil said.
"할 수 있어요." 어린 악마가 말했다

"Then do so."
"그럼 그렇게 해줘"

The devil bent toward the earth / and began searching for
악마는 땅을 향해 숙였다 / 그리고 뿌리를 찾기 시작했다 /

roots, / and when he found them / he gave them to Ivan, /
그리고 그가 뿌리를 찾았을 때 / 그것을 이반에게 주었다 /

saying: "If you will swallow some of these /
이렇게 말하면서. "만일 당신이 이 뿌리를 조금만 삼켜도 /

you will be immediately cured / of any disease /
당신은 즉시 고칠 수 있습니다 / 어떤 병이든지 /

you are afflicted with."
당신이 고통 받는"

Ivan did / as he was told, / and obtained instant relief.
이반은 했다 / 들은 대로 / 그러자 즉시 편해졌다

---

grasp ~을 잡다 in appearance 외관상으로, 걷보기에 disgust 혐오감을 불러일으키다, 싫어지다
exclaim 소리치다, 외치다 nasty 역겨운, 불쾌한 proceed 시작하다 swallow 삼키다 afflict 고통을 주다
instant 즉시의, 즉각 relief (통증의) 완화, 안심

"I beg of you / to let me go now," the little devil pleaded.
"부탁합니다 / 이제 저를 놔주도록" 어린 악마가 간청했다

"I will pass into the earth, / never to return."
"저는 땅속으로 들어가서 / 절대로 돌아오지 않을 것입니다"

"Very well, you may go, / and God bless you."
"좋아, 가도 좋아 / 그리고 신께서 축복하시길 바랄께"

And as Ivan pronounced / the name of God, /
그리고 이반이 말했을 때 / 신의 이름을 /

the small devil disappeared / into the earth / like a flash, /
작은 악마는 사라졌다 / 땅속으로 / 눈 깜짝할 사이에 /

and only a slight opening / in the ground / remained.
그리고 작은 구멍만이 / 땅 위에 / 남아있었다

Ivan placed in his hat / what roots he had left, /
이반은 모자 안에 놓았다 / 먹고 남은 뿌리를 /

and proceeded to plow.
그리고 밭을 갈기 시작했다.

Soon finishing his work, / he turned his plow over /
곧 일을 끝마치고 / 그는 쟁기를 엎어 놓고 /

and returned home.
집으로 돌아갔다

When he reached the house / he found /
집에 도착했을 때 / 그는 발견했다 /

his brother Simeon and his wife seated / at the supper-table.
세몬 형과 형수가 앉아있는 것을 / 저녁식사 테이블에

His estate had been confiscated, /
그의 재산은 몰수되었다 /

and he himself had barely escaped execution /
그리고 그는 가까스로 처형되는 것을 피했다 /

by making his way out of prison.
감옥에서 빠져나와서

Now he had nothing to live on / and had come back /
이제 그는 먹고 살 것이 없었다 / 그래서 돌아왔다 /

to his father for support.
아버지한테 도움을 받으러

Turning to Ivan / he said: /
이반 쪽으로 몸을 돌리면서 / 그가 말했다 /

112   Tolstoy's Short Stories

"I came to ask / you to take care of us /
"나는 부탁하려 왔어 / 네가 우리를 돌봐 달라고 /

until I can find something to do."
내가 뭔가 할 일을 찾을 때까지"

"Very well," Ivan replied, / "you may remain with us."
"좋아요," 이반은 대답했다 / "우리와 함께 머무르세요."

Just as Ivan was about to sit down / at the table /
이반이 앉으려했던 바로 그 때에 / 테이블에 /

Simeon's wife made a wry face, /
세몬의 아내는 얼굴을 찡그렸다 /

indicating / that she did not like /
나타내면서 / 그녀가 싫어한다는 것을 /

the smell of Ivan's sheep-skin coat.
이반의 양가죽 코트 냄새를

She turned to her husband / and said, /
그녀는 자기 남편 쪽으로 몸을 돌리면서 / 말했다 /

"I shall not sit / at the table / with a peasant /
"나는 앉지 않을 거야 / 식탁에 / 소작농과 함께 /

who smells like that."
저런 냄새가 나는"

Simeon the soldier turned to his brother / and said: /
군인인 세몬은 자기 동생 쪽으로 몸을 돌리면서 / 말했다 /

"My lady objects / to the smell of your clothes.
"내 아내가 싫어해 / 네 옷 냄새를

You may eat in the porch."
너는 현관에서 먹어라"

Ivan said: "Very well, it is all the same to me.
이반이 말했다 "좋아요, 저한테는 마찬가지예요

I will soon have to go / and feed my horse / any way."
저는 곧 가서 / 말에게 먹이를 줘야하거든요 / 어쨌든"

Ivan took some bread / in one hand, /
이반은 빵을 약간 잡았고 / 한 손에 /

and his coat / in the other, / and left the room.
코트를 잡았다 / 다른 손으로 / 그리고 나서 방을 나갔다

plead 간청하다 pronounce 확실히 말하다, 발음하다 disappear 사라지다 like a flash 눈 깜짝할 사이에
remain ~머무르다, 체재하다 confiscate (재산을) 몰수하다 barely 겨우, 간신히 escape 모면하다, 피하다
execution 사형 wry face 찡그린 얼굴 object ~을 싫어하다

Chapter 4

The small devil finished with Simeon / that night, /
세몬을 맡았던 작은 악마는 일을 마쳤다 / 그날 밤에 /

and according to agreement / went to the assistance of his
그리고 합의한 대로 / 동료를 돕기 위해 갔다 /

comrade / who took charge of Ivan, /
이반을 맡고 있던 /

that he might help / to conquer the Fool.
그가 도와주기 위하여 / 바보를 동료가 정복하는 것을

He went to the field / and searched everywhere, /
그는 밭으로 가서 / 모든 곳을 찾아봤다 /

but could find nothing but the hole / through which /
그러나 구멍만 발견할 수 있었다 / 그 구멍으로 /

the small devil had disappeared.
작은 악마가 사라져버렸던.

"Well, this is strange," he said, /
"음, 이건 이상한데" 그가 말했다 /

"something bad must have happened / to my companion, /
"좋지 않은 일이 일어난 것이 틀림없군 / 내 동료에게 /

and I will have to take his place / and continue /
그러면 내가 그를 대신해야 겠군 / 그리고 계속해야 겠군 /

the work he began.
그가 시작한 일을

The Fool is through with his plowing, /
바보가 밭가는 일을 끝냈어 /

so I must look for / some other means / of destroying him.
그러니까 나는 찾아 봐야 겠어 / 뭔가 다른 수단을 / 그를 파멸시킬 수 있는.

I must overflow his meadow / and prevent /
나는 그의 초원에 물이 넘치게 해서 / 그래서 방해해야지 /

him from cutting the grass."
그가 풀 베는 것을"

So the little devil overflowed the meadow /
그래서 작은 악마는 초원에 물을 넘치게 했다 /

with muddy water, / and, when Ivan went /
진흙탕 물로 / 그리고 이반이 가서 /

at dawn next morning / with his scythe / and sharpened /
새벽에 다음날 아침 / 큰 낫을 갖고 / 날을 간 다음에 /

and tried to cut the grass, / he found /
풀을 베려고 했을 때 / 그는 알았다 /

that it resisted all his efforts /
풀은 그의 모든 시도에 저항했고(아무리 노력도 베어지지 않았고) /

and would not yield to the implement / as usual.
풀은 연장에 굴복하려 하지 않는 것을(풀이 베어지지 않는 다는 것을) / 평소 때처럼.

Many times Ivan tried to cut the grass, /
여러 번 이반은 풀을 베려고 시도했지만 /

but always without success.
매번 성공하지 못했다

At last becoming weary of the effort, / he decided /
마침내 애를 쓰느라 지쳤기 때문에 / 그는 결심했다 /

to return home / and have his scythe again sharpened, /
집으로 돌아가서 / 큰 낫을 다시 갈기로 /

and also to eat a lot of bread, / saying: /
그리고 또한 빵도 많이 먹기로 (결심했다) / 그리고 이렇게 말했다 /

"I will come back here / and will not leave /
"나는 여기 다시 올 거야 / 그리고 떠나지 않을 거야 /

until I have mown all the meadow, /
초원을 다 벨 때까지 /

even if it should take a whole week."
비록 그 일이 1주일이 걸릴 지라도"

Hearing this, / the little devil became thoughtful, / saying: /
이 말을 듣고 / 작은 악마는 생각에 잠겼다 / 그리고 이렇게 말했다 /

"That Ivan is a hard case, / and I must think /
"이반은 상대하기가 어려운 별난 놈인걸, / 그러면 나는 생각해내야만 해 /

of some other way of conquering him."
그를 정복할 다른 방법을"

Ivan soon returned / with his sharpened scythe /
이반은 곧 돌아와서 / 날을 간 큰 낫을 갖고 /

and started to mow.
풀을 베기 시작했다

---

agreement 동의, 합의 comrade 친구, 동료 take charge of ~을 떠맡다, 담당하다 conquer 정복하다
nothing but 단지, ~만 companion 동료, 친구 through ~을 끝낸 overflow ~을 넘치게 하다, 범람시키다
meadow 초원, 목초지 muddy 진흙투성이의 scythe (긴 자루의) 큰 낫 resist ~에 저항하다 yield ~에 굴복하다
weary 지친, 힘이 빠진 mow (잔디, 풀을) 깎다(mow-mowed-mown) thoughtful 생각에 잠긴 case 별난 사람, 괴짜

The small devil hid himself / in the grass, /
작은 악마는 몸을 숨겼다 / 풀 속에 /

and as the point of the scythe came down / he buried it /
그리고 큰 낫의 끝이 내려왔을 때 / 그는 낫의 끝을 묻었다 /

in the earth / and made it almost impossible /
땅속에 / 그래서 (뭔가를) 불가능하게 했다 /

for Ivan to move the implement.
이반이 연장을 움직이는 것을

He, however, succeeded in mowing all /
그러나 그는 모든 풀을 베는 데 성공했다 /

but one small spot in the swamp, /
늪의 작은 부분을 제외하고는 /

where again the small devil hid himself, / saying: /
그곳에 다시 작은 악마가 숨어있었다 / 그리고 이렇게 말했다 /

"Even if he should cut my hands / I will prevent /
"비록 그가 내 손을 벤다고 해도 / 나는 못하게 할 거야 /

him from accomplishing his work."
그가 일을 완수하는 것을"

When Ivan came to the swamp / he found /
이반이 늪으로 왔을 때 / 그는 발견했다 /

that the grass was not very thick.
풀이 아주 두껍지 않다는 것을

Still, the scythe would not work, /
여전히 큰 낫이 말을 듣지 않았다 /

which / made him so angry / that he worked /
이런 일은 / 이반을 너무 화나게 해서 / 그는 일했다 /

with all his might, / and one powerful blow / cut off /
있는 힘을 다하여 / 그래서 낫을 세게 내려치자 / 잘랐다 /

a portion of the small devil's tail, /
작은 악마의 꼬리 부분을 /

who had hidden himself there.
(어떤 악마?) 거기(늪지)에 몸을 숨기고 있던

Despite the little devil's efforts / he succeeded /
작은 악마의 노력에도 불구하고 / 그는 성공했다 /

in finishing his work.
일을 끝내는데

He returned home / and ordered /
그는 집에 돌아왔다 / 그리고 지시했다 /

his sister to gather up the grass / while he went /
여동생에게 풀을 모으라고 / 그가 간 동안에 /

to another field / to cut rye.
다른 밭으로 / 호밀을 베러

But the devil preceded him there, / and fixed the rye /
그러나 악마는 그보다 먼저 그곳에 갔다 / 그리고 호밀을 고정시켜놓았다 /

in such a manner that it was almost impossible /
거의 불가능 하도록 /

for Ivan to cut it.
이반이 호밀을 잘라내는 것이

However, after continuous hard labor / he succeeded, /
그러나 계속해서 열심히 일해서 / 그는 성공했다 /

and when he was through with the rye / he said to himself: /
그리고 이반이 호밀을 다 베었을 때 / 그는 혼잣말을 했다 /

"Now I will start to mow oats."
"이제 귀리를 베기 시작해야겠군."

On hearing this, / the little devil thought to himself: /
이 말을 듣자마자 / 작은 악마는 혼자 생각했다 /

"I could not prevent / him from mowing the rye, /
"내가 못하게 할 수가 없겠군 / 그가 호밀을 베는 것을 /

but I will surely stop / him from mowing the oats /
하지만 나는 틀림없이 못하게 할 거야 / 그가 귀리를 베는 것을 /

when the morning comes."
아침이 오면"

Early next day, / when the devil came to the field, /
다음날 아침 일찍 / 악마가 밭으로 왔을 때 /

he found / that the oats had been already mowed.
그는 발견했다 / 귀리가 이미 베어진 것을

Ivan did it / during the night, / so as to avoid the loss /
이반이 그 일을 했다 / 밤사이에 / 피해를 막기 위하여 /

that might have resulted from the grain being too ripe and
(어떤 피해?) 곡식이 너무 익거나 마르면 발생할 수 있는(피해)

dry.

---

swamp 늪, 소택지 accomplish (일, 임무를) 완수하다, 완성하다 blow 강타, 타격 portion 부분, 몫 rye 호밀
precede ~보다 앞서다, 먼저가다 oat 귀리 prevent ~을 막다, 방해하다

Seeing / that Ivan again had escaped him, /
보았기 때문에 / 이반이 또다시 그의 방해로부터 피한 것을 /

the little devil became greatly enraged, / saying: /
작은 악마는 엄청나게 분노했다 / 그래서 이렇게 말했다 /

"He cut me all over / and made me tired, that fool.
"그는 내 몸에 온갖 상처를 냈고 / 지치게 만들었어, 저 바보가

I did not meet such misfortune / even on the battle-field.
이런 불운한 경우는 맛보지 못했는데 / 심지어 전쟁터에서도

He does not even sleep," and the devil began to swear.
그는 잠도 안 자는군" 그리고 악마는 맹세하기 시작했다

"I cannot beat him," / he continued.
"나는 그를 이길(당해낼) 수가 없어" / 그는 계속해서 말했다

"I will go now to the heaps / and make everything rotten."
"나는 지금 (곡식) 더미로 가서 / 몽땅 썩게 만들어야지"

Key Expression

on 동사+ing; ~하자마자

"a book on the desk"(책상위에 있는 책)에 전치사 "on"이 사용된다. 책과 책상이라는 두 물체가 서로 붙어 있다는 "접촉"의 의미를 표현하고자 "on"이라는 전치사를 사용하였다. 또한 어떤 사건이 발생하자마자 다음 사건이 일어나는 경우가 있다. 이런 경우엔 마치 두 사건이 서로 붙어 있는 느낌이다. 그래서 "on 동사+ing"라는 표현은 "~하자마자", "바로 ~할 때"라고 해석한다.

On hearing this, the little devil thought to himself.
이 말을 듣자마자 / 작은 악마는 혼자 생각했다

enraged 화내는 misfortune 불행 swear 맹세하나 heap (곡식) 더미, 축적

So he went to a heap of the new-mown grain /
그래서 그는 새로 벤 곡식 더미로 가서 /

and began his fiendish work.
잔인한 짓을 시작했다

After wetting it / he built a fire and warmed himself, /
더미를 적신 다음에 / 불을 붙여서 몸을 따뜻하게 했다

and soon was fast asleep. Ivan harnessed his horse, /
그랬더니 금방 잠들어버렸다. 이반은 말에 마구를 채웠다 /

and, with his sister, / went to bring / the rye home /
그리고 여동생과 함께 / 가지러 갔다 / 귀리를 집으로 /

from the field. After lifting a couple of sheaves /
밭에서. 두 개의 묶음을 들어올린 다음 /

from the first heap / his pitchfork came into contact /
첫 번째 더미에서 / 그의 갈퀴가 닿게 되었다 /

with the little devil's back, / which caused him to howl /
작은 악마의 등에 / 이런 일은 그 악마가 소리를 지르게 만들었고 /

with pain / and to jump around in every direction.
고통스럽게 / 그리고 사방으로 펄쩍 뛰어다니게 (만들었다)

Ivan exclaimed: / "See here! What nasty thing!
이반이 소리쳤다 / "어라! 정말로 징그러운 놈이야!

You again here?" "I am another one!" said the little devil.
너 또 여기에 (있어)?" "나는 다른 애야!" 작은 악마가 말했다

"That was my brother. I am the one /
그것(전에 만난 악마)은 내 형제였어. 나는 악마야 /

who was sent to your brother Simeon."
당신 형인 세몬에게 보내졌던

"Well," said Ivan, "it doesn't matter /
"그래" 이반이 말했다. "상관 없어 /

who you are. I will fix you all the same."
네가 누구이든. 너도 똑같이 혼내줄게"

As Ivan was about to strike the first blow / the devil pleaded:
이반이 처음 때리려고 할 때 / 악마는 간청했다

"Let me go / and I will do you no more harm. I will do /
"나를 놔줘 / 그러면 더 이상 해롭게 안할게. 내가 할게 /

whatever you wish." "What can you do for me?" asked Ivan.
당신이 원하는 건 뭐든지" "나한테 뭘 해줄 수 있는데?" 이반이 물어봤다

fiendish 잔인한, 악마 같은 harness 마구를 채우다 sheaf (추수한 곡물의) 단, 묶음 howl 큰소리로 외치다, 고함치다 fix 혼내주다

"I can make soldiers / from almost anything."
"나는 군사를 만들 수 있어 / 무엇을 가지고라도"

"And what will they be good for?"
"그러면 군사가 어디에다 쓰지?"

"Oh, they will do everything / for you!"
"오, 군사들은 뭐든지 할 거야 / 너를 위해"

"Can they sing?"
"그들이 노래를 부를 수 있니?"

"They can."
"부를 수 있지."

"Well, make them."
"그러면 만들어줘."

"Take a bunch of straw / and scatter it / on the ground, /
"한 다발의 지푸라기를 잡으세요 / 그리고 뿌리세요 / 땅에다 /

and see / if each straw will not turn into a soldier."
그리고 지켜보세요 / 지푸라기 하나가 한 명의 군사로 변하는지"

Ivan shook the straws / on the ground, /
이반은 지푸라기들을 흔들었다 / 땅에 대고 /

and, as he expected, / each straw turned into a soldier, /
그랬더니 그가 예상한 대로 / 지푸라기 한 개가 한명의 군사로 변했다 /

and they began marching / with a band at their head.
그리고 그들은 행진하기 시작했다 / 악단이 선두에 서서

"That was well done! How it will delight /
"근사한데! 얼마나 기쁘게 할까 /

the village maidens!" he exclaimed.
마을 처녀들을!" 그가 소리쳤다

The small devil now said:
작은 악마가 이제 말했다

"Let me go. You do not need me any longer."
"나를 놔줘. 내가 더 이상 필요 없잖아."

Key Expression

matter; 중요하다

"matter"라는 단어가 명사로 쓰이면, "일", "사건", "문제"라는 의미가 있다. 이런 의미 외에도 동사로 사용되면, "중요하다"라는 의미가 있다.

It doesn't matter who you are. 상관이 없어 / 네가 누구이든
Power doesn't matter much to him. 권력은 중요하지 않다 / 그에게

---

good for ~에 사용되다 turn into ~을 바꾸다, 변하다 maiden 처녀 exclaim 큰소리로 외치다, 소리치다

Tolstoy's Short Stories

But Ivan said: "No, I will not let you go just yet.
그러나 이반은 말했다 "아니, 나는 아직 널 놔주지 않을 거야.

You have converted / the straw into soldiers, /
네가 변하게 했어 / 지푸라기를 군사로 /

and now I want / you to turn them again into straw, /
그러면 이제는 원해 / 네가 군사를 다시 짚으로 변하게 하길 /

as I cannot afford to lose it, / but I want it /
나는 짚이 없으면 안 되기 때문이야 / 하지만 짚을 원해 /

with the grain on."
낱알이 붙어 있는"

The devil replied:
악마가 대답했다

"Say: / 'So many soldiers, so much straw.'"
"이렇게 말해봐, / 군사들 숫자만큼 지푸라기 숫자가 되어라"

Ivan did as he was told, / and got back /
이반은 들은 대로 했다 / 그러자 다시 얻었다 /

his rye with the straw.
호밀이 있는 지푸라기를

The small devil again begged / for his release.
작은 악마가 다시 애원했다 / 풀어달라고

Ivan, / taking him from the pitchfork, / said: /
이반은 / 갈퀴에서 악마를 떼어내면서 / 이렇게 말했다 /

"With God's blessing / you may depart."
"신의 은총으로 / 너는 떠나도 돼."

And, as before / at the mention of God's name, /
그리고 전과 같이 / 신의 이름을 말했을 때 /

the little devil disappeared into the earth / like a flash, /
작은 악마는 땅속으로 사라졌다 / 번개같이 /

and nothing was left / but the hole /
그리고 아무것도 남지 않았다 /

to show where he had gone.
구멍을 제외하곤 / 어디로 그가 사라졌는지 보여주는

---

convert 바꾸다 depart 떠나다 mention 언급, 말함

Soon afterward / Ivan returned home, /
이 사건 이후 곧 / 이반이 집으로 돌아오자 /

to find / his brother Tarras and his wife there.
발견했다 / 타라스 형과 형수가 집에 있는 것을

Tarras could not pay his debts, / and was forced to flee /
타라스는 빚을 갚을 수가 없었다 / 그래서 어쩔 수 없이 도망치고 /

from his creditors / and seek refuge / under his father's
빚쟁이들로부터 / 도피처를 찾았다 / 아버지 집에서.

roof. Seeing Ivan, he said: / "Well, Ivan, may we stay here /
이반을 보자 그가 말했다 / "어, 이반, 여기 있어도 되겠니 /

until I start in some new business?"
내가 사업을 새로 시작할 때까지"

Ivan replied / as he had before to Simeon: /
이반은 대답했다 / 세몬에게 전에 했던 것처럼 /

"Yes, you are perfectly welcome to stay here /
"응, 이곳에 있어도 좋아 /

as long as it suits you." With that announcement /
마음에 맞으면 그렇게 말하면서 /

he removed his coat / and seated himself /
그는 코트를 벗고 / 앉았다 /

at the supper-table with the others. But Tarras's wife
다른 사람들과 함께 저녁 식사 테이블에 / 그러나 타라스의 아내는 싫어했다 /

objected to / the smell of his clothes, saying: /
이반의 옷 냄새를 / 그래서 이렇게 말했다 /

"I cannot eat with a fool, / neither can I stand / the smell."
"나는 바보와 같이 먹을 수 없고 / 게다가 나는 견딜 수가 없어 / 냄새도"

Then Tarras said: / "Ivan, from your clothes /
그러자 타라스는 말했다 / "이반, 네 옷에서 /

there comes a bad smell. Go and eat by yourself /
고약한 냄새가 난다 / 가서 너 혼자 먹어라 /

in the porch." "Very well," said Ivan, / and he took some
현관에서" "좋아" 이반이 말했다 / 그리고 그는 빵을 갖고 나갔다 /

bread and went out / as ordered / saying, /
시키는 대로 / 이렇게 말하면서 /

"It is time for me / to feed my mare."
줄 시간이야 / 말에게 사료를

---

be forced to 어쩔 수 없이 ~하다 creditor 빚쟁이, 채권자 refuge 도피처, 피난처 welcome ~해도 좋은
as long as ~하는 한 suit 마음에 들다, 편리하나 mare 암말

Key Expression

at the mention of; ~라고 말하는 순간에, 말할 때

"at the sight of"는 "~를 보는 순간에"라는 의미이며, "at the mention of"는 "~를 말하는 순간에"라는 의미로 사용된다. 동사의 성질이 있는 "sight"나 "mention" 같은 명사가 "at the" 다음에 오면, 어떤 사건이 발생하는 시간이나 때를 나타낸다.

At the mention of God's name, the little devil disappeared into the earth like a flash.
신의 이름을 말했을 때 / 작은 악마는 땅속으로 사라졌다 / 번개같이

Quiz 6

A. 내용 이해하기
다음 문장을 읽고 본문의 내용과 맞으면 T(True), 틀리면 F(False)를 쓰세요.

1. Ivan went on with his work in spite of the pain in his stomach.
2. Ivan's stomach pain was immediately relieved, after he swallowed some roots that a little devil gave to him.
3. As soon as Ivan mentioned the name of God, the devil disappeared into the earth.
4. Simeon and his wife visited Ivan's house on vacation.

B. 단어
다음 제시된 단어의 설명을 읽고, 어떤 단어의 정의를 설명하는지 아래의 박스에서 찾아 써 보세요.

1. a person or bank that you owe money to
2. an unmarried woman or girl
3. to shout something angrily; utter long, mournful, plaintive sound
4. a group of straw tied together; a number of pieces of paper held together
5. vow; to promise that you will do something
6. to stop something from happening
7. a part of a whole; a part of something larger
8. a very wet area of ground; a lowland region saturated with water
9. to cut down grass with a scythe
10. a field with wild grass; a tract of grassland

---

howl portion swear maiden mow

creditor sheaf swamp meadow prevent

Answer A. 1. T 2. T 3. T 4. F
B. 1. creditor 2. maiden 3. howl 4. sheaf 5. swear 6. prevent 7. portion 8. swamp 9. mow
10. meadow

C. 직독직해

아래에 제시된 문장을 직독직해로 해석해보세요.

1. Ivan having succeeded / in plowing all / but a small portion of his land, / he returned the next day / to finish it.

   →

2. "I could not prevent / him from mowing the rye, / but I will surely stop / him from mowing the oats / when the morning comes."

   →

3. "Take a bunch of straw / and scatter it / on the ground, / and see / if each straw will not turn into a soldier."

   →

4. At the mention of God's name, / the little devil disappeared into the earth / like a flash, / and nothing was left / but the hole / to show where he had gone.

   →

D. 동시통역

아래에 제시된 직독직해를 보고, 영어로 말해보세요.

1. 이제 그는 먹고 살 것이 없었다 / 그래서 돌아왔다 / 아버지한테 도움을 받으러.

   →

2. "그래" 이반이 말했다, "상관이 없어 / 네가 누구이든. 너도 똑같이 혼내줄게"

   →

3. 네가 변하게 했어 / 지푸라기를 군사로 / 그러면 이제는 원해 / 네가 군사를 다시 짚으로 변하게 하길

   →

4. "나는 바보와 같이 먹을 수 없고 / 게다가 나는 견딜 수가 없어 / 냄새도"

   →

Answer

C. 1. 이반은 성공했다 / 모든 밭을 가는 일에 / 자기 땅의 작은 부분을 제외하고 / 그는 다음날 돌아왔다 / 그 일을 끝내려고. 2. "나는 막을 수가 없었지 / 그가 호밀을 베는 것을 / 그러나 나는 틀림없이 못하게 할 거야 / 그가 귀리를 베는 것을 / 아침이 오면" 3. "한 다발의 지푸라기를 잡으세요 / 그리고 뿌리세요 / 땅에다 / 그리고 지켜보세요 / 지푸라기 하나가 한 명의 군사로 변하는지" 4. 신의 이름을 말했을 때 / 작은 악마는 땅속으로 사라졌다 / 번개같이 / 그리고 아무것도 남지 않았다 / 구멍을 제외하곤 / 어디로 그가 사라졌는지 보여주는

D. 1. Now he had nothing to live on / and had come back / to his father for support.

2. "Well," said Ivan, "it doesn't matter / who you are. I will fix you all the same."

3. You have converted / the straw into soldiers, / and now I want / you to turn them again into straw.

4. "I cannot eat with a fool, / neither can I stand / the smell."

Chapter 5

The small devil / who had charge of Tarras / finished with
작은 악마가 / 타라스를 맡았던 / 일을 끝냈다 /

him / that night, / and according to agreement /
그날 밤에 / 그리고 약속한 대로 /

proceeded to the assistance of the other two /
다른 두 악마를 도와주러 갔다 /

to help them conquer Ivan.
두 악마가 이반을 정복하는 것을 돕기 위해서

Arriving at the plowed field / he looked around for his
간 밭에 도착해서 / 그는 자기 동료들을 찾아보았다 /

comrades, / but found only the hole /
하지만 구멍만을 발견했다 /

through which one had disappeared.
그 구멍으로 악마가 사라져버렸던.

In the meadow he discovered / the severed tail of the other, /
초원에서 그는 발견했다 / 다른 동료의 잘린 꼬리를 /

and in the rye-field found / yet another hole.
그리고 호밀 밭에서 발견했다 / 또 다른 구멍을

"Well," he thought, / "it is quite clear /
"음" 그는 생각했다 / "틀림없이 (무엇이?) /

that my comrades have met with some great misfortune, /
내 동료들이 엄청난 불행을 당한 것이/

and that I will have to take their places / and arrange /
그러면 나는 그들을 대신해서 / 준비해야겠군 /

the feud between the brothers."
형제들 사이의 다툼이 일어나도록"

The small devil then went / in search of Ivan.
그래서 작은 악마는 갔다 / 이반을 찾으러

But he, / having finished with the field, /
그러나 그는 / 밭일을 끝낸 다음에 /

was nowhere to be found.
어디서도 찾을 수가 없었다.

He had gone to the forest / to cut logs /
그는 숲으로 갔다 / 나무를 베러 /

to build homes for his brothers, / as they found /
형제들이 살 집을 지을 /   그들은 불편하다고 생각했기 때문이었다 /

it inconvenient / for so many to live / under the same roof.
                       그렇게 많은 사람들이 사는 것이 / 같은 지붕 아래에서

The small devil at last discovered / Ivan's whereabouts.
작은 악마는 마침내 발견했다 /   이반이 어디 있는지

Going to the forest, / he climbed into the branches of the
숲으로 가서 /   그는 나무 가지로 올라갔다 /

trees / and began to interfere / with Ivan's work.
          그리고 방해하기 시작했다 /   이반이 하는 일을

Ivan cut down a tree, / but it failed to fall to the ground, /
이반이 나무를 한 그루 잘랐다 / 하지만 나무는 땅바닥에 쓰러지지 않았다 /

becoming entangled / in the branches of other trees.
엉켜버렸다 /   다른 나무의 가지에 (땅에 쓰러지지 않았다)

Finally he succeeded / in getting it down /
드디어 그는 성공했다 /   나무를 땅에 떨어뜨리는 일에 /

after a hard struggle. In chopping down the next tree /
열심히 노력해서   다음 나무를 벨 때도 /

he met with the same difficulties, / and also with the third.
그는 똑같은 어려움에 부딪혔다 /   그리고 세 번째 나무도 그랬다

Ivan had thought / he could cut down fifty trees /
이반은 예상했었다 /   50그루를 벨 수 있을 것이라고 /

in a day, / but he succeeded in chopping only ten /
하루에 /   그러나 단지 10그루만 벨 수 있었다 /

before darkness. He put an end to his labors / for a time.
날이 어두워지기 전에.   그는 일을 멈추었다 /   잠시 동안

He was now exhausted, / and, perspiring profusely, /
그는 이제 지쳤다 /   그리고 땀을 엄청 흘렸기 때문에 /

he sat down / alone in the woods / to rest.
그는 앉았다 /   숲속에 홀로 /   쉬려고

---

plow (밭을) 갈다 severed 잘린, 절단된 comrade 친구, 동료 misfortune 불행 arrange 준비하다, 조정하다
feud (형제간의) 다툼, 불화 inconvenient 불편한 whereabouts 사람이 있는 곳, 행방 interfere 방해하다,
간섭하다 entangled 얽힌, 엉켜버린 perspire 땀을 흘리다 profusely 엄청나게, 많이

But he soon resumed his work, /
하지만 그는 곧 일을 다시 시작해서 /

cutting down one more tree.
한 그루를 더 베었다

However, the effort gave him a pain in his back, /
하지만 (나무를 베려고) 고생했기 때문에 등이 아팠다 /

and he was obliged to rest again.
그래서 다시 쉴 수밖에 없었다

Seeing this, / the small devil was full of joy.
이것을 보고 / 작은 악마는 매우 기뻤다

"Well," he thought, / "now he is exhausted /
"음" 그는 생각했다 / "이제 그(이반)는 지쳤고 /

and will stop work, / and I will rest also."
일을 중지할 거야 / 그러면 나도 쉬어야지"

He then seated himself on some branches /
그런 다음 그는 나뭇가지에 앉아서 /

and congratulated himself.
자랑스럽게 생각했다

However, Ivan again arose, / took his axe, /
그러나 이반은 다시 일어나서 / 도끼를 잡았다

and gave the tree a terrific blow / from the opposite side, /
그리고 세게 나무를 (도끼로) 찍었다 / 나무의 반대편에서 /

which felled it / instantly to the ground, /
그래서 그 나무를 쓰러뜨렸다 / 곧바로 땅으로 /

carrying the little devil with it.
작은 악마와 함께

And Ivan, / proceeding to cut the branches, /
그리고 이반이 / 가지를 자르기 시작했을 때 /

found the devil alive.
악마가 살아있는 것을 발견했다.

Very much astonished, / Ivan exclaimed: /
엄청 놀래서 / 이반은 소리쳤다 /

"Look you! Such nasty thing! Are you again here?"
"야, 너! 엄청 징그러운 놈이 군! 너도 또 여기에 있냐?"

"I am another one," replied the devil.
"나는 다른 애야" 악마가 대답했다

"I was with your brother Tarras."
"나는 네 형 타라스에 붙어 있었던 놈이에요."

Tolstoy's Short Stories

"Well," said Ivan, "that makes no difference. I will fix you."
"음" 이반이 말했다 "그건 상관없어. 내가 너를 혼내주마."

And he was about to strike him a blow / with the axe /
그리고 그는 악마를 내리치려고 했다 / 도끼로 /

when the devil pleaded:
악마가 간청할 때 /

"Do not kill me, / and whatever you wish / you shall have."
"날 죽이지 마 / 그러면 네가 원하는 것은 / 뭐든지 줄게"

Ivan asked, "What can you do?"
이반이 물었다. "뭘 해줄 수 있는데?"

"I can make for you / all the money / you wish."
"저는 당신을 위해 만들 수 있어요 / 모든 돈을 / 네가 원하는 만큼"

Ivan then told the devil / to go ahead.
이반은 그러자 악마에게 말했다 / 계속 이야기해보라고

So the devil began to explain / to him /
그래서 악마는 설명하기 시작했다 / 그에게 /

how he might become rich.
어떻게 이반이 부자가 될 수 있는지

"Take," / said he to Ivan, /
"잡아요" / 악마가 이반에게 말했다 /

"the leaves of his oak tree / and rub them in your hands, /
"떡갈나무 잎을 / 그리고 손으로 문질러요 /

and the gold will fall to the ground."
그러면 황금이 땅에 떨어질 거예요"

Ivan did / as he was told, /
이반은 했다 / 들은 대로 /

and immediately the gold began to drop / about his feet.
그러자 즉시 황금이 떨어지기 시작했다 / 그의 발 주위에

He remarked: /
그가 말했다 /

"This will be a fine trick / to amuse the village boys with."
"이것은 묘기가 될 것이에요 / 마을 소년들을 즐겁게 해줄"

"Can I leave?" asked the devil, / to which Ivan replied, /
"이제 가도 돼요?" 악마가 이반에게 물었다 / 악마의 말에 이반이 대답했다 /

"With God's blessing / you may go."
"신의 은총으로 / 넌 가도 돼"

resume 일을 다시시작하다 be obliged to ~하지 않을 수 없다 joy 기쁨 congratulate oneself 자랑스럽게 생각하다 instantly 곧바로, 즉시 proceed ~을 시작하다 astonish ~을 놀라게 하다 fix 혼내주다 remark 말을 하다 amuse 즐겁게 하다

At the mention of the name of God /
신의 이름을 말하는 순간 /

the devil disappeared into the earth.
악마는 땅 속으로 사라져버렸다

Key Expression

사물이 주어로 사용되는 무생물주어란?

무생물 주어란 사람이 아닌 사물, 사건이 문장의 주어로 사용된 경우이다. 무생물 주어가 있는 문장을 자연스럽게 해석하려다보면 시간 낭비를 할 수도 있다. 그렇기 때문에 영어 문장을 있는 그대로 받아들이는 습관(직역)을 길러야 한다. 즉 직역을 통하여 무생물 주어가 사용된 문장을 영어식 사고로 받아들이는 훈련을 해야 한다. 그렇지 않으면, 무생물 주어가 사용된 문장을 만날 때마다 영어 표현에 대한 거리감을 느끼며 문장을 자연스럽게 해석하려다보면, 그 문장을 이해하는데 많은 시간이 걸린다.

The effort gave him a pain in his back.
나무를 베려는 노력은 / 그에게 통증을 주었다 / (어디에?) 그의 등에
(나무를 베려고 고생했기 때문에 등이 아팠다)

Chapter 6

The brothers, / having finished their houses, /
형제들은 / 각자 집을 다 지은 다음에 /

moved into their new houses / and lived apart /
자신의 새 집으로 이사 가서 / 떨어져 살았다 /

from their father and brother.
자기 아버지와 형제와

Ivan, / when he had completed his plowing, /
이반은 / 밭갈이를 마친 후 /

made a great feast, / to which / he invited his brothers, /
큰 잔치를 벌였다 / 그 잔치에 / 이반은 형제들을 초대했고 /

telling them / that he had plenty of beer / for them to
그리고 형제들에게 말했다 / 맥주가 많이 있다고 / 그들이 마실.

drink. The brothers, however, declined /
그러나 형제들은 거절했다 /

Ivan's invitation, / saying, / "We have seen the beer /
이반의 초대를 / 이렇게 말하면서 / "우리는 맥주를 이미 봤어 /

that peasants drink, / and want none of it."
소작농들이 마시는 / 그리고 마시고 싶지 않아"

Ivan then gathered around him /
그러자 이반은 모았다 /

all the peasants in the village / and with them drank beer /
마을의 모든 소작농들을 / 그리고 그들과 함께 맥주를 마셨다 /

until he became intoxicated.
그가 취할 때까지

He went to / a street gathering of the village boys and
그는 갔다 / 마을 소년과 소녀가 길가에 모여 있는 곳으로 /

girls, / and told them / they must sing his praises, /
그러고 나서 말했다 / 아이들이 자신을 칭찬하는 노래를 불러야 한다고 /

saying / that in return he would show them / such sights /
그리고 말했다 / 보답으로 아이들에게 보여주겠다고 / 새로운 구경거리를 /

as they had never before seen in their lives.
아이들이 평생 보지 못했던

move into 집으로 이사 가다 complete (일을) 마치다, 완성하다 feast 잔치, 연회 decline 거절하다
invitation 초대, 초청 intoxicated 술에 취한 sight 색다른 것, 구경거리

The little girls laughed / and began to sing songs /
어린 소녀들이 웃음을 터뜨리더니 / 노래를 부르기 시작했다 /

praising Ivan, / and when they had finished / they said:
이반을 칭송하는 / 그리고 그들이 노래를 마쳤을 때 / 그들은 말했다 /

"Very well, now give us / what you said you would."
"좋아요. 이제 우리한테 줘 / 네가 해준다고 말한 것을.

Ivan replied, / "I will soon show you," /
이반이 대답했다 / "내가 너희들에게 곧 보여줄게" /

and, taking an empty bag in his hand, /
그리고는 빈 자루를 손으로 잡고 /

he started for the woods.
그는 숲속으로 가버렸다

The little girls laughed / as they said,
어린 소녀들은 비웃었다 / 말하면서,

"What a fool he is!" / and they forgot all about him.
"정말로 바보 같으니라고!" / 그리고 이반에 대해서는 새까맣게 잊었다.

Some time after / Ivan suddenly appeared / among them /
얼마 후에 / 이반이 갑자기 나타났다 / 아이들에게 /

carrying in his hand the bag, / which / was now filled.
손에 자루를 들고 / 그런데 그 자루는 / 이제는 (뭔가로) 채워져 있었다.

"Shall I divide this with you?" he said.
"이것을 너희들에게 나눠줄까?" 그가 말했다

"Yes, divide!" they sang in chorus.
"네, 나눠줘요!" 아이들이 이구동성으로 말했다.

So Ivan put his hand into the bag / and drew out some gold
그러자 이반은 가방 안으로 손을 넣었고 / 금화를 꺼냈다 /

coins, / which / he scattered / among them.
그리고 그 금화를 / 그는 뿌렸다 / 아이들에게

"It's magic!" they cried / as they ran to gather up /
"마술이다!" 그들은 외쳤다 / 주우러 달려가면서 /

the precious pieces.
금화를

---

praise 칭송하다, 칭찬하다 divide 나누다, 분배하다 in chorus 이구동성으로 scatter 뿌리다, 흩어지게 하다

The peasants then appeared / on the scene /
그러자 소작농들도 나타났다 / 현장(그곳)에

and began to fight / among themselves /
그리고 싸우기 시작했다 / 서로 /

for the possession of the yellow objects.
노란 물건을 가지려고

In the fight / one old woman was nearly crushed to death.
서로 다툴 때 / 어느 할머니가 거의 깔려 죽을 뻔했다.

Ivan laughed and was greatly amused / at the sight /
이반은 웃었고 아주 재미있었다 / 보고서 /

of so many persons quarrelling / over a few pieces of gold.
그렇게 많은 사람들이 싸우는 모습을 / 금 조각 몇 개 때문에

"Oh! You little fools," he said, /
"오! 어리석은 사람들!" 그가 말했다 /

"why did you almost crush the life out of /
"왜 당신들이 깔려 죽을 뻔하게 하니 /

the old grandmother? Be more gentle. I have plenty more, /
늙은 할머니를? 점잖게 구세요 전 많이 있어요 /

and I will give them to you."
그리고 당신들에게 줄게요"

He began throwing / about / more of the coins.
그는 던지기 시작했다 / 여기저기로 / 더 많은 동전을

The people gathered around him, /
사람들이 이반의 주위에 모였다 /

and Ivan continued throwing / until he emptied his bag.
그리고 이반은 계속 던졌다 / 자루가 빌 때까지

They clamored for more, / but Ivan replied: /
사람들이 더 달라고 외쳤다 / 하지만 이반은 대답했다 /

"The gold is all gone. Another time I will give you more.
"금화가 떨어졌어요. 다음에 더 드릴게요

Now we will resume / our singing and dancing."
이제는 다시 시작합시다 / 노래와 춤을"

The little children sang, / but Ivan said to them,
어린이들이 노래했다 / 그러나 이반은 아이들에게 말했다

"Your songs are no good."
"너희 노래는 좋지 않아."

scene (사건의) 현장, 장소 possession 소유 object 물건 quarrel 말다툼하다, ~와 싸우다 crush ~을 눌러 부수다, 뭉개다 clamor 큰소리로 외치다, ~을 요구하다

The children said, / "Then show us / how to sing better."
아이들이 말했다 / "그러면 가르쳐주세요 / 어떻게 더 잘 부르는지"

To this Ivan replied, / "I will show you /
이 말에 이반은 대답했다 / "내가 보여주지 /

people who can sing better than you."
너희보다 더 잘 부르는 사람을"

With this remark / Ivan went to the barn /
이렇게 말을 하면서 / 이반은 헛간으로 들어가서 /

and found a bundle of straw.
짚더미를 찾았다

He did / as the little devil had directed him, /
그는 했다 / 작은 악마가 가르쳐준 대로 /

and presently a regiment of soldiers / appeared /
그리고 즉시 많은 군사들이 / 나타났다 /

in the village street, / and he ordered /
마을 거리에 / 그러자 그는 명령했다 /

them to sing and dance.
그들에게 노래하고 춤추라고

The people were astonished / and could not understand /
사람들은 놀랬고 / 이해할 수 없었다 /

how Ivan had produced / the soldiers.
어떻게 이반이 만들어 냈는지 / 군사들을

They sang for some time, / to the great delight of the
군사들은 한동안 노래했다 / 마을사람들이 아주 기쁠 정도로

villagers. When Ivan commanded / them to stop /
이반이 명령했을 때 / 그들에게 중지하라고 /

they instantly ceased. Ivan then ordered / them off to the
그들은 즉시 멈췄다 그러자 이반은 명령했다 / 그들에게 헛간으로 사라지라고 /

barn, / telling / the astonished and mystified peasants /
그리고 말했다 / 놀라고 어리둥절해하는 소작농들에게는 /

that they must not follow him.
자신을 따라오지 말라고

Reaching the barn, / he turned the soldiers again into straw /
헛간에 도착하자 / 그는 군사들을 다시 지푸라기로 만들었다 /

and went home / to sleep off / the effects of the alcohol.
그리고 집으로 갔다 / 잠으로 풀려고 / 술기운을

remark 언급, 논평 barn 헛간 direct 가르치다, 안내하다 presently 즉시, 머지않아 a regiment of 많은, 다수의 to the great delight of ~을 매우 기쁘게 instantly 즉시, 곧 cease 멈추다, 정지하다 mystify 어리둥절하게 하다 sleep off 잠으로 떨쳐 버리다 effect 영향, 작용

134 Tolstoy's Short Stories

Key Expression

sleep off ; 잠으로 (술기운이나 스트레스)를 풀다

숙어를 무조건 암기만 하면, 매우 힘들며 곧 잊어버리기 쉽다. 예를 들어 "sleep off"를 보면, 두 단어가 어떤 의미로 쓰일지 생각해본다. 우선 "sleep"은 잠을 자다는 의미이고, "off"에는 분리의 의미가 있다. 잠을 자면서 고민거리, 가벼운 두통, 숙취를 떨쳐버리는 상황을 상상해보면, "sleep off"라는 숙어가 쉽게 이해된다.

He went home to sleep off the effects of the alcohol.
그는 집으로 갔다 / 잠으로 풀려고 / 술기운을

Quiz 7

A. 내용 이해하기
다음 문장을 읽고 본문의 내용과 맞으면 T(True), 틀리면 F(False)를 쓰세요.

1. The small devil went to help his comrades to conquer Ivan.

2. Ivan was very amused at the sight of many villagers quarreling over a few pieces of gold.

3. The small devil was full of joy because Ivan did not stop working.

4. Ivan's brothers held a great feast for the peasants in the village because they had plenty of beer.

B. 단어
다음 제시된 단어의 설명을 읽고, 어떤 단어의 정의를 설명하는지 아래의 박스에서 찾아 써 보세요.

1. confused or puzzled mentally

2. a brief expression of opinion or comment; something that you say to express an opinion

3. to demand something loudly; to make a loud noise

4. the place where an accident happened

5. under the influence of alcohol; drunk

6. to say no politely when someone invites you somewhere; refuse

7. to make someone laugh or smile from pleasure

8. to say something suddenly from surprise

9. greatly surprised

10. to intrude in the affairs of others; to deliberately get involved in a situation that does not concern you

---

exclaim scene clamor intoxicated amuse

mystified astonished remark interfere decline

Answer

A. 1. T 2. F 3. F 4. F

B. 1. mystified 2. remark 3. clamor 4. scene 5. intoxicated 6. decline 7. amuse 8. exclaim 9. astonished 10. interfere

C. 직독직해

아래에 제시된 문장을 직독직해로 해석해보세요.

1. According to agreement / the small devil proceeded to the assistance of the other two / to help them conquer Ivan.

    →

2. He had gone to the forest / to cut logs / to build homes for his brothers, / as they found / it inconvenient / for so many to live / under the same roof.

    →

3. So Ivan put his hand into the bag / and drew out some gold coins, / which / he scattered / among them.

    →

4. He was now exhausted, / and, perspiring profusely, / he sat down / alone in the woods / to rest.

    →

D. 동시통역

아래에 제시된 직독직해를 보고, 영어로 말해보세요.

1. "내가 보여주지 / 너희보다 더 잘 부르는 사람을"

    →

2. 사람들이 이반의 주위에 모였다 / 그리고 이반은 계속 던졌다 / 자루가 빌 때까지.

    →

3. "우리는 맥주를 이미 봤어 / 소작농들이 마시는 / 그리고 마시고 싶지 않아"

    →

4. "이것은 묘기가 될 것이에요 / 마을 소년들을 즐겁게 해줄"

    →

Answer

C. 1. 약속한 대로 / 작은 악마가 다른 두 악마를 도와주러 갔다 / 두 악마가 이반을 정복하는 것을 돕기 위해서. 2. 그는 숲으로 갔다 / 나무를 베러 / 형제들이 살 집을 지을 / 그들은 불편하다고 생각했기 때문이었다 / 그렇게 많은 사람들이 사는 것이 / 같은 지붕 아래에서. 3. 그러자 이반은 가방 안으로 손을 넣었고 / 금화를 꺼냈다 / 그리고 그 금화를 / 그는 뿌렸다 / 아이들에게. 4. 그는 이제 지쳤다 / 그리고 땀을 엄청 흘렸기 때문에 / 그는 앉았다 / 숲속에 홀로 / 쉬려고

D. 1. "I will show you / people who can sing better than you."

2. The people gathered around him, / and Ivan continued throwing / until he emptied his bag.

3. "We have seen the beer / that peasants drink, / and want none of it."

4. "This will be a fine trick / to amuse the village boys with."

Chapter 7

The next morning Ivan's exploits were the talk of the
다음날 아침 이반의 영웅적인 행위는 마을의 이야깃 거리가 되었다 /

village, / and news of the wonderful things / he had done /
그리고 신기한 일에 대한 소식은 / 그가 행한 /

reached the ears of his brother Simeon, /
세몬 형의 귀에 전달되었다 /

who / immediately went to Ivan / to learn all about it.
그러자 그는 / 즉시 이반에게 갔다 / 자초지종을 알아보려고.

"Explain to me," he said.
"내게 설명해 봐" 그가 말했다

"Where did you bring / the soldiers, / and where did you
"어디에서 너는 데리고 왔어 / 군사들을 / 그리고 어디로 데려간 거야?"

take them?" "Why do you wish to know?" asked Ivan.
"왜 알고 싶은 거야?" 이반이 물었다

"Why, with soldiers / we can do almost anything /
"글쎄, 군사들이 있으면 / 우리는 거의 뭐든지 할 수 있어 /

we wish — / whole kingdoms can be conquered,"
우리가 원하는 / 왕국 전체를 정복할 수도 있어"

replied Simeon.
세몬이 대답했다

This information greatly surprised / Ivan, / who said: /
이 소식(말)은 엄청나게 놀라게 했다 / 이반을 / 그래서 그는 말했다 /

"Well, why did you not tell me / about this before?
"그럼, 왜 내게 말해주지 않았지 / 이런 것을 전에?

I can make as many / as you want."
나는 얼마든지 만들 수 있거든 / 형이 원하는 만큼"

Ivan then took / his brother to the barn, / as he said: /
그 다음에 이반은 데리고 갔다 / 자기 형을 헛간으로 / 그는 이렇게 말하면서 /

"I am willing to create the soldiers, /
"내가 기꺼이 군사들을 만들어 줄께 /

but you must take them away from here.
하지만 형은 여기서 군사들을 데려가야 해

It will be necessary to feed / them, /
먹여야 할 필요가 있어 / 군사들을 /

and all the food in the village / would last them /
마을에 있는 모든 음식으론 / 그들은 버틸 수 있어 /

only one day."
단지 하루만"

Simeon promised to do / as Ivan wished.
세몬은 하겠다고 약속했다 / 이반이 바라는 대로

So Ivan proceeded / to convert the straw into soldiers.
그러자 이반은 시작했다 / 지푸라기를 군사로 변하게 하는 일을

Out of one bundle of straw / he made an entire regiment.
지푸라기 더미 한 개로 / 그는 1개 연대를 만들었다

In fact, so many soldiers appeared /
실제로 수많은 군사들이 나타났다 /

as if there was not a vacant spot / in the field.
마치 빈 곳이라고는 하나도 없었던 것처럼 / 밭에

Turning to Simeon Ivan said, / "Well, is that enough?"
세몬 쪽으로 몸을 돌리면서 이반은 말했다 / "자, 이걸로 충분해?"

Beaming with joy, / Simeon replied: /
기뻐서 환하게 미소 지으며 / 세몬이 대답했다 /

"Enough! enough! Thank you, Ivan!"
"충분해! 충분해! 고맙다, 이반!"

"Glad / you are satisfied," / said Ivan, /
"기뻐요 / 형이 만족한다니까" / 이반이 말했다 /

"and if you wish more / I will make them for you.
"그리고 더 원하면 / 더 만들어줄게

I have plenty of straw now."
나는 지금 지푸라기가 많이 있어"

Simeon divided / his soldiers into battalions and
세몬은 나눴다 / 자기 군사들을 대대와 연대로 /

regiments, / and after having drilled them /
그리고 그들을 훈련시킨 다음에 /

he went away / to fight and conquer.
그는 떠났다 / 싸우고 정복하기 위해서

---

exploit 영웅적인 행위, 위업 conquer 정복하다 be willing to 기꺼이 ~하다 last 견디게 하다, 살아남게 하다
convert 바꾸다, 변하게 하다 bundle 더미 regiment 연대(3~4개 대대로 구성되어 있으며, 1500~2500명 정도임)
vacant 빈, 텅 빈 spot 장소 battalion 대대 (3~4개 중대로 300~600명 정도임) drill 훈련시키다

Simeon had just left the village / with his soldiers /
세몬이 마을을 떠났다 / 자기 군사들을 데리고 /

when Tarras, the other brother appeared / before Ivan.
다른 형인 타라스도 나타났을 때 / 이반 앞에

He had also heard / of the previous day's performance /
그도 들었다 / 전날에 있었던 놀라운 일에 대해 /

and wanted to learn / the secret of his power.
그래서 알고 싶어 했다 / 놀라운 능력의 비밀을

He sought Ivan, saying: /
그는 이반을 찾아와서, 말했다 /

"Tell me / where you got / that much gold, /
"말해 줘 / 어디서 네가 구했는지 / 그렇게 많은 금을 /

for if I had plenty of money / I could with its assistance
왜냐하면 내가 돈이 많으면 / 나는 그 돈의 도움으로 모을 수 있어 /

gather in / all the wealth in the world."
/ 이 세상의 모든 부를"

Key Expression ♥

조동사 다음엔 동사 원형

조동사 다음에는 동사 원형이 온다는 문법 규칙은 기초 문법에 속한다. 이 규칙만 제대로 활용하면, 아래에 있는 다소 생소한 문장을 쉽게 이해할 수 있다. 즉 "could"와 "gather"를 연결하기만 하면, 어렵게 느껴지는 문장도 쉽게 이해할 수 있다는 것이다.

If I had plenty of money I could with its assistance gather in all the wealth in the world.
내가 돈이 많으면 / 나는 그 돈의 도움으로 모을 수 있어 / 이 세상의 모든 부를

previous 전의, 과거의 assistance 도움, 조력

Ivan was greatly surprised / on hearing this statement, /
이반은 매우 놀랐다 / 이 말을 들었을 때 /

and said: / "You should have told me this / before, /
그래서 이렇게 말했다 / "그런 말을 내게 했어야지 / 전에 /

for I can make for you / as much money / as you wish."
나는 형에게 만들어 줄 수 있어 / 많은 돈을 / 형이 원하는 만큼"

Tarras was delighted, and he said, /
타라스는 기뻐서 말했다 /

"You might get me / about three barrels full of money."
"나에게 만들어줘 / 세 통 정도의 돈을"

"Well," said Ivan, "we will go to the woods, or, /
"좋아" 이반이 말했다 "우리는 숲으로 가거나 /

better still, / we will harness the horse, /
더 좋은 방법은 / 말에 마구를 채우는 거야 /

as we could not possibly carry / so much money ourselves."
우리는 아마 옮길 수 없을 테니까 / 그렇게 많은 돈은"

The brothers went to the woods /
두 형제는 숲으로 갔고 /

and Ivan proceeded to gather / the oak leaves, /
이반은 주워 모으기 시작했다 / 떡갈나무 잎을 /

which / he rubbed / between his hands, /
그리고 나무 잎을 / 그는 비볐다 / 양손으로 /

the dust falling to the ground /
(그러자) (나뭇잎) 부스러기가 땅으로 떨어졌고 /

and turning into gold pieces / as quickly as it fell.
금화로 변했다 / 떨어지자마자 곧

When quite a pile had accumulated /
상당히 많은 양의 금 더미가 모였을 때 /

Ivan turned to Tarras and asked /
이반은 타라스 쪽으로 몸을 돌리면서 물었다 /

if he had rubbed enough leaves into money. /
그가 충분한 양의 나뭇잎을 비벼서 돈으로 만들었는지 /

Tarras replied: /
그러자 타라스가 대답했다 /

"Thank you, Ivan. That will be sufficient for this time."
"고마워, 이반. 이것으로 충분해 / 이번엔"

statement 말, 발언 barrel 나무 통 possibly 아마 pile 더미 accumulate (물건이) 쌓이다, 모이다

Ivan then said: / "If you wish more, / come to me /
그러자 이반이 말했다 / "더 원하면 / 내게로 와 /

and I will rub / as much as you want, / for there are plenty
그러면 (비벼) 만들게 / 형이 원하는 만큼 많은 양을 / 잎은 많으니까"

of leaves." Tarras, / with his wagon filled with gold, /
타라스는 / 마차에 금을 가득 싣고 /

rode away to the city / to engage in trade /
도시로 갔다 / 장사를 하여 /

and increase his wealth. Both brothers went their way, /
재산을 늘리려고 / 두 형제는 각자의 길을 갔다 /

Simeon to fight and Tarras to trade.
세몬은 싸우러 타라스는 장사하러

Simeon's soldiers conquered a kingdom / for him /
세몬의 군사들은 왕국을 정복했고 / 그를 위해 /

and Tarras made plenty of money.
타라스는 많은 돈을 벌었다

Some time afterward / the two brothers met and confessed
얼마의 시간이 흐른 뒤 / 두 형제는 만나서 서로에게 털어놨다 /

to each other / from where sprang their prosperity, /
어디에서 그들의 번영이 나왔는지 /

but they were not yet satisfied.
그러나 그들은 아직도 만족하지 않았다

Simeon said: "I have conquered a kingdom /
세몬이 말했다 "나는 왕국을 정복했고 /

and enjoy a very pleasant life, / but I have not sufficient
아주 즐거운 삶을 살고 있다고 / 그러나 나는 충분한 돈이 없어 /

money / to procure food for my soldiers." /
내 군사들을 먹일 음식을 마련할"

Tarras confessed / that he was the possessor of enormous
타라스는 고백했다 / 그가 어마어마한 재산을 소유한 사람이라고 /

wealth, / but the care of it / caused him much uneasiness.
그러나 재산을 관리하다보니 / 그에게 많은 불안감이 생겼다

"Let us go again to our brother," / said Simeon.
"우리 동생한테 다시 가자" / 세몬이 말했다

"I will order / him to make more soldiers /
"내가 요구할 거야 / 이반에게 군사를 더 만들라고 /

and will give them to you, / and you may then tell him /
그리고 너에게 군사들을 줄께 / 그런 다음 너는 이반에게 말해 /

that he must make more money /
그가 돈을 더 만들어야 한다고 /

so that we can buy food / for them."
그러면 우리는 살 수 있잖아 / 군사들을 먹일 음식을"

They went again to Ivan, / and Simeon said: /
그들은 다시 이반에게 갔고 / 세몬이 말했다 /

"I have not sufficient soldiers.
"나는 병사가 부족해.

I want / you to make me / at least two divisions more."
나는 바래 / 네가 나에게 만들어 주길 / 최소한 사단 두 개를"

Key Expression

should have +동사의 과거분사; ~했어야만 했는데

"should have +과거분사"로 과거에 일어나지 않은 사건에 대한 후회하는 감정을 표현한다.
즉 어떤 일을 했어야 했지만 사실 그런 일이 일어나지 않은 경우에 이 표현을 사용한다.

You should have told me this before.
너는 나에게 말했어야 했는데 / 이것을 미리

---

engage ~에 종사하다 trade 장사, 무역 confess 고백하다, 비밀을 털어 놓다 prosperity 번영, 번성
sufficient 충분한 procure ~을 얻다, 손에 넣다 enormous 엄청난, 거대한
division 사단(4개의 연대로 구성되어 있으며 1만 명 내외임)

But Ivan shook his head / as he said: /
그러나 이반은 고개를 저었다 / 이렇게 말하면서 /

"I will not create soldiers / for nothing.
"나는 군사를 만들지 않을 거야 / 공짜로

You must pay me / for doing it."
형은 대가를 지불해야 해 / 군사를 만들어 주면"

"Well, but you promised," said Simeon.
"어, 그러나 네가 약속했잖아" 세몬이 말했다

"I know I did," replied Ivan, /
"나도 내가 약속한 것을 알아" 이반이 대답했다 /

"but I have changed my mind / since that time."
"그러나 마음이 바꿨어 / 그 이후로"

"But, fool, why will you not do / as you promised?"
"하지만, 바보야, 왜 하지 않지 / 네가 약속한대로"

"For the reason / that your soldiers kill men, /
"그 이유는 / 형의 군사들이 사람들을 죽였기 때문이야 /

and I will not make any more / for such a cruel purpose."
그리고 나는 군사를 만들지는 않을 거야 / 그런 잔혹한 목적을 위하여"

With this reply / Ivan remained stubborn /
이렇게 대답하면서 / 이반은 완고했고 /

and would not create any more soldiers.
군사를 더 이상 만들지 않았다

Tarras next approached Ivan / and ordered /
타라스는 다음에 이반에게 다가가서 / 요구했다 /

him to make more money, / but, as in the case of Simeon, /
그에게 돈을 더 만들어달라고 / 그러나 세몬의 경우처럼 /

Ivan only shook his head, / as he said: /
이반은 고개를 젓기만 했다 / 이렇게 말하면서 /

"I will not make you any money / unless you pay me for
"나는 돈을 만들어 주지 않을 거야 / 형이 나에게 대가를 지불하지 않으면

doing it. I cannot work / without pay."
일을 할 수는 없다고 / 공짜로"

Tarras then reminded him / of his promise.
그러자 타라스는 이반에게 생각나게 했다 / 자신의 약속을

"I know / I promised," / replied Ivan, /
"나도 알아 / 내가 약속한 것을" / 이반이 대답했다 /

"but still I must refuse / to do as you wish."
"그러나 그래도 나는 거절해야 해 / 형이 원하는 대로 하는 것을"

"But why, fool, will you not fulfill your promise?"
"하지만 왜 바보야, 너는 네 약속을 지키려 하지 않아?"

asked Tarras.
타라스가 물었다

"For the reason / that your gold was the means /
"그 이유는 / 형의 황금은 수단이었기 때문이야 /

of depriving Mikhailovna of her cow."
미하일로브나에게서 암소를 빼앗는"

"But how did that happen?" inquired Tarras.
"어떻게 그런 일이 일어난 거지?" 타라스가 물었다

"It happened in this way," said Ivan.
"이런 식으로 일어났지" 이반이 말했다

"Mikhailovna always kept a cow, /
"미카일로브나는 항상 암소를 갖고 있어서 /

and her children had plenty of milk / to drink.
그녀의 아이들은 우유가 많았지 / 마실 수 있는

But some time ago / one of her boys came to me /
그런데 얼마 전에 / 그녀의 아들 중 한 명이 내게 와서 /

to beg for some milk.
우유를 좀 달라고 했어

And I asked him, / 'Where is your cow?' He replied, /
그래서 내가 그에게 물었지 / '너희 암소는 어디 있냐?' 그 아이가 대답했다 /

'A clerk of Tarras came to our home /
'타라스의 종업원 한 명이 저희 집에 왔어요 /

and offered three gold pieces / for our mother.
그리고 금화 3냥을 주었어요 / 엄마에게

She could not resist the temptation, /
우리 엄마는 유혹을 견디지 못했고 /

and now we have no milk / to drink.'
이제 저희는 우유가 없어요 / 마실만 한'

I gave you the gold pieces / for your pleasure, /
나는 형에게 금화를 줬어 / 형이 기뻐하라고 /

and you put them to such poor use /
그런데 형은 금화를 매우 고약한 용도로 사용했지 /

---

stubborn 완고한, 고집 센 remind 생각나게 하다, 상기시켜주다 refuse 거절하다 fulfill (약속을) 이루다, 실현하다
deprive ~을 빼앗다 inquire ~을 묻다 clerk 종업원, 점원 temptation 유혹

that I will not give you any more."
그래서 나는 더 이상 주지 않을 거야"

The brothers, / on hearing this, / took their departure to
형제들은 / 이 말을 듣자 / 의논하기 위해서 떠났다 (뭘 의논해?) /

discuss / as to the best plan / to settle their troubles.
가장 좋은 계획에 대하여 / 자신들의 문제를 해결할 수 있는

Simeon said: / "Let us arrange it in this way.
세몬이 말했다 / "이런 식으로 결정하자

I will give you / the half of my kingdom, and soldiers /
내가 너에게 줄게 / 내 왕국의 절반과 군사를 /

to keep guard over your wealth. And you give me money /
네 재산을 지킬 그리고 너는 내게 돈을 줘 /

to feed the soldiers in my half of the kingdom."
내 반쪽짜리 왕국의 군사들을 먹일"

To this arrangement Tarras agreed, /
이 타협안에 타라스는 동의했고 /

and both the brothers became rulers and very happy.
두 형제는 둘 다 지배자가 되어서 매우 행복했다

Key Expression

resist; 견디다, 참다

"resist" 동사가 부정문과 함께 쓰이면, 어떤 것을 참을 수 없거나 견딜 수 없다는 의미가 된다.
Our mother could not resist the temptation. 엄마는 유혹을 뿌리칠 수 없었어요.
I can't resist chocolates. 나는 초콜릿만 보면 참을 수 없어요.

departure 출발, 떠남 as to ~에 대하여 arrange 정하다, 결정하다 arrangement 합의(안)

Quiz 8

A. 내용 이해하기

다음 문장을 읽고 본문의 내용과 맞으면 T(True), 틀리면 F(False)를 쓰세요.

1. Ivan was willing to create soldiers for his brother for the second time.
2. Ivan drilled soldiers to fight and conquer his neighboring kingdom.
3. Simeon had not sufficient money to procure food for his family.
4. Tarras asked his brother to create more money by magic.

B. 단어

다음 제시된 단어의 설명을 읽고, 어떤 단어의 정의를 설명하는지 아래의 박스에서 찾아서 보세요.

1. a brilliant or heroic act or deed
2. to change something into another form; to turn something into another state
3. a number of things or objects tied together
4. not being used or empty
5. aid; help or support
6. something said or declared to give an opinion
7. a large container with a flat top and bottom made of wood or metal
8. to be doing something for a long time or to become involved in an activity
9. to disclose something; to admit that you have done something
10. determined not to change your opinion; firmly resolved or determined

---

assistance barrel convert confess vacant

exploit bundle engage stubborn statement

Answer

A. 1. F 2. F 3. F 4. T

B. 1. exploit 2. convert 3. bundle 4. vacant 5. assistance 6. statement 7. barrel 8. engage 9. confess 10. stubborn

C. 직독직해

아래에 제시된 문장을 직독직해로 해석해보세요.

1. News of the wonderful things / he had done / reached the ears of his brother Simeon, / who / immediately went to Ivan / to learn all about it.

   →

2. Simeon divided / his soldiers into battalions and regiments, / and after having drilled them / he went away / to fight and conquer.

   →

3. Tarras next approached Ivan / and ordered / him to make more money, / but, as in the case of Simeon, / Ivan only shook his head.

   →

4. Tarras confessed / that he was the possessor of enormous wealth, / but the care of it / caused him much uneasiness.

   →

D. 동시통역

아래에 제시된 직독직해를 보고, 영어로 말해보세요.

1. "어디에서 너는 데리고 왔어 / 군사들을 / 그리고 어디로 데려간 거야?"

   →

2. "내가 기꺼이 군사들을 만들어 줄께 / 하지만 형은 여기서 군사들을 데려가야 해.

   →

3. "그런 말을 내게 했어야지 / 전에, / 나는 형에게 만들어 줄 수 있어 / 많은 돈을 / 형이 원하는 만큼"

   →

4. 내가 너에게 줄게 / 내 왕국의 절반과 군사를 / 네 재산을 지킬

   →

Answer C. 1. 신기한 일에 대한 소식은 / 그가 행한 / 세몬 형의 귀에 전달되었다 / 그러자 그는 / 즉시 이반에게 갔다 / 자초지종을 알아보려고. 2. 세몬은 나눴다 / 자기 군사들을 대대와 연대로 / 그리고 그들을 훈련시킨 다음에 / 그는 떠났다 / 싸우고 정복하기 위해서. 3. 타라스는 다음에 이반에게 다가가서 / 요구했다 / 그에게 돈을 더 만들어달라고 / 그러나 세몬의 경우처럼 / 이반은 고개를 젓기만 했다 4. 타라스는 고백했다 / 그가 어마어마한 재산을 소유한 사람이라고 / 그러나 재산을 관리하다보니 / 그에게 많은 불안감이 생겼다.

D. 1. "Where did you bring / the soldiers, / and where did you take them?"

2. "I am willing to create the soldiers, / but you must take them away from here.

3. "You should have told me this / before, / for I can make for you / as much money / as you wish."

4. I will give you / the half of my kingdom, and soldiers / to keep guard over your wealth.

Chapter 8

Ivan stayed on the farm / and worked to support /
이반은 농장에 남았다 / 그리고 돌보기 위해 일했다 /

his father, mother, and dumb sister.
아버지, 어머니, 그리고 벙어리 여동생을

One day it happened / that the old dog, /
어느날 이런 일이 있었다 / 늙은 개가 /

which had grown up on the farm, /
농장에서 키웠던 /

was taken sick, / when Ivan thought / he was dying, /
병에 걸렸던 일이 / 그때 이반은 생각했다 / 개가 죽어가고 있다고 /

and, taking pity on the animal, /
게다가 개를 불쌍히 여겼기 때문에 /

placed some bread in his hat / and carried it to him.
모자에 빵을 좀 담았고 / 그 빵을 개에게 가지고 갔다.

As he fed the bread to his dog, / the root / which the little
그가 개에게 빵을 주고 있었을 때 / 뿌리가 / (어떤 뿌리?) 작은 악마가 주었던 /

devil had given him / fell out of his pocket.
주머니에서 떨어졌다

The old dog swallowed it / with the bread /
늙은 개는 뿌리를 삼켰다 / 빵과 함께 /

and was almost instantly cured.
그러자 거의 즉시 (병에서) 나았다

He jumped up and began to wag his tail /
개는 껑충 뛰었고 꼬리를 흔들기 시작했다 /

as an expression of joy. Ivan's father and mother, /
기쁨을 표현하듯이 이반의 아버지와 어머니는 /

seeing the dog cured so quickly, / asked / by what means /
개가 빨리 나아지는 것을 보자 / 물어봤다 / 어떤 방법으로 /

he had performed such a miracle.
그가 그런 기적을 일으켰는지

Ivan replied: / "I have some roots / which would cure any
이반이 대답했다 / "저는 뿌리가 있었어요 / 그 뿌리는 어떤 병이든 고칠 수 있는 /

disease, / and the dog swallowed one of them."
그리고 개가 그 뿌리 중에서 하나를 삼켰어요"

At about that time / the Czar's daughter became ill, /
그 무렵에 / 러시아 황제의 딸이 병에 걸렸다 /

and her father had it announced / in every city, town,
그래서 그녀의 아버지는 알렸다 / 모든 도시, 읍내 그리고 마을에 /

and village / that whosoever would cure her /
(뭐라고 알렸나?) 누구든지 딸을 살리는 자라면 /

would be richly rewarded.
큰 상을 받을 것이라고

And if the lucky person was a single man /
그리고 만일 그 행운아가 미혼이라면 /

he would give her in marriage / to him.
딸을 시집보내겠다고 / 그에게

This announcement, of course, / appeared in Ivan's village.
이 발표는 물론 / 이반의 마을에도 알려졌다.

Ivan's father and mother called him / and said: /
이반의 아버지와 어머니는 이반을 불러서 / 이렇게 말했다 /

"If you have any of those wonderful roots, /
"네가 그 신비로운 뿌리를 갖고 있다면 /

go and cure / the Czar's daughter. You will be much
가서 치료해라 / 황제의 딸을 / 너는 훨씬 더 행복해질 것이다 /

happier / for having performed such a kind act /
그런 자비로운 행동을 한다면 /

indeed, you will be made happy / for all your after life."
참으로 너는 행복해질 것이다 / 남은 여생동안"

"Very well," said Ivan.
"좋아요" 이반이 말했다

And he immediately made ready / for the journey.
그리고 그는 즉시 준비를 했다 / 여행을 떠날

Key Expression

비교급을 강조하는 "much"

"much"는 비교급을 나타내는 형용사나 부사 앞에 오면 "훨씬"이라는 의미가 있다. "much" 이외에도 비교급 형용사나 부사를 강조하는 말은 "still, far, even"등이 있다.

You will be much happier for having performed such a kind act.
너는 훨씬 더 행복해질 것이다 / 그런 자비로운 행동을 한다면

---

swallow 삼키다 instantly 즉시, 곧 wag (꼬리를) 흔들다 perform ~을 행하다, 하다 Czar 러시아의 황제
announce 발표하다, 알리다

As he reached the porch / on his way out /
그가 현관에 갔을 때 / 그가 길을 떠나려고 /

he saw a poor woman / standing directly in front of his
그는 불쌍한 여인을 봤다 / 바로 그의 집 앞에 서있고 /

house / and holding a broken arm.
부러진 팔을 하고 있는

The woman approached him, / saying: /
그 여인은 이반에게 다가와서 / 이렇게 말했다 /

"I was told / that you could cure me, /
"저는 들었어요 / 당신이 절 고칠 수 있다고 /

and will you please do so, / as I am powerless /
그리고 그렇게 해주시겠어요 / 저는 힘이 없으니까요 /

to do anything for myself?" Ivan replied:
혼자서 어떤 것도 할" 이반이 대답했다

"Very well, my poor woman. I will help you / if I can."
"좋아요, 불쌍한 여인이여. 내가 도와줄게요 / 할 수 있다면"

He took out a root / which / he handed to the poor woman /
그는 뿌리 하나를 꺼냈다 / 그리고 그것을 / 그는 불쌍한 여인에게 건네주었고 /

and told her / to swallow it.
그녀에게 말했다 / 그것을 삼키라고

She did / as Ivan told her / and was instantly cured, /
그녀는 했고 / 이반이 말한 대로 / 금세 병이 나았다 /

and went away rejoicing / that her arm had been healed.
그리고 기뻐하면서 떠났다 / 자신의 팔이 치료되어

Ivan's father and mother came out /
이반의 아버지와 어머니는 나왔다 /

to wish him good luck / on his journey, /
아들에게 축복하려고 / 여행을 떠나는

and to them he told / the story of the poor woman, /
그리고 부모님에게 이반은 말했다 / 부모님에게 불쌍한 여인의 이야기를 /

saying / that he had given her his last root.
그때 그는 말했다 / 그가 그녀에게 마지막 뿌리를 줘버렸다고

On hearing this / his parents were much distressed, /
이 이야기를 듣자마자 / 그의 부모는 많이 괴로워했다 /

as they now believed / him to be without the means /
그들은 이제 믿었기 때문이었다 / 이반은 방법이 없다고 /

of curing the Czar's daughter, / and began to scold him.
황제의 딸을 고칠 / 그래서 그에게 야단치기 시작했다

152   Tolstoy's Short Stories

"You had pity for a beggar / and gave no thought to the
"너는 거지는 동정하면서 / 황제의 딸은 생각하지도 않았구나" /

Czar's daughter," / they said.
그들이 말했다

"I have pity for the Czar's daughter also," / replied Ivan, /
"저는 황제의 딸도 동정해요" / 이반이 대답했다 /

after which / he harnessed his horse to his wagon /
이런 말을 한 후 / 그가 말을 마차에 채우고 /

and got ready for his departure.
그리고 출발할 준비를 했다

Just then his parents said: /
바로 그때 그의 부모는 말했다 /

"Where are you going, / you fool / -to cure the Czar's
"너 어디로 가니, / 이 바보야 / 황제의 딸을 고친다고 /

daughter, / and without anything to do it with?"
치료할 방법도 없으면서"

"Very well," replied Ivan, / as he drove away.
"걱정 마세요" 이반은 대답했다 / 떠나면서

---

approach ~에게 다가가다 heal (병을) 낫게 하다, 고치다 distressed 괴로워하는, 고민하는 means 수단, 방법
scold 야단치다, 혼내주다 harness (말을 마구로) 마차에 매다 whereupon 그리고 그 후

In due time / he arrived at the palace, /
머지않아 / 그가 왕궁에 도착했다 /

and the moment he appeared / on the balcony /
그리고 그가 나타났던 순간에 / 발코니에 /

the Czar's daughter was cured.
황제의 딸은 치료되었다

The Czar was overjoyed / and ordered /
황제는 아주 기뻐했고 / 명령했다 /

Ivan to be brought / into his presence.
이반을 데려오라고 / 황제 앞으로

He dressed him in the richest robes /
그는 이반에게 가장 값비싼 옷을 입혔고 /

and addressed him as his son-in-law.
그를 사위라고 불렀다

Ivan was married to the Czar's daughter, /
이반은 황제의 딸과 결혼했다 /

and, the Czar dying soon after, / Ivan became ruler.
그리고 황제는 얼마 되지 않아 죽고 / 이반이 통치자가 되었다

Thus the three brothers became rulers /
이렇게 해서 삼형제가 통치자가 되었다 /

in different kingdoms.
다른 왕국의

Key Expression

명사 뒤에 오는 현재분사

"동사ing" 형태는 두 가지 역할을 한다. 그것은 동명사와 현재분사이다. 현재 분사가 단독으로 사용되면 명사 앞에 온다. 하지만 아래에 있는 예문처럼 현재분사 다음에 수식하는 어구가 따라 오면, 명사 뒤에 온다.

He saw a poor woman standing directly in front of his house and holding a broken arm.
그는 불쌍한 여인을 봤다 / 바로 그의 집 앞에 서있었고 / 부러진 팔을 하고 있는.

in due time 곧, 머지않아 presence 알현, (남의) 앞, 면전 address ~를 ~라고 칭하다, 부르다

Chapter 9

The brothers lived and reigned.
형제는 살았고 통치했다

Simeon, / the eldest brother, / with his straw soldiers /
세몬은 / 첫째 형인 / 지푸라기 군사들로 /

took the genuine soldiers prisoner / and trained all alike.
진짜 군사들을 포로로 잡아서 / 똑같이 훈련시켰다

He was feared by every one.
모두 그를 무서워했다

Tarras, the other brother, did not squander / the gold /
또다른 형인 타라스는 낭비하지 않았다 / 금을 /

he obtained from Ivan, / but instead greatly increased his
그가 이반으로부터 얻은 / 그러나 (낭비하는) 대신 재산을 엄청나게 불렸다 /

wealth, / and at the same time lived well.
그리고 동시에 유복하게 살았다.

He kept his money in large trunks, / and, while having
그는 돈을 큰 가방에 보관했다 / 그리고 더 많이 가졌지만 /

more / than he knew what to do with, /
그가 쓰려고 하는 것보다 /

still continued to collect / money from his subjects.
여전히 계속 긁어모았다 / 백성들로부터 돈을

The people had to work / for the money to pay the taxes /
백성들은 일해야만 했다 / 세금을 낼 돈을 마련하려고 /

which Tarras levied on them, /
타라스가 백성들에게 부과한 (세금을) /

and life was made burdensome to them.
그래서 그들의 생활은 힘들었다.

Ivan the Fool did not enjoy / his wealth and power /
바보 이반은 즐기지 않았다 / 부와 권력을 /

to the same extent as did his brothers.
자기 형들과 같은 정도로.

As soon as his father-in-law, the late Czar, was buried, /
자기장인, 전 황제를 안장하자마자 /

he discarded / the Imperial robes /
그는 벗어 버렸다 / 황제의 관복을 /

which had fallen to him /
자기에게 주어졌던 /

and told his wife / to put them away, /
그리고 아내에게 말했다 / 관복을 치우라고 /

as he had no further use for them.
그는 더 이상 그것이 필요 없기 때문에

Having cast aside the insignia of his rank, /
그의 신분의 징표(황제의 관복)를 벗어던진 다음 /

he once more donned his peasant garb /
그는 다시 한번 자신의 소작농 옷을 입었고 /

and went back to his old work.
예전처럼 일하기 시작했다.

"I felt lonesome," he said, /
"나는 외로워" 그가 말했다 /

"and began to grow enormously stout, /
"그리고 엄청나게 뚱뚱해지기 시작했어 /

and yet I had no appetite, / and neither could I sleep."
그렇지만 식욕이 없고 / 잠을 잘 수도 없어"

Ivan sent for / his father, mother, and dumb sister, /
이반은 데리러 사람을 보냈다 / 자기 아버지, 어머니, 그리고 벙어리 여동생을 /

and brought them to live with him, /
그리고 그들을 데려와서 자신과 함께 살았다 /

and they worked with him / at whatever he chose to do.
그리고 그들은 이반과 함께 일했다 / 이반이 하려고 선택한 어떤 일이라도

The people soon learned / that Ivan was a fool.
백성들은 곧 알았다 / 이반이 바보라는 것을

His wife one day said to him, /
그의 아내가 어느 날 이반에게 말했다 /

"The people say you are a fool, Ivan."
"백성들이 당신이 바보라고 말해요, 이반"

"Well, let them think so / if they wish," he replied.
"음, 그렇게 생각하라고 해 / 원한다면" 그가 대답했다

---

reign 통치하다 squander 낭비하다, 헛되이 쓰다 subject 백성 levy (세금을) 부과하다, 징수하다
burdensome 번거로운, 무거운 짐이 되는 discard 버리다 Imperial 황제의 insignia 표시, 기장 rank 지위, 신분
don ~을 입다, 신다 garb 복장, 옷 enormously 엄청나게, 매우 stout 뚱뚱한, 살찐 appetite 식욕

His wife pondered / this reply for some time, /
그의 아내는 곰곰이 생각해보았다 / 이 대답을 한동안 /

and at last decided / that if Ivan was a fool /
그리고 마침내 결정했다 / 이반이 바보라면 /

she also was one, / and that it would be useless /
자신도 바보라고 / 그리고 부질없을 것이라고 (결정했다) /

to go contrary to her husband, /
남편의 뜻을 거스르는 것은 /

thinking affectionately of the old proverb that /
인자하게도 옛 속담을 생각했기 때문에 (어떤 속담?) /

"where the needle goes / there goes the thread also."
"바늘 가는 곳에(데) / 실도 간다

She therefore cast aside her magnificent robes, /
그래서 그녀는 자신의 화려한 옷을 벗어던졌다 /

and, putting them into the trunk / with Ivan's, /
그리고 가방에 넣고 / 이반의 황제의 관복과 함께 /

dressed herself in cheap clothing / and joined her dumb
싸구려 옷을 입고서 / 벙어리 시누이와 합세했다 /

sister-in-law, / with the intention of learning to work.
/ 일하는 것을 배울 작정으로.

She succeeded so well / that she soon became a great help /
그녀는 훌륭하게 성공해서 / 그녀는 곧 큰 도움이 되었다 /

to Ivan. Seeing that Ivan was a fool, /
이반에게. 이반이 바보라는 것을 알자 /

all the wise men left the kingdom /
모든 현명한 사람들은 왕국을 떠났으며 /

and only the fools remained. They had no money, /
오직 바보들만이 남았다 그들은 돈이 없었고 /

their wealth consisting only of the products of their labor.
그들의 재산은 오직 노동의 결과로 생긴(노동으로만 생산된) 것이었다

But they lived peacefully together, /
그러나 그들은 평화롭게 함께 살았고 /

supported themselves in comfort, /
편안하게 서로 도왔다 /

and had plenty to spare / for the needy and afflicted.
그리고 나누어 줄만큼 풍부했다 / 가난하고 고통 받는 사람들에게

---

ponder 곰곰이 생각하다 go contrary (~의 뜻을) 거스르다, 거역하다 affectionately 다정하게, 인자하게
intention 의도, 작정 product 결과, 산물 spare ~을 나눠주다 needy 가난한 afflict 고통을 주다, 괴롭히다

158 Tolstoy's Short Stories

Key Expression

the +형용사(분사); ~한 사람들

"the +형용사(분사)"는 복수 보통명사로 쓰이면, "~한 사람들"이라는 의미가 된다. 그래서 아래 예문에 있는 "the needy and afflicted"는 "가난하고 고통 받는 사람들"이라는 의미로 쓰였다.

They had plenty to spare for the needy and afflicted.
그들은 나누어 줄만큼 풍부했다 / 가난하고 고통 받는 사람들에게.

Quiz 9

A. 내용 이해하기
다음 문장을 읽고 본문의 내용과 맞으면 T(True), 틀리면 F(False)를 쓰세요.

1. Ivan's sister left the farm and became a merchant in order to support his father.
2. Ivan's old dog could perform a miracle because the dog swallowed the root which the devil had given to Ivan.
3. Because Ivan cured the Czar's daughter, he could marry her.
4. Tarras wasted all his gold he obtained from Ivan by gambling.

B. 단어
다음 제시된 단어의 설명을 읽고, 어떤 단어의 정의를 설명하는지 아래의 박스에서 찾아 써 보세요.

1. to make food or drink to pass through the mouth into the stomach
2. to move many times from one side to the other or up and down
3. immediately; at once
4. to do something; carry out
5. to restore to health; cure
6. unhappy or greatly worried; very upset
7. to use an official name or particular title when you speak to someone
8. one who is under the rule of a king or queen
9. to get rid of something that you no longer need; to throw away
10. to think about something with care for a long time; to consider something carefully

---

distressed ponder address perform wag

swallow discard instantly heal subject

Answer
A. 1. F 2. F 3. T 4. F
B. 1. swallow 2. wag 3. instantly 4. perform 5. heal 6. distressed 7. address 8. subject 9. discard 10. ponder

C. 직독직해

아래에 제시된 문장을 직독직해로 해석해보세요.

1. As he fed the bread to his dog, / the root / which the little devil had given him / fell out of his pocket.

   →

2. But they lived peacefully together, / supported themselves in comfort, / and had plenty to spare / for the needy and afflicted.

   →

3. The people had to work / for the money to pay the taxes / which Tarras levied on them, / and life was made burdensome to them.

   →

4. The Czar was overjoyed / and ordered / Ivan to be brought / into his presence.

   →

D. 동시통역

아래에 제시된 직독직해를 보고, 영어로 말해보세요.

1. "너는 거지는 동정하면서 / 황제의 딸은 생각하지도 않았구나" / 그들이 말했다.

   →

2. 세몬은 / 첫째 형인 / 지푸라기 군사들로 / 진짜 군사들을 포로로 잡아서 / 똑같이 훈련시켰다.

   →

3. "을, 그렇게 생각하라고 해 / 원한다면" 그가 대답했다.

   →

4. 그래서 그녀는 자신의 화려한 옷을 벗어던졌다 / 그리고 가방에 넣었다 / 이반의 황제의 관복과 함께

   →

Answer
C. 1. 그가 개에게 빵을 주고 있었을 때 / 뿌리가 / (어떤 뿌리?) 작은 악마가 주었던 / 주머니에서 떨어졌다. 2. 그러나 그들은 평화롭게 함께 살았고 / 편안하게 서로 도왔다 / 그리고 나누어 줄만큼 풍부했다 / 가난하고 고통 받는 사람들에게. 3. 백성들은 일해야만 했다 / 세금을 낼 돈을 마련하려고 / 타라스가 백성들에게 부과한 (세금을) / 그래서 그들의 생활은 힘들었다. 4. 황제는 아주 기뻐했고 / 명령했다 / 이반을 데려오라고 / 황제 앞으로
D. 1. "You had pity for a beggar / and gave no thought to the Czar's daughter," / they said.
2. Simeon, / the eldest brother, / with his straw soldiers / took the genuine soldiers prisoner / and trained all alike.
3. "Well, let them think so / if they wish," he replied.
4. She therefore cast aside her magnificent robes, / and, putting them into the trunk / with Ivan's.

Chapter 10

The old devil grew tired / of waiting for the good news /
늙은 악마는 차츰 지쳤다 / 희소식을 기다리다가 /

which he expected / the little devils to bring him.
(어떤 소식?) 그는 기대했었던 / 작은 악마들이 가져올 것이라고

He waited in vain / to hear of the ruin of the brothers, /
그는 헛되게 기다렸다 / 형제들을 파멸시켰다는 소식을 들으려고 /

so he went in search of the emissaries /
그래서 그는 밀사들을 찾아 갔다 /

which he had sent / to perform that work for him.
자신이 보냈던(밀사를) / 자신을 위해서 그 일을 대신하라고.

After looking around for some time, /
한동안 찾아보고 /

and seeing nothing but the three holes in the ground, /
땅에 구멍 3개만 있는 것을 보자 /

he decided / that they had not succeeded in their work /
그는 판단했다 / 그들이 맡은 일에 성공하지 못했다고 /

and that / he would have to do it himself.
그래서 (그는 판단했다) / 자신이 스스로 해야겠다고

The old devil next went in search of the brothers, /
다음으로 늙은 악마는 형제들을 찾으러 갔다 /

but he could learn nothing / of their whereabouts.
그러나 그는 전혀 알 수가 없었다 / 그들의 행방을

After some time he found / them in their different
얼마 후에 그는 알게 되었다 / 형제들이 각자의 왕국에 있다는 것을 /

kingdoms, / contented and happy.
(그리고) 만족하면서 행복하게 지내고 있는 것을

This greatly incensed / the old devil, / and he said, /
이런 일은 매우 분노하게 했다 / 늙은 악마를 / 그래서 그는 말했다 /

"I will now have to accomplish / their mission myself."
"이제는 내가 해야겠네 / 그들의 임무를 직접"

He first visited / Simeon the soldier, /
그는 먼저 찾아갔다 / 군인인 세몬을 /

and appeared before him as a general, / saying: /
그리고 그의 앞에 장군모습으로 나타나서 / 이렇게 말했다 /

"You, Simeon, are a great warrior, /
"세몬, 당신은 대단한 용사입니다 /

and I also have had considerable experience in warfare, /
그리고 저 역시 상당한 전쟁 경험이 있습니다 /

and am desirous of serving you."
그리고 당신을 모시고 싶습니다"

Simeon questioned the disguised devil, /
세몬은 변장한 악마에게 질문을 했다 /

and seeing that he was an intelligent man
그리고 그가 영리한 사람이라고 생각했기 때문에 /

took him into his service.
그가 (군에서) 복무하도록 받아들였다

The new General taught Simeon /
신임 장군은 세몬에게 가르쳐주었다 /

how to strengthen his army / until it became very powerful.
어떻게 군대의 힘을 기르는지 / 아주 강해질 때까지

New implements of warfare were introduced.
새로운 전쟁 장비(무기)가 소개되었다

Cannons capable of throwing one hundred balls a minute /
1분에 1백발을 쏠 수 있는 대포가 /

were also constructed, / and these, / it was expected, /
또한 만들어졌다 / 그리고 이 대포는 / 기대됐다 /

would be of deadly effect in battle.
전투에서 치명적인 영향을 끼칠 것으로

Simeon, / on the advice of his new General, / ordered /
세몬은 / 신임 장군의 조언에 따라 / 명령했다 /

all young men above a certain age / to report for drill.
일정 나이 이상의 모든 젊은이들에게 / 훈련에 참여하기 위해 출두하라는

On the same advice / Simeon established gun-shops, /
동일한 조언에 따라 / 세몬은 총포를 만드는 공장을 세웠다 /

where immense numbers of cannons and rifles were made.
그곳에서 어마어마한 양의 대포와 총을 만들었다

---

emissary 사자, 밀사 whereabouts 행방, 사람이 있는 곳 contented 만족한 incense 분노하게 하다, 성나게 하다 accomplish (목적을) 달성하다, (임무를) 완수하다 warrior 전사 considerable 상당한, 꽤 많은 desirous 원하는, 열망하는 disguise 변장하다 intelligent 영리한, 지적인 implement 도구, 장비 warfare 전쟁 cannon 대포 construct 조립하다, 만들다 report 출두하다, 나가다 establish 설립하다, 설치하다

The next move of the new General /
신임 장군의 다음 조치는 /

was to have Simeon declare war / against the neighboring
세몬으로 하여금 선전포고를 하게 하는 것이었다 /   이웃 왕국에

kingdom. This he did, / and with his immense army /
세몬은 이대로 했고 /   그의 거대한 군대로 /

marched into the adjoining territory, /
인접한 (다른 나라) 영토로 행군해 들어갔다 /

which / he pillaged and burned, /
그리고 그 영토를 / 그는 약탈하고 방화했다 /

destroying more than half the enemy's soldiers.
(그리고) 적군의 병사들을 반 이상 죽였다

Key Expression !

grow; (차츰) ~하게 되다(상태변화)

동물이나 식물이 성장하는 모습을 표현할 때, "grow"가 쓰인다. 시간이 지나면 동식물이 성장하거나 발육하고 그 모습은 변한다. 또한 "grow" 동사 다음에 형용사가 오면, 시간이 지남에 따라 상태가 변하는 의미를 표현할 수 있다.

The old devil grew tired of waiting for the good news.
늙은 악마는 차츰 지쳤다 / 희소식을 기다리다가.
He began to grow richer.
그는 더욱더 부유해졌다.

---

move 조치 immense 거대한, 막대한 adjoining 인접한 territory 영토 pillage 약탈하다
destroy 죽이다, 전멸시키다

This so frightened / the ruler of that country /
이것은 매우 놀라게 만들었다 /   그 나라 통치자를 /

that he willingly gave up / half of his kingdom /
그래서 그는 기꺼이 포기했다 /   자기 왕국의 절반을 /

to save the other half.
남은 절반을 살리려고.

Simeon, overjoyed at his success, / declared his intention /
세몬은 자신의 성공을 매우 기뻐했고 /   자신의 계획을 발표했다 /

of marching into Indian territory /
인도 땅에도 진격해서 /

and subduing the Viceroy of that country.
인도의 총독을 정복하려는

But Simeon's intentions / reached the ears of the Indian
그러나 세몬의 계획은 /   인도의 통치자의 귀에 들어갔다 /

ruler, / who / prepared to do battle with him.
          그래서 그는 / 세몬과 싸울 준비를 했다

In addition to having secured / all the latest implements of
마련한데다가 /   최신예 전쟁 장비를 /

warfare, / he added / still others of his own invention.
          그는 추가했다 /   자신이 발명한 전쟁 무기도

He ordered / all boys over fourteen and all single women /
그는 명령했다 /   14세 이상의 모든 소년과 모든 미혼 여성들을 /

to be drafted into the army, / until it became much larger /
군대로 징집하도록 /   자신의 군대가 훨씬 커질 때까지 /

than Simeon's. His cannons and rifles were of the same
세몬의 군대보다   그의 대포와 총은 똑같은 모델로 만든 것이었다 /

pattern / as Simeon's, / and he invented a flying-machine /
          세몬의 것과 /   그리고 그는 하늘을 나는 기계(비행기)를 발명했다 /

from which / bombs could be thrown / into the enemy's
그 기계로 /   폭탄을 떨어뜨릴 수 있는 /   적군의 진지로

camp. Simeon went forth to conquer the Viceroy /
세몬은 총독을 정복하러 갔다 /

with full confidence / in his own powers to succeed.
자신감으로 가득 차서 /   자신의 힘으로 성공할 수 있다는.

---

overjoyed 매우 기쁜 declare ~을 발표하다, 밝히다 subdue 정복하다 Viceroy 총독, 태수
in addition to ~에 더하여 secure 얻다, 손에 넣다 draft ~을 징병하다, 징집하다 camp 진지, 진영

This time luck forsook him, / and instead of being the
이번에는 운이 그를 저버렸다 / 그리고 정복자가 되는 대신에 /

conqueror / he was himself conquered.
그가 정복당했다

The Indian ruler had so arranged his army /
인도의 통치자는 자신의 군대를 잘 배치해서 /

that Simeon could not even get / within shooting distance, /
세몬은 들어갈 수가 없었다 / 사정거리 안으로 /

while the bombs / from the flying-machine /
한편 폭탄이 / 비행기에서 떨어뜨리는 /

carried destruction and terror in their path,
(세몬의 군대가 진격하는) 길에 파괴와 공포를 가져왔고 /

completely routing his army, / so that Simeon was left alone.
완전히 세몬의 군대를 완패시켰었다 / 그래서 세몬이 혼자 남았다

The Viceroy took possession of his kingdom /
총독은 세몬의 왕국을 손에 넣었고 /

and Simeon had to run for his life.
세몬은 목숨을 구하기 위해 필사적으로 도망가야만 했다

Having finished with Simeon, / the old devil next
세몬을 해치우자 / 늙은 악마는 다음에 접근했다 /

approached / Tarras. He appeared before him /
타라스에게. 그는 타라스 앞에 나타났다 /

disguised as one of the merchants of his kingdom,
타라스의 왕국의 상인으로 위장하고 /

and established factories / and began to make money.
그리고 공장을 설립하고 / 돈을 벌기 시작했다

The "merchant" paid the highest price /
그 상인은 최고로 높은 가격을 지불했다 /

for everything he purchased, / and the people ran after him /
자신이 사들이는 모든 물건에 / 그래서 사람들은 그에게 달려갔다 /

to sell their goods. Through this "merchant" /
물건을 팔려고 이 상인을 통해서 /

they were enabled to make plenty of money,
사람들은 많은 돈을 벌 수 있었다 /

paying up all their arrears of taxes /
그래서 밀린 세금 전부를 갚았다 /

as well as the others when they came due.
지불기한이 된 다른 것(부채)뿐만 아니라

Key Expression

전치사 + 관계대명사

관계대명사 앞에 전치사가 있는 경우가 있다. 전치사와 관계대명사가 합쳐지면, 더욱더 어려운 문장처럼 느껴질 때가 있다. 이런 문장을 보면, 과감하게 관계대명사 앞에 나온 명사와 전치사의 의미를 합쳐본다. 아래에 있는 예문의 "from which"의 경우 선행사인 "flying machine"(비행기)와 "from"을 합쳐보면, "그 비행기에서"라는 의미가 된다.

He invented a flying-machine from which bombs could be thrown into the enemy's camp.
그는 하늘을 나는 기계(비행기)를 발명했다 / 그 기계에서 / 폭탄을 떨어뜨릴 수 있는 / 적군의 진지로

---

forsake ~을 버리다 conquer 정복하다 arrange 배치하다 shooting distance 사정거리 rout ~을 패주시키다, 완패시키다 take possession of ~을 손에 넣다 disguise 변장하다 purchase 구입하다, 사다 goods 상품, 제품 arrears 연체금 due 지불만기가 되어

Tarras was overjoyed / at this condition of affairs /
타라스는 매우 기뻤다 / 이러한 상황 때문에 /

and said: / "Thanks to this merchant, /
그래서 이렇게 말했다 / "이 상인 덕분에 /

now I will have more money / than before, /
이제 나는 돈을 더 많이 갖게 될 거야 / 전보다 /

and life will be much more pleasant for me."
그리고 인생도 훨씬 더 즐거워질 거야."

He wished to erect new buildings, /
그는 새 건물을 짓길 바랬다 /

and advertised for workmen, / offering the highest prices /
그래서 일군을 모집하는 광고를 했고 / 가장 높은 임금을 제시하면서 /

for all kinds of labor.
모든 노동에 대해서

Tarras thought / the people would be as anxious to work /
타라스는 생각했었다 / 사람들이 일하고 싶어 할 것이라고 /

as formerly, / but instead he was much surprised /
예전처럼 / 그러나 그 대신에 무척 놀랐다 /

to learn / that they were working for the "merchant."
알았기 때문에 (무엇을?) / 사람들이 '상인'을 위해서 일하고 있다는 것을

To make them to leave the "merchant," /
사람들이 그 '상인'을 떠나도록 하려고 /

he increased his offers, / but the merchant, equal to the
그는 호가(임금)를 높였다 / 그러나 상인도 비상상황에 적합하게 /

emergency, / also raised the wages of his workmen.
자신도 일꾼의 임금을 올려주었다

Tarras, having plenty of money, / increased the offers still
타라스는 돈이 많았던 / 임금을 더욱더 올렸다 /

more, / but the "merchant" raised them still higher /
그러나 그 '상인'은 임금을 더욱더 높이 올렸다 /

and got the better of him.
그래서 타라스를 이겼다

Thus, defeated at every point, /
이렇게 모든 면에서(완전히) 패배를 당했기 때문에 /

Tarras was compelled to abandon / the idea of building.
타라스는 단념할 수밖에 없었다 / 건물을 지으려던 계획을

Tarras next announced / that he intended laying out
다음에 타라스는 발표했다 / 정원을 만들고 분수를 세운다고 /

168 Tolstoy's Short Stories

gardens and erecting fountains, /

and the work was to be commenced / in the fall, /
그리고 작업은 시작할 예정이었다 / 가을에 /

but no one came / to offer his services, /
그러나 아무도 오지 않았다 / 일하러 /

and again he was obliged to forgo / his intentions.
그래서 다시 그는 단념할 수밖에 없었다 / 자신의 계획을

Winter set in, / and Tarras wanted some sable fur /
겨울이 시작되었고 / 타라스는 검은담비의 모피가 갖고 싶었다 /

with which / to line his great-coat, /
그 모피로 / 자신의 근사한 외투에 안감을 댈 수 있는 /

and he sent his man / to procure it for him.
그래서 그는 자신의 부하를 보냈다 / 모피를 구해오라고

But the servant returned without it, / saying: /
그러나 하인은 모피 없이 돌아와서 / 이렇게 말했다 /

"There are no sables to be had. The 'merchant' has bought
"검은 담비의 모피가 없어요. 그 '상인'이 몽땅 사들였어요 /

them all, / paying a very high price for them."
아주 높은 값을 지불하면서."

Tarras needed horses / and sent a messenger /
타라스는 말이 필요해서 / 심부름꾼을 보냈다 /

to purchase them, / but he returned with the same story /
말을 사오라고 / 그러나 그 부하는 돌아와서 똑같은 이야기를 했다 /

as on former occasions / that none were to be found, /
이전의 경우와 / 말이 한 마리도 보이지 않는다고 /

the "merchant" having bought them all / to carry water /
그 '상인'은 모두 사들였다 / 물을 운반하려고 /

for an artificial pond / he was constructing.
인공 연못에 필요한 / 자신이 만들고 있는

---

affair 사건, 사태 erect (건물을) 세우다, 조립하다 advertise 광고하다 anxious 열망하여, 매우 ~하고 싶은
emergency 비상 get the better of ~을 이기다, ~보다 한수 위다 defeat 패배시키다 commence 시작하다
forgo 그만두다, 단념하다 sable 검은 담비 line 안감을 대다 procure 얻다, 확보하다 occasion 경우, 때
artificial 인공의

Tarras was at last compelled to suspend any business, /
타라스는 마침내 (하려던) 어떤 일이든지 중지하지 않을 수 없었다 /

as he could not find any one / willing to work for him.
그는 사람을 찾을 수 없었기 때문에 / 자신을 위해서 일하려고 하는

They had all gone / over to the "merchant's" side.
그들은 모두 가버렸다 / 그 '상인'의 편으로

The only dealings / the people had with Tarras /
유일한 거래는 / 사람들이 타라스와 했던 /

were when they went to pay their taxes.
세금을 내러갈 때였다

His money accumulated so fast / that he could not find a
그의 돈은 아주 빨리 모아졌다 / 그래서 장소를 찾을 수가 없었다 /

place / to put it, / and his life became miserable.
돈을 놓을 / 그리고 그의 삶은 비참하게 됐다

He abandoned all ideas / of entering upon the new venture, /
그는 모든 계획을 단념했다 / 새로운 모험적 사업에 뛰어드는 /

and only thought of / how to exist peaceably.
그리고 생각하기만 했다 / 어떻게 평화롭게 살 것인지

He found it difficult / to form plans and live in peace, /
그는 어렵다는 것을 알았다 (뭐가?) / 계획을 세우고 평화롭게 지내는 것이 /

for his plans always hit / an fresh obstacles.
왜냐하면 그의 계획은 늘 부딪쳤기 때문이었다 / 새로운 장애물에

Even his cooks, coachmen, and all his other servants /
그의 요리사, 마부, 그리고 모든 하인들이 /

forsook him / and joined the "merchant."
그를 저버렸고 / 그 '상인'에게 갔다

With all his wealth / he had nothing to eat, /
자신의 모든 재산이 있으면서도 / 그는 먹을 것이 없었다 /

and when he went to market / he found /
그리고 그가 시장에 갔을 때 / 그는 알았다 /

the "merchant" had been there / before him /
그 '상인'이 시장에 왔었다는 것을 / 자기보다 먼저 /

and had bought up all the provisions.
그리고 그가 모든 식량을 사갔다는 것을 (알았다)

Still, the people continued to bring / him money.
여전히 사람들은 계속 가져왔다 / 그에게 돈을

170　Tolstoy's Short Stories

Tarras at last became so indignant / that he ordered /
타라스는 마침내 너무나 화가 나서 / 그는 명령했다 /

the "merchant" out of his kingdom.
그 '상인'에게 자신의 왕국에서 나가라고

He left, but settled / just outside the boundary line, /
그는 떠났지만 정착했다 / 국경선 바로 바깥에 /

and continued his business / with the same result as before, /
그리고 사업을 계속하여 / 예전과 같았다 /

and Tarras was frequently forced to go /
그래서 타라스는 자주 지내야만 했다 /

without food for days.
음식 없이 여러 날 동안

It was rumored / that the "merchant" wanted to buy /
소문까지 나돌았다 / 그 '상인'이 사고 싶어 한다는 (소문까지) /

even Tarras himself. On hearing this / Tarras became very
타라스까지 / 이 소문을 들었을 때 / 타라스는 엄청나게 놀랐고 /

much alarmed / and could not decide / what to do.
/ 결정할 수 없었다 / 어떻게 해야 할지

About this time / his brother Simeon arrived in the
이 무렵에 / 그의 형인 세몬이 왕국에 도착해서 /

kingdom, / and said: / "Help me, / for I have been defeated
말했다 / "날 도와줘 / 내가 패배당하고 멸망했어 /

and ruined / by the Indian Viceroy."
/ 인도의 총독한테"

Tarras replied: / "How can I help you, /
타라스가 대답했다 / "내가 어떻게 형을 돕지 /

when I have had no food myself / for two days?"
난 내가 먹을 음식도 없는데 / 이틀 째"

> ### Key Expression
>
> **With all; ~이 있으면서, ~임에도 불구하고**
>
> "with all"은 "in spite of"와 같은 의미로 사용된다. "in spite of"는 "despite"와 같은 의미를 지녔지만 더 격식을 차린 표현이다.
>
> With all his wealth he had nothing to eat.
> 자신의 모든 재산이 있으면서도 / 그는 먹을 것이 없었다.

suspend ~을 중지하다 dealing 상거래, 매매 accumulate 모으다, 축적하다 miserable 비참한 abandon 단념하다, 포기하다 obstacle 장애물, 난관 provisions 식량, 양식 frequently 자주, 종종 alarm 놀라게 하다

Quiz 10

A. 내용 이해하기
다음 문장을 읽고 본문의 내용과 맞으면 T(True), 틀리면 F(False)를 쓰세요.

1. Simeon ordered all subjects to report for drill.
2. Simeon invaded the neighboring kingdom with his army.
3. The Old Devil who disguised himself as a businessman helped Simeon to erect new buildings.
4. Tarras succeeded in buying some sable fur for his wife.

B. 단어
다음 제시된 단어의 설명을 읽고, 어떤 단어의 정의를 설명하는지 아래의 박스에서 찾아 써 보세요.

1. A person who is sent on a mission to represent the interests of another or perform a special task
2. very angry; infuriated
3. large enough to have an effect; large in amount or degree
4. neighboring; being next to something
5. to steal a lot of things from a place in a war and do a lot of damage
6. to make somebody join the armed forces for compulsory service
7. to defeat somebody overwhelmingly in a battle
8. an unpaid overdue debt; being late in paying something that someone should pay regularly
9. to begin something
10. to gradually get more and more money or possessions over a period of time

---

accumulate arrears draft rout incensed pillage

emissary commence adjoining considerable

Answer
A. 1. F 2. T 3. F 4. F
B. 1. emissary 2. incensed 3. considerable 4. adjoining 5. pillage 6. draft 7. rout 8. arrears 9. commence 10. accumulate

C. 직독직해

아래에 제시된 문장을 직독직해로 해석해보세요.

1. After looking around for some time, / and seeing nothing but the three holes in the ground, / he decided / that they had not succeeded in their work.

    →

2. Winter set in, / and Tarras wanted some sable fur / with which / to line his great-coat.

    →

3. His money accumulated so fast / that he could not find a place / to put it, / and his life became miserable.

    →

4. He left, but settled / just outside the boundary line, / and continued his business / with the same result as before.

    →

D. 동시통역

아래에 제시된 직독직해를 보고, 영어로 말해보세요.

1. "이제는 내가 해야겠네 / 그들의 임무를 직접"

    →

2. 이것은 매우 놀라게 만들었다 / 그 나라 통치자를 / 그래서 그는 기꺼이 포기했다 / 자기 왕국의 절반을 / 남은 절반을 살리려고.

    →

3. "이 상인 덕분에 / 이제 나는 돈을 더 많이 갖게 될 거야 / 전보다

    →

4. 타라스가 대답했다 / "내가 어떻게 형을 돕지 / 난 내가 먹을 음식도 없는데 / 이틀째"

    →

Answer

C. 1. 한동안 찾아보고 / 땅에 구멍 3개만 있는 것을 보자 / 그는 판단했다 / 그들이 맡은 일에 성공하지 못했다고 2. 겨울이 시작되었고 / 타라스는 검은담비의 모피가 갖고 싶었다 / 그 모피로 / 자신의 근사한 외투에 안감을 댈 수 있는 3. 그의 돈은 아주 빨리 모아졌다 / 그래서 장소를 찾을 수가 없었다 / 돈을 놓을 / 그리고 그의 삶은 비참하게 됐다. 4. 그는 떠났지만 정착했다 / 국경선 바로 바깥에 / 그리고 사업을 계속하여 / 예전과 같았다

D. 1. "I will now have to accomplish their mission myself."
2. This so frightened / the ruler of that country / that he willingly gave up / half of his kingdom / to save the other half. 3. "Thanks to this merchant, / now I will have more money / than before.
4. Tarras replied: / "How can I help you, / when I have had no food myself / for two days?"

Chapter 11

The old devil, / having finished with the second brother, /
늙은 악마는 / 두 번째 형제를 해치우자 /

went to Ivan the Fool.
바보 이반에게 갔다

This time he disguised himself as a General, /
이번에도 그는 변장했다 / 장군으로 /

the same as in the case of Simeon, /
세몬의 경우와 마찬가지로 /

and, appearing before Ivan, / said: /
그리고 이반 앞에 나타나 / 이렇게 말했다 /

"Get an army together. It is disgraceful / for the ruler of a
"군대를 만드세요. 수치스러운 일입니다 / 왕국의 통치자가 /

kingdom / to be without an army. You call / your people to
군대도 없이 지내는 것은 발표하세요 / 백성들에게 모이라고 /

assemble, / and I will form them / into a fine large army."
그러면 제가 만들어 드리겠습니다 / 훌륭한 대규모 군대로"

Ivan took the supposed General's advice, / and said: /
이반은 장군이라고 추정되는 사람의 조언을 받아들이면서 / 이렇게 말했다 /

"Well, you may form / my people into an army, /
"흠, 그대는 만들어 보게 / 내 백성들을 군대로 /

but you must also teach / them to sing the songs / I like."
하지만 그대는 가르쳐야 돼 / 그들이 노래를 부르도록 / 내가 좋아하는"

The old devil then went through / Ivan's kingdom /
그러자 늙은 악마는 찾아다녔다 / 이반의 왕국을 /

to find recruits for the army, saying: /
군대를 만들 신병을 찾으러, / 이렇게 말하면서 /

"Come, shave your heads, join the army, /
"자, 머리를 깎고, 군대에 입대하라 /

and I will give each of you / a red hat and plenty of vodka."
그러면 나는 너희들에게 줄게 / 빨간 모자와 많은 보드카(술)를"

At this the fools only laughed, and said: /
이 말을 듣고 바보들은 웃기만 하고 / 이렇게 말했다 /

"We can have / all the vodka / we want, /
"우리는 마실 수 있어 / 모든 술을 / 원하기만 하면 /

for we distill it ourselves. And our little girls make /
우리가 직접 술을 만들 수 있으니까 / 그리고 어린 소녀들이 만들어 주는 걸 /

all the hats we want, / of any color we please.
우리가 원하는 모든 모자를 / 마음에 드는 어떤 색으로든지.

Thus was the devil foiled / in securing recruits /
이렇게 악마는 실패했다 / 신병을 모집하는 일에 /

for his army. So he returned to Ivan and said: /
군대를 만들려고 그래서 악마는 이반에게 돌아가서 말했다 /

"Your fools will not volunteer to be soldiers.
"당신의 백성들이 지원하지 않습니다 / 군사가 되려고

It will therefore be necessary / to force them."
그래서 필요할 것입니다 / 강제로 징집할"

"Very well," replied Ivan, / "you may use force /
"그러지," 이반이 대답했다 / "무력을 사용해도 좋아 /

if you want to." The old devil then announced /
원한다면" 늙은 악마는 그래서 발표했다 /

that all the fools must become soldiers, /
모든 바보들이 군사가 되어야 한다고 /

and those who refused, / Ivan would punish with death.
그리고 거역하는 자들을 / 이반이 사형으로 처벌할 것이라고.

The fools went to the General and said: /
바보들은 장군에게 가서 말했다 /

"You tell us / that Ivan will punish with death /
"당신은 우리에게 말했지요 / 이반이 사형으로 처벌할 것 이라고 /

all those / who refuse to become soldiers, /
모든 사람들을 / 군사가 되길 거역하는 /

but have omitted to state / what will be done /
하지만 말하지 않았어요 / 어떻게 된다는 것을 /

with us soldiers. We have been told / that we are only to be
군대에 입대하면. 들리는 소문에 의하면 / 우리는 결국 목숨만 잃게 될 것이라고

killed." "Yes, that is true," was the reply.
하던데요" "그래, 그건 사실이야" 라고 대답했다

The fools on hearing this / became stubborn /
이 말을 들은 바보들은 / 고집을 부렸고 /

and refused to go.
군에 입대하길 거부했다

disguise 변장하다, 가장하다 disgraceful 면목 없는, 수치스러운 supposed ~라고 추정되는, ~라고 생각되는
recruit 신병 distill 증류하다, (위스키를) 증류하여 만들다 foil 실패하게 하다, 좌절시키다 omit 생략하다
state 말하다, 진술하다 stubborn 고집 센, 완고한

"Better kill us now / if we cannot avoid death, /
"지금 우리를 죽이는 것이 낫지요 / 우리가 죽음을 피할 수 없다면, /

but we will not become soldiers," / they declared.
하지만 우리는 군사가 되지 않을 거예요" /   그들은 주장했다

"Oh! you fools," / said the old devil, /
"오, 너희들은 바보다" /   늙은 악마가 말했다 /

"soldiers may and may not be killed.
"군사들은 죽을 수도 죽지 않을 수도 있다

But if you disobey / Ivan's orders / you will certainly die."
하지만 만일 너희들이 따르지 않으면 / 이반의 명령에 / 너희들은 틀림없이 사형을 당할 거야"

The fools remained absorbed in thought / for some time /
바보들은 생각에 잠겨있었다 /   잠시 동안 /

and finally went to Ivan / to question him /
그리고 마침내 이반에게 갔다 /   그에게 물어보려고 /

in regard to the matter.
이 문제에 대하여

On arriving at his house / they said: /
이반의 집에 도착했을 때 /   그들은 말했다 /

"A General came to us / with an order from you /
"장군이 우리에게 왔다 /   당신의 명령으로 /

that we were all to become soldiers, and if we refused /
우리 모두가 군사가 되어야 한다는 /   그리고 만일 우리가 거역하면 /

you were to punish us with death. Is it true?"
당신이 우리를 사형으로 처벌한다고(말했어요)   그게 사실입니까?"

Ivan began to laugh heartily / on hearing this, and said:
이반은 배꼽을 잡고 큰소리로 웃기 시작했다 / 이 말을 듣자,   그리고 이렇게 말했다.

"Well, how I alone can punish / you with death / is /
"흠, 어찌 나 홀로 벌을 줄 수 있는지가 / 너희들을 사형시키는 / (그것은)

something I cannot understand.
내가 이해할 수 없는 것이다

If I was not a fool myself / I would be able to explain /
내가 바보가 아니라면 /   내가 설명할 수 있을 텐데 /

it to you, but as I am a fool / I cannot."
상황을 너희들에게 / 하지만 내가 바보이기 때문에 / 설명할 수 없군"

declare 주장 하다, ~을 밝히다 disobey ~에 따르지 않다, 거역하다 absorbed in thought 생각에 잠긴
in regard to ~에 대하여 heartily 마음껏, 실컷

"Well, then, we will not go," / they said.
"그렇다면 우리는 군대에 가지 않을 것입니다" / 그들은 말했다

"Very well," replied Ivan, /
"그럼 그렇게 해라" 이반이 대답했다 /

"you need not become soldiers / unless you wish to."
"너희들은 군사가 될 필요가 없다 / 만일 너희들이 원하지 않으면"

The old devil, / seeing his schemes about to prove failures, /
늙은 악마는 / 그의 계획이 실패할 것이라는 것을 알고 /

went to the ruler of a neighboring kingdom /
이웃왕국의 통치자에게 가서 /

and became his friend, / saying: /
그의 친구가 되었다 / 그리고 이렇게 말했다 /

"Let us go and conquer / Ivan's kingdom.
"가서 정복하자 / 이반의 왕국을

He has no money, but he has plenty / of cattle, provisions,
그는 돈이 없지만 그는 많이 있다 / 가축, 식량, 그리고 다양한 것들이 /

and various other things / that would be useful to us."
우리에게 유용한"

The neighboring kingdom's ruler gathered /
이웃왕국의 통치자는 모았다 /

his large army together, / and equipping it /
거대한 군대를 / 그리고 준비한 후 /

with cannons and rifles, / crossed the boundary line /
대포와 총을 / 국경선을 넘어서 /

into Ivan's kingdom. The people went to Ivan and said: /
이반의 왕국으로 들어왔다. 백성들은 이반에게 가서 / 말했다 /

"The ruler of our neighboring kingdom is here /
"이웃왕국의 통치자가 쳐들어옵니다 /

with a large army / to fight us."
대군을 몰고 / 우리와 싸우려고"

"Let them come," / replied Ivan.
"올 테면 오라고 해" / 이반이 대답했다.

The neighboring kingdom's ruler, /
이웃왕국의 통치자는 /

after crossing the line into Ivan's kingdom, /
국경을 넘고 이반의 왕국으로 침입한 후 /

could not find any soldiers / to fight against.
병사를 찾을 수 없었다 / 대적해 싸울만한

After waiting some time / and none appearing, /
잠시 기다렸지만 / 어떤 군사도 나타나지 않자 /

he sent his own warriors / to attack the villages.
그는 자신의 전사들을 보냈다 / 마을을 공격하려고

They soon reached the first village, / which /
전사들은 곧 첫 번째 마을에 도착하였다 / 그리고 그 마을을 /

they began to plunder. The fools looked calmly on, /
약탈하기 시작했다 바보들은 냉정하게 바라보기만 했고 /

offering not the least resistance / when their cattle and
최소한의 저항도 하지 않았다 / 가축과 식량이 빼앗길 때

provisions were being taken from them.

On the contrary, they invited the soldiers /
그와는 반대로 바보들은 군사들을 초대했다 /

to come and live with them, / saying: /
여기로 와서 함께 살자고 / 이렇게 말하면서 /

"If you, dear friends, find it is difficult / to earn a living /
"이봐요, 어렵다면 / 생계를 유지하는 것이 /

in your own land, come and live with us.
당신의 나라에서 / 여기로 와서 우리와 함께 삽시다

We have plenty of food."
우리는 먹을 것이 많아요."

The soldiers decided to remain with the people, /
군사들은 (이반 왕국의) 백성들과 함께 있기로 결정했다 /

finding them happy and prosperous,
그들이 행복하게 살고 번영하는 것을 알고서 /

with enough surplus food / to supply many of their
여분의 음식이 충분하였기에 / 많은 이웃에게 줄 정도로

neighbors. They were much surprised /
그들은 매우 놀랐다 /

at the cordial greetings / which they everywhere received, /
진심으로 인사를 하는 것을 보고 / 그들이 어디를 가든지 받았던 /

and, returning to their ruler, / they said: /
그래서 자신들의 통치자에게 돌아가서 / 말하였다 /

---

scheme 계획, 획책 boundary 경계(선) attack 공격하다 plunder 약탈하다 on the contrary 그와는 반대로,
그렇기는커녕 prosperous 번영하는, 성공한 supply 주다, 공급하다 cordial 진심에서 우러나는

"We cannot fight / with these people.
"우리는 전쟁할 수 없어요 / 이런 사람들과

Take us to another place. We would much prefer /
우리를 다른 곳으로 데려가세요.   우리는 훨씬 더 좋아해요 /

the dangers of actual warfare /
실제로 전쟁하는 위험을 /

to this unsoldierly method / of subduing the village."
이렇게 군사답지 않는 방법보다 /   마을을 정복하는"

The neighboring kingdom's ruler, / becoming enraged, /
이웃 왕국의 통치자는 /   격분하였기 때문에 /

ordered the soldiers / to destroy the whole kingdom, /
군사들에게 명령했다   왕국 전체를 파괴하고, /

plunder the villages, / burn the houses and provisions, /
마을을 약탈하고, /   가옥과 식량을 불태우고 /

and slaughter the cattle.
가축을 학살하라고(명령했다)

"Should you disobey / my orders," / said he, /
"만일 너희들이 거역한다면 / 내 명령에 /   그는 말했다 /

"I will have every one of you executed."
"나는 너희들 모두가 사형 당하게 할 거야."

The soldiers, / becoming frightened, / started to do as
군사들은 /   겁을 먹고 /   명령받은 대로 하기 시작했다 /

they were ordered, / but the fools wept bitterly, /
    하지만 바보들은 격렬하게 울었고 /

offering no resistance, / men, women, and children all
아무런 저항을 하지 않았다 /   (그리고) 남자와 여자, 어린아이들 모두가 함께

joining in the general lamentation.
매우 슬퍼했다

"Why do you treat us / so cruelly?" / they cried /
"왜 당신네들은 우리를 대해요 /   그렇게 잔인하게" /   그들은 소리쳤다 /

to the invading soldiers.
침략하는 군사들에게

"Why do you wish / to destroy everything / we have?
"왜 당신네들은 바래요 /   모든 것을 파괴하길 /   우리가 가진

If you have more need / of these things / than we have, /
만일 당신네들이 더 필요하다면 /   이런 것들이 /   우리가 가진 것보다 /

why not take them with you / and leave us in peace?"
왜 가져가지 않지요 / 우리를 평화롭게 내버려두지 (않나요)"

The soldiers, / becoming saddened with remorse, /
군사들은 / 양심의 가책으로 슬퍼졌기 때문에 /

refused further to pursue / their path of destruction, /
더 따라가길 거절했다 / 파괴의 길을 /

and the entire army scattered / in many directions.
그리고 군대전체가 흩어졌다 / 사방으로

Key Expression

to 부정사의 형용사적 용법

"to + 동사원형"을 to 부정사라고 부른다. 이런패턴의 동사가 바로 앞에 있는 명사를 더 자세히 설명하면, 형용사처럼 사용된 것이다. 그래서 "to 부정사"의 형용사적 용법이라고 말한다.

The neighboring kingdom's ruler, after crossing the line into Ivan's kingdom, could not find any soldiers to fight against.
이웃왕국의 통치자는 / 국경을 넘고 이반의 왕국으로 침입한 후 / 병사를 찾을 수 없었다 / 대적해 싸울만한(병사를)

---

subdue 정복하다 enraged 노한, 분노한 slaughter 학살하다, 죽이다 execute 사형시키다
frightened 겁먹은 bitterly 몹시, 통렬히 lamentation 비탄, 애도 remorse 양심의 가책
pursue ~을 추구하다, 계속하다 destruction 파괴

Chapter 12

The old devil, / failing to ruin Ivan's kingdom with soldiers, /
늙은 악마는 / 군사들로 이반의 왕국을 몰락시키지 못했기 때문에 /

transformed himself into a nobleman, /
자신을 귀족으로 모습으로 바꾸었고 /

dressed exquisitely, / and became one of Ivan's subjects, /
우아하게 옷을 입었고 / 이반의 백성이 되었다 /

with the intention of ruining his kingdom /
그의 왕국을 파괴할 의도로 /

as he had done with that of Tarras.
그가 타라스의 왕국에서 했던 것처럼

The "nobleman" said to Ivan: /
'귀족'은 이반에게 말했다 /

"I desire / to teach you wisdom / and to serve you.
"저는 바래요 / 당신에게 지혜를 가르치고 / 당신에게 봉사하길.

I will build you / a palace and factories."
저는 당신에게 지어드리겠습니다 / 궁전과 공장을"

"Very well," / said Ivan, / "you may live with us."
"매우 좋은 생각이네" / 이반은 말했다 / "그대는 우리와 함께 사시오."

The next day the "nobleman" appeared / on the Square /
다음날 '귀족'은 나타났다 / 광장에 /

with a sack of gold in his hand /
금화가든 자루를 손에 들고 /

and a plan for building a palace, /
그리고 궁전을 지을 설계도를 들고 /

saying to the people: / "You are living like pigs, /
그리고 사람들에게 말했다 / "당신들은 돼지와 같은 생활을 하고 있어요 /

and I am going to teach you / how to live decently.
내가 여러분들에게 가르쳐줄게요 / 어떻게 품위 있게 사는지.

You are to build a palace / for me according to this plan.
여러분들은 궁전을 지어주세요 / 나에게 이설계도에 따라

I will superintend the work / myself, /
내가 작업을 감독할게요 / 직접 /

and will pay you for your services / in gold," /
그리고 여러분이 일하면 지불할게요 / 금화로" /

182 Tolstoy's Short Stories

showing them / at the same time / the contents of his sack.
사람들에게 보여주면서 / 동시에 / 자루에 들어있는 내용물을

The fools were amused.
바보들은 즐거워했다

They had never before seen any money.
전에 그들은 돈이라는 것을 본적이 없었다

Their business was conducted entirely /
상거래는 오로지 이루어졌다 /

by exchange of farm products /
농작물을 교환하거나 /

or by hiring themselves out to work by the day /
또는 일당으로 일하는 방식으로만 /

in return for whatever they most needed.
그들이 가장 필요한 것과 맞바꾸기 위해

They therefore glanced at the gold pieces /
그러므로 그들은 금화를 보았다 /

with amazement, / and said,
놀라서 / 그리고 말했다 /

"What nice toys they would be / to play with!"
"정말로 멋진 장난감이네 / 갖고 놀기에"

In return for the gold / they gave their services /
금과 맞바꾸기 위해 / 그들은 노동력을 제공했고 /

and brought the "nobleman" / the produce of their farms.
'귀족'에게 가져왔다 / 농장에서 기른 농산물을.

The old devil was overjoyed / as he thought, /
늙은 악마는 매우 기뻤다 / 그는 이렇게 생각했기 때문에 /

"Now my plan is going well / and I will be able to ruin /
"이제 내 계획이 잘 진행되고 있군 / 그리고 파멸시킬 수 있겠지 /

the Fool / as I did his brothers."
바보 이반을 / 그의 형제들을 파멸시킨 것처럼"

The fools obtained sufficient gold /
바보들은 충분한 금화를 얻었다 /

to distribute among the entire community, /
마을 전체가 나눠 가질 수 있을 만큼 /

---

ruin 몰락시키다, 파멸시키다 transform ~을 ~로 바꾸다 nobleman 귀족 exquisitely 우아하게, 고상하게
subject 백성 superintend 감독하다 content 내용물 amused 즐거워하는 work by the day 일당으로 일하다,
날품으로 일하다 in return for ~와 맞바꾸기 위해 glance ~을 힐긋 보다 with amazement 놀라서
overjoyed 매우 기뻐하는 obtain ~을 얻다 sufficient 충분한 distribute 나누어 주다, 분배하다

the women and young girls of the village / wearing /
마을의 여인들과 어린 소녀들은 / 달고 있었다 /

much of it as ornaments, / while to the children they gave
대부분의 금화를 장식품으로 / 한편 바보들은 아이들에게 금화를 주었다 /

some pieces / to play with on the streets.
 길거리에서 가지고 놀 수 있도록.

When they had secured / all they wanted, /
바보들이 얻었을 때 / 그들이 원하는 모든 것을 /

they stopped working / and the "noblemen" did not get /
그들은 더 이상 일하지 않았다 / 그래서 '귀족'은 할 수 없었다 /

his palace more than half finished.
그의 궁전이 반 이상 완성되게

He had neither / provisions nor cattle, /
그는 없었다 / 식량도 가축도 /

and ordered the people / to bring him both.
그래서 사람들에게 명령했다 / 그에게 식량이나 가축을 가져오라고

He directed them also / to go on with /
그는 또한 그들에게 명령했다 / 진행하라고 /

the building of the palace and factories.
궁전과 공장을 짓는 일을

He promised to pay them / liberally in gold /
그는 그들에게 지불하겠다고 약속했다 / 금화로 넉넉히 /

for everything they did. No one responded to his call.
그들이 하는 모든 일에 대한 답례로. 아무도 그의 명령에 응하지 않았다

Only once in awhile a little boy or girl /
단지 가끔씩 어린 소년이나 소녀가 /

would call to exchange / eggs for his gold.
교환하려고 그를 방문했다 / 계란을 금화로

Thus was the "nobleman" deserted, /
이렇게 '귀족'은 버림받았고 /

and, having nothing to eat, / he went to the village /
그리고 먹을 것이 아무것도 없었기 때문에 / 그는 마을로 갔다 /

to procure some provisions / for his dinner.
양식을 얻으려고 / 저녁식사에 필요한

He went to one house / and offered gold /
그는 한 집으로 가서 / 금화를 주었다 /

in return for a chicken, / but was refused, /
닭 한 마리와 맞바꾸려고 / 하지만 거절당했고 /

the owner saying: / "We have enough of that already /
집주인은 이렇게 말해서 / "우리는 이미 금화가 충분해요 /

and do not want any more."
그래서 더 이상 원하지 않아요"

Key Expression

to 부정사의 부사적 용법; 목적

부사는 동사를 더 자세히 설명하는 역할을 한다. "to +동사원형"이 앞에 나온 동사, 부사, 형용사를 더 자세히 설명하면, 부사처럼 사용된 것이다. 그래서 "to 부정사"의 부사적 용법이라고 말한다. 예를 들어 아래의 예문의 경우, 그는 마을로 갔는데 왜 갔는지 이유나 원인을 설명한다. 또는 그가 마을에 간 목적을 설명하기 때문에 부사적 용법이라고 부를 수 있다.

He went to the village to procure some provisions for his dinner.
그는 마을로 갔다 / (왜 갔나?) 양식을 얻으려고 / 저녁식사에 필요한.

---

ornament 장식품 secure 얻다, 손에 넣다 direct 명령하다, 지시하다 liberally 후하게, 넉넉히
respond 응하다, 응답하다 deserted 버림받은

He next went to a fisherman / to buy some herring, /
다음에 그는 어부에게 갔다 / 청어를 사러 /

when he, too, refused to accept / his gold /
그때 어부도 받지 않았다 / 금화를 /

in return for fish, saying:
생선과 맞바꾸는 / 이렇게 말하면서 /

"I do not wish it, / my dear man. I have no children /
"저는 금화가 필요없어요 / 나리 저는 아이가 없어요 /

to whom I can give it / to play with.
금화를 줄 수 있는 / 가지고 놀도록

I have three pieces / which I keep / as curiosities only."
저는 금화 3냥이 있어요 / 그것들을 제가 보관하고 있지요 / 단지 진기한 물건이므로"

He then went to a peasant / to buy bread, /
그래서 그는 농부에게 갔어요 / 빵을 사러 /

but he also refused to accept / the gold. "I have no use for
하지만 그도 또한 받지 않았다 / 금화를 "나는 필요가 없어요,"

it," said he. "But if you are begging / in the name of Christ, /
그는 말했다. "하지만 당신이 구걸한다면 / 예수의 이름으로 /

I will tell my wife / to cut a piece of bread / for you."
제 집사람한테 말해볼게요 / 빵 한 조각을 자르라고 / 당신을 위해"

The old devil was so angry / that he ran away from the
늙은 악마는 너무나 화가 나서 / 그는 농부의 집에서 뛰쳐나왔다 /

peasant, / spitting and cursing as he went.
침을 뱉고 욕을 하면서 / 그가 떠나면서

Not only did the offer to accept / in the name of Christ /
받겠다는 제의가 / 예수의 이름으로 /

anger him, / but the very mention of the name /
그를 분노하게 했을 뿐만 아니라 / 예수 이름을 말한 것 자체가 /

was like the thrust of a knife / in his throat.
칼로 찌르는 것 같았다 / 그의 목에

The old devil did not succeed / in getting any bread, /
늙은 악마는 성공하지 못했다 / 빵을 얻는 일에 /

and in his efforts / to secure other articles of food /
그리고 그가 시도할 때 / 다른 식료품을 얻으려고 /

he met with the same failure.
그는 또한 실패했다

The people had all the gold / they wanted /
사람들은 모든 금화를 가지게 되었다 / 그들이 갖길 원했던 /

and what pieces they had / they regarded / as curiosities.
게다가 그들이 소유하고 있던 금화를 / 그들은 생각했다 / 진기한 물건이라고

They said to the old devil: / "If you bring us /
그들은 늙은 악마에게 말했다 / "만일 당신이 우리에게 가지고 오거나 /

something else in exchange for food, / or come to beg /
음식과 맞바꿀 뭔가 다른 것을 / 또는 구걸한다면 /

in the name of Christ, / we will give you / all you want."
예수의 이름으로 / 우리는 당신에게 줄게 / 당신이 원하는 모든 것을"

But the old devil had nothing but gold, /
하지만 늙은 악마는 단지 금화만 있었다 /

and was too lazy to work.
그리고 일을 하기에는 너무 게을렀다

He was unable to accept anything / for Christ's sake, /
그는 어떤 것도 받을 수 없었다 / 예수의 이름으로 /

so he was greatly enraged.
그래서 그는 매우 화가 났다

"What else do you want?" he said. /
"다른 뭔가 필요한 것이 있어?" 그는 말했다 /

"I will give you gold / with which /
"내가 금화를 줄게 / 금화로 /

you can buy everything / you want, /
뭐든지 살수 있지 / 원하는 /

and you need labor no longer."
(금화가 있으면) 더 이상 일할 필요가 없어"

But the fools would not accept / his gold, /
하지만 바보들은 받으려하지 않았다 / 그의 금화를 /

nor listen to him.
게다가 그의 말에 경청하지도 않았다.

Thus the old devil was obliged to go to sleep / hungry.
그래서 늙은 악마는 잠자리에 들 수밖에 없었다 / 배고픈 채로

Tidings of this condition of affairs /
이런 일에 대한 소식이 /

soon reached the ears of Ivan.
곧 이반의 귀에 이르렀다

herring 청어 curiosity 진기한 물건, 골동품 article 물품, 상품 enraged 분노한
be obliged to 어쩔 수 없이 ~하다 tidings 소식, 정보

The people went to him and said: /
사람들이 그에게 가서 말했다 /

"What shell we do? This nobleman came to us.
"어떻게 할까요? 귀족이 우리에게 왔어요

He is well dressed. He wishes to eat and drink well, /
그는 잘 차려입었어요. 그는 잘 먹고 마시길 원해요 /

but is unwilling to work, / and does not beg for food /
하지만 일을 하려하지 않지요 / 그리고 음식을 구걸하지도 않지요 /

for Christ's sake. He only offers / every one gold pieces.
예수의 이름으로. 그는 그저 주기만 하지요 / 모든 사람들에게 금화를

At first we gave him / everything he wanted, /
처음에 우리는 그에게 주었어요 / 그가 원하는 모든 것을 /

taking the gold pieces.
금화를 받고

But now we have enough of them /
하지만 우리는 이제 금화가 충분해요 /

and refuse to accept any more from him.
그래서 더 이상 금화를 받지 않아요

What shall we do with him? He may die of hunger!"
어떻게 해야 할까요? 그는 굶어 죽을 수 있어요!"

Ivan heard all / they had to say, / and told them /
이반은 다 들었다 / 그들이 해야 할 말을 / 그리고 그들에게 말했다 /

to employ him / as a shepherd, taking turns / in doing so.
그를 고용하라고 / 양치기로 / 그리고 마을 사람끼리 번갈아 가면서 / 그를 고용하라고

The old devil saw no other way / out of the difficulty /
늙은 악마는 다른 방안을 찾을 수 없었다 / 곤경에서 빠져나갈 수 있는 /

and was obliged to submit.

It soon came the old devil's turn / to go to Ivan's house /
곧 늙은 악마의 차례가 돌아왔다 / 이반의 집에 가서 /

to look after his sheep.
그의 양을 돌볼(차례가)

He went there / to dinner / and found /
그는 이반의 집으로 갔다 / 식사하러 / 그리고 발견했다 /

Ivan's dumb sister preparing / the meal.
이반의 벙어리 여동생이 준비하고 있는 것을 / 식사를

She was often cheated / by the lazy people, /
그녀는 자주 속았다 /   게으름뱅이들에게 /

who while they did not work, / yet ate up all the food.
그들은 일을 하지 않지만   모든 음식을 먹어치웠던(게으름뱅이에 의해 속았다)

But she learned to know / the lazy people /
하지만 그녀는 알아보는 방법을 배웠다 / 게으름뱅이를 /

from the condition of their hands.
손의 상태를 보고

Key Expression

목적어처럼 쓰이는 관계대명사 which

관계대명사 "which"가 목적어로 쓰이면, 두 가지 조건을 충족시켜야 한다. 첫째 관계대명사 다음에 주어 동사가 온다. 그리고 "which" 다음에 타동사가 나와야 한다. 아래 예문에서 "which"가 목적어로 사용되었기 때문에 "그것들을"이라고 해석한다.

I have three pieces which I keep as curiosities only.
저는 금화 3닢이 있어요 / 그것들을 제가 보관하고 있지요 / 단지 진기한 물건이므로

submit 굴복하다

Those with great calluses on their hands / she invited first
손에 굳은살이 박인 사람들을 / 그녀는 먼저 식탁으로

to the table, / and those having smooth white hands /
초대했고 / 그리고 부드럽고 흰 손을 가진 사람들은 /

had to take what was left.
(남이 먹다) 남은 음식을 먹어야만 했다

The old devil took a seat at the table, / but the dumb girl, /
늙은 악마는 식탁에 앉았다 / 하지만 벙어리 처녀는 /

taking his hands, / looked at them, / and seeing /
그의 손을 잡고 / 손을 들여다보았다 / 그리고 보았기 때문에 /

them white and clean, and with long nails, / swore at him
손이 희고 깨끗하고, 긴 손톱이 있다는 것을 / 그에게 욕설을 퍼붓고

and told him to leave the table.
그에게 식탁에서 물러나라고 말했다

Ivan's wife said to the old devil: /
이반의 아내는 늙은 악마에게 말했다 /

"You must excuse / my sister-in-law.
"너그럽게 용서해줘야 해요 / 내 시누이를

She will not allow / any one to sit at the table /
그녀는 허락하지 않지요 / 누구라도 식탁에 앉는 것을 /

whose hands have not been hardened / by toil, /
그 사람의 손에 굳은살이 없으면 / 노동으로 인해 /

so you will have to wait / until the dinner is over /
그래서 기다려야 해요 / 식사가 끝날 때까지 /

and then you can have / leftovers.
그러면 당신은 먹을 수 있지요 / 남이 먹다 남은 음식을

With it you must be satisfied."
그것(남은 음식)이라도 만족해야 되요."

The old devil was very much offended /
늙은 악마는 매우 화가 났다 /

that he was made to eat / what is left, /
그가 먹어야만 했기에 / (남이 먹다) 남은 음식을 /

and complained to Ivan, / saying: /
이반에게 불평했다 / 이렇게 말하면서 /

"The foolish law / you have in your kingdom, /
"어리석은 법은 / 당신의 왕국에 있는 /

that all persons must work, / is surely the invention of fools.
모든 사람들이 일을 해야 한다는 (법은) 틀림없이 바보들이 만든 것이지요

People who work for a living /
생계를 위해 일하는 사람들은 /

are not always forced to labor / with their hands.
항상 일해야만 하는 것은 아니지요 /   손으로

Do you think / wise men labor so?"
생각해요 /   영리한 사람이 손으로 노동한다고"

Ivan replied: / "Well, what do fools know about it?
이반이 대답했다 /   "흠, 바보들이 뭘 알아요?

We all work / with our hands."
우리 모두 일해요 /   손으로"

"And for that reason / you are fools,"
"그렇게 때문에 /   당신들은 바보에요,"

replied the old devil.
늙은 악마가 대답했다.

"I can teach you / how to use your brains, /
"나는 가르쳐줄 수 있지요 / 머리를 사용하는 법을 /

and you will find / such labor more beneficial."
그리고 당신은 알게 될 거예요 / 지적 노동이 더 이롭다는 것을"

Ivan was surprised / at hearing this, / and said:
이반은 놀랐다 /   이런 말을 듣고서 /   그리고 말했다

"Well, it is perhaps not without good reason /
"흠, 아마 충분한 이유가 있네요 /

that we are called fools."
우리가 바보라고 불리는 것은"

"It is not so easy / to work with the brain," /
"쉽지 않지요 /   머리로 노동을 하는 것은" /

the old devil said.
늙은 악마가 말했다

"You will not give me anything to eat /
"당신은 나에게 먹을 것을 주려하지 않을 것입니다 /

because my hands have not the appearance /
네 손에 모습이 없다고 /

of being toil-hardened, / but you must understand /
노동으로 굳어진 /   하지만 알아야 해요 /

callus (피부의) 굳은 살, 못 toil 힘든 일, 수고 leftover 남은 음식, 나머지 complain 불평하다
beneficial 유익한, 이로운

that it is much harder / to do brain-work, /
훨씬 더 어렵다는 것을 / 머리로 노동하는 것이 /

and sometimes the head feels like bursting /
그리고 때로는 머리가 깨질 것 같지요 /

with the effort of thinking."
생각하려고 애를 쓰면"

"Then why do you not select / some light work /
"그렇다면 왜 당신은 선택하지 않지요 / 좀더 쉬운 일을 /

that you can perform / with your hands?" / Ivan asked.
당신이 할 수 있는 / 손으로" / 이반이 물었다

The devil said: "I torment myself / with brain-work /
악마는 말했다 / "제가 제 자신을 괴롭히지요 / 머리로 노동하기 때문에 /

because I have pity / for you fools.
왜냐하면 나는 불쌍히 여겨요 / 당신 같은 바보들을

If I did not torture myself, / people like you /
만일 제가 자신을 괴롭히지 않으면 / 당신 같은 사람들은 /

would remain fools / for all eternity.
바보로 남아 있을 것입니다 / 영원히

I have exercised my brain a great deal / during my life, /
저는 머리를 많이 사용해봤어요 / 평생 동안 /

and now I am able to teach you."
그래서 이제 저는 당신을 가르칠 수 있어요."

Ivan was greatly surprised and said: /
이반은 매우 놀라서 말했다 /

"Very well, teach us. Then when our hands are tired /
"매우 좋아요, 가르쳐줘요. 그러면 우리의 손이 피곤할 때 /

we can use our heads / to replace them."
우리는 머리를 사용할 수 있지요 / 손을 대신할 수 있는"

The old devil promised / to instruct the people, /
늙은 악마는 약속했다 / 사람들에게 가르쳐주기를 /

and Ivan announced the fact / throughout his kingdom.
그래서 이반은 그 사실을 알렸다 / 온 왕국에

The devil was willing to teach / all those / who came to
악마는 기꺼이 가르쳐주었다 / 모든 사람을 / 그에게 찾아온 /

him / how to use the head / instead of the hands, / so as
어떻게 머리를 사용하는지 / 손대신 /

to produce more / with the former / than with the latter.
더 많이 생산하기위하여 / 전자(머리)로 / 후자(손)보다

In Ivan's kingdom there was / a high tower, /
이반의 왕국에 있었다 /   그 높은 망루에

which was reached / by a long, narrow ladder /
갈 수 있었다 /   좁고 긴 사다리로 /

leading up to the balcony. Ivan told the old devil /
전망대까지 이르는.   이반은 늙은 악마에게 말했다 /

that every one could see him / from the top of the tower.
모든 사람들이 그를 볼 수 있다고 /   망루 꼭대기에 있으면

Key Expression

those(who); ~한 사람들 instead of; ~대신에

so as to +동사원형; ~하기 위하여(in order to +동사원형)

the former; 전자 the latter; 후자

The devil was willing to teach / all those who came to him / how to use the head / instead of the hands, / so as to produce more / with the former / than with the latter.
악마는 기꺼이 가르쳐주었다 / 그에게 찾아 온 모든 사람들을 / 어떻게 머리를 사용하는지 / 손대신 / 더 많이 생산하기위하여 / 전자(머리)로 / 후자(손)보다

burst 터지다, 파열하다 effort 고생, 수고 select 선택하다 torment 괴롭히다 eternity 영원 instruct 가르치다
balcony 발코니, 전망대

So the old devil went up / to the balcony /
그래서 늙은 악마는 올라갔다 / 전망대까지 /

and addressed the people.
그리고 사람들에게 연설을 했다

The fools came in great crowds / to hear /
바보들은 큰 무리를 지어왔다 / 듣기 위해 /

what the old devil had to say, / thinking /
늙은 악마가 말하는 것을 / (그들은) 생각했기 때문에 /

that he really meant to tell /
악마가 정말로 말해줄 것이라고 /

them how to work with the head.
그들에게 머리로 일하는 방법을

But the old devil only told them in words / what to do, /
하지만 늙은 악마는 단지 입으로만 말해주었다 / 어떻게 머리를 사용하는지 /

and did not give them any practical instruction.
그리고 실행 가능한 설명은 없었다

He said / that men working only with their hands /
그는 말했다 / 손으로만 일하는 사람은 /

could not make a living. The fools did not understand /
생계를 유지할 수 없다고. 바보들은 이해하지 못했다 /

what he said to them / and looked at him /
그가 설명하는 것을 / 그래서 그를 쳐다보았다 /

in amazement, and then departed / for their daily work.
놀라서, 그리고 나서 떠났다 / 일상적인 일을 하러

The old devil addressed them / for two days /
늙은 악마는 그들에게 연설했다 / 이틀 동안 /

from the balcony, / Then feeling hungry, /
전망대에서 / 그러자 배가 고파졌기 때문에 /

he asked the people / to bring him some bread.
그는 사람들에게 부탁했다 / 그에게 빵을 가져오라고

But they only laughed at him and said: /
하지만 사람들은 단지 비웃으면서 말했다 /

"if you could work better / with your head /
"만일 당신이 일을 더 잘한다면 / 머리로 /

than with your hands, / you could also find bread /
손으로 보다 / 당신도 빵을 찾을 수 있을 것이다 /

for yourself."
스스로"

194　Tolstoy's Short Stories

He addressed the people / for yet another day, /
그는 사람들에게 연설을 했다 / 또 다시 하루 동안 /

and they went to hear him / from curiosity, /
그래서 사람들은 그의 말을 들으러 갔다 / 호기심으로 /

but soon left him / to return to their work.
하지만 곧 그를 떠났다 / 자신들의 일터로 돌아가려고

Ivan asked, / "Well, did the nobleman work / with his
이반은 물었다 / "흠, 귀족은 일했나요 / 머리로"

head?" "Not yet," they said, / "so far he has only talked."
"아직은 아닙니다." 그들은 말했다 / "지금까지 그는 단지 말만했어요."

One day, / while the old devil was standing /
어느 날 / 늙은 악마가 서있던 동안 /

on the balcony, / he became weak, / and, falling down, /
전망대에 / 그는 약해졌다 / 그래서 굴러 떨어질 때 /

hurt his head against a pole.
그의 머리를 기둥에 부딪쳤다

Seeing this, / one of the fools ran to Ivan's wife /
이것을 본 / 바보 한명은 이반의 아내에게 달려가서 /

and said, / "The gentleman has at last commenced /
말했다 / "귀족이 마침내 시작했다고 /

to work with his head." She ran to the field / to tell Ivan, /
머리로 일하기" 그녀는 밭으로 달려가서 / 이반에게 말했다 /

who was much surprised, and said, /
그랬더니 그는 매우 놀라서 말했다 /

"Let us go and see him."
"가서 봅시다."

He turned his horses' heads / in the direction of the tower, /
그는 말 머리를 돌렸다 / 망루가 있는 방향으로 /

where the old devil / remained weak from hunger /
망루에서 늙은 악마는 / 굶주림으로 쇠약해져 있었고

and was still suspended / from the pole, /
여전히 매달려 있었다 / 기둥에 /

with his body swaying back and forth /
그의 몸이 앞뒤로 흔들리면서 /

address ~에게 연설을 하다, 강연을 하다 practical 실용적인, 실행 가능한 instruction 설명, 가르침
in amazement 놀라서 depart 떠나다 from curiosity 호기심으로 commence 시작하다 suspend 매달다, 걸다
sway 흔들리다

and his head striking the lower part of the pole /
그리고 그의 머리는 기둥 아랫부분에 부딪치면서 /

each time it came in contact with it.
머리가 기둥에 닿을 때마다

While Ivan was looking, / the old devil started to slide
이반이 쳐다보고 있을 동안에 / 늙은 악마는 미끄러져 내려가기 시작했다 /

down / the steps head-first.
계단을 머리부터

"Well," said Ivan, / "he told the truth after all /
"그렇구나," 이반이 말했다 / "그는 결국 진실을 말했네 /

—that sometimes from this kind of work /
때로는 이런 종류의 일(머리로 하는 일)을 하면 /

the head bursts.
머리가 깨질 수 있다는(진실을)

This is far worse / than calluses on the hands."
이건 훨씬 더 나쁘잖아 / 손에 굳은살 보다"

The old devil fell / to the ground head-first.
늙은 악마는 떨어졌다 / 땅바닥으로 머리부터

Ivan approached him, / but at that instant the ground
이반은 그에게 다가갔다 / 하지만 그 순간에 땅은 갈라지더니 /

opened / and the devil disappeared, / leaving only a hole /
악마는 사라졌다 / 단지 구멍만 남기고 /

to show where he had gone.
그가 어디로 갔는지 보여주는

Ivan scratched his head and said: /
이반은 머리를 긁적거리면서 말했다 /

"See here. What a nasty thing! This is yet another devil.
"여기를 봐. 정말로 고약한 놈이네! 이건 또 다른 악마네

He looks like / the father of the little ones."
그놈은 보여 / 작은 악마들의 아비처럼"

Ivan still lives, / and people flock to his kingdom.
이반은 아직도 살아있으며 / 사람들은 그의 왕국으로 몰려간다

His brothers come to him / and he feeds them.
그의 형제들도 그에게 와서 / 그는 그들을 먹여 살린다

To every one / who comes to him and says, /
모든 사람들에게 / 그에게 와서 말하는 /

"Give us food," / he replies: /
"우리를 먹여살려주세요" 라고 / 그는 이렇게 대답한다 /

196   Tolstoy's Short Stories

"Very well, you are welcome.
"그래 좋아. 이곳에서 살아도 좋아

We have plenty of everything."
우리는 모든 것이 풍요로워."

There is only one unchangeable custom /
단지 변하지 않는 한 가지 관습이 있다 /

observed in Ivan's kingdom.
이반의 왕국에서 지켜지는

The man with toil-hardened hands /
노동으로 손에 굳은살이 박인 사람은 /

is always given a seat at the table, /
늘 식탁에 앉을 좌석이 있다 /

while the possessor of soft white hands /
한편 부드럽고 하얀 손을 가진 사람은 /

must be contented / with leftovers.
만족해야 된다 /   (남이 먹다) 남은 음식에

Key Expression

명사를 수식하는 과거분사

현재 분사와 마찬가지로 과거분사도 명사 뒤에서 명사를 수식한다. 명사를 수식한다는 말은 명사를 더 자세히 설명하는 것이다. 아래 예문의 "unchangeable"은 명사인 "custom" 앞에서 명사를 수식한다. 또한 "observed"는 과거분사로 "custom" 뒤에서 그 명사를 수식한다.

There is only one unchangeable custom observed in Ivan's kingdom.
단지 변하지 않는 한 가지 관습이 있다 / 이반의 왕국에서 지켜지는

---

flock 몰려들다 observe (관습, 습관을) 따르다, 지키다 possessor 소유자 contented 만족한

Quiz 11

A. 내용 이해하기
다음 문장을 읽고 본문의 내용과 맞으면 T(True), 틀리면 F(False)를 쓰세요.

1. The soldiers invading Ivan's kingdom did not plunder the villages.
2. Ivan's people invited the invading soldiers to live with them.
3. The Old Devil was very contented to eat leftovers.
4. Ivan's subjects learned how to use their heads on the devil's practical instructions.

B. 단어
다음 제시된 단어의 설명을 읽고, 어떤 단어의 정의를 설명하는지 아래의 박스에서 찾아 써 보세요.

1. to observe or direct; to have responsibility for ensuring that something is carried out properly
2. to steal a large amount of property from a place while fighting in a war
3. a strange or odd object
4. to give in to somebody; to agree to obey a person
5. hard work done over a long period of time that makes you very tired
6. to cause someone physical pain or make him suffer a lot
7. time without beginning or end
8. a feeling of great surprise
9. to teach a person something; to tell somebody to do something in a formal way
10. a person who has or owns something

---

possessor submit eternity torment instruct
amazement toil superintend curiosity plunder

Answer

A. 1. F 2. T 3. F 4. F

B. 1. superintend 2. plunder 3. curiosity 4. submit 5. toil 6. torment 7. eternity 8. amazement 9. instruct 10. possessor

C. 직독직해

아래에 제시된 문장을 직독직해로 해석해보세요.

1. The fools remained absorbed in thought / for some time / and finally went to Ivan / to question him / in regard to the matter.

   →

2. The soldiers, / becoming saddened with remorse, / refused further to pursue / their path of destruction, / and the entire army scattered / in many directions.

   →

3. He promised to pay them / liberally in gold / for everything they did.

   →

4. The old devil saw no other way / out of the difficulty / and was obliged to submit.

   →

D. 동시통역

아래에 제시된 직독직해를 보고, 영어로 말해보세요.

1. 수치스러운 일입니다 / 왕국의 통치자가 / 군대도 없이 지내는 것은.

   →

2. "당신은 우리에게 말했지요 / 이반이 사형으로 처벌할 것 이라고 / 모든 사람들을 / 군사가 되길 거역하는

   →

3. 이반이 쳐다보고 있을 동안에 / 늙은 악마는 미끄러져 내려가기 시작했다 / 계단을 머리부터.

   →

4. "만일 당신이 일을 더 잘한다면 / 머리로 / 손으로 보다 / 당신도 빵을 찾을 수 있을 것이다 / 스스로"

   →

Answer   C. 1. 바보들은 생각에 잠겨있었다 / 잠시 동안 / 그리고 마침내 이반에게 갔다 / 그에게 물어보려고 / 이 문제에 대하여. 2. 군사들은 / 양심의 가책으로 슬퍼졌기 때문에 / 더 따라가길 거절했다 / 파괴의 길을 / 그리고 군대전체가 흩어졌다 / 사방으로. 3. 그는 그들에게 지불하겠다고 약속했다 / 금화로 넉넉히 / 그들이 하는 모든 일에 대한 답례로. 4. 늙은 악마는 다른 방안을 찾을 수 없었다 / 곤경에서 빠져나갈 수 있는 / 그래서 굴복할 수밖에 없었다.

D. 1. It is disgraceful / for the ruler of a kingdom / to be without an army. 2. "You tell us / that Ivan will punish with death / all those / who refuse to become soldiers. 3. While Ivan was looking, / the old devil started to slide down / the steps head-first. 4. "if you could work better / with your head / than with your hands, / you could also find bread / for yourself."

Tolstoy's Short Stories를
다시 읽어보세요.

What Men Live By

Chapter 1

A shoemaker named Simon, who had neither house nor land of his own, lived with his wife and children in a peasant's hut, and earned his living by his work. Work was cheap, but bread was expensive, and what he earned he spent for food. The man and his wife had but one sheepskin coat between them for winter wear, and even that was torn to tatters, and this was the second year he had been wanting to buy sheep-skins for a new coat. Before winter Simon saved up a little money: a three-rouble note lay hidden in his wife's box, and five roubles and twenty kopeks were owed to him by customers in the village.

So one morning he prepared to go to the village to buy the sheep-skins for his coat. He put on over his shirt his wife's wadded jacket, and over that he put his own cloth coat. He took the three-rouble note in his pocket, cut himself a stick to serve as a staff, and started off after breakfast. "I'll collect the five roubles that are owed to me," thought he, "add the three I have got, and that will be enough to buy sheep-skins for the winter coat."

He came to the village and called at a peasant's hut, but the man was not at home. The peasant's wife promised that the money should be paid next week, but she could not pay it herself. Then Simon called on another peasant, but this one swore he had no money, and would only pay twenty kopeks which he owed for a pair of boots Simon had mended. Simon then tried to buy the sheep-skins on credit, but the fur dealer refused to sell on credit. "Bring your money," said he, "then you may pick the best skins we have. We know what debt-collecting is like." So all the business the shoemaker did was to get the twenty kopeks for boots he had mended, and to take a pair of felt boots a peasant gave him to sole with leather. Simon felt downhearted. He spent the twenty kopeks on vodka, and started homewards without having bought any skins. In the morning he had felt the frost. But now, after drinking the vodka, he felt warm, even without a sheep-skin. He trudged along, striking his stick on the frozen earth with one hand, swinging the felt boots with the other, and talking to himself.

Chapter 2

"I'm quite warm," said he, "though I have no sheep-skin.
I've had a drop, and it runs through all my veins.
I need no sheep-skins.
I walk along and all my vexation is forgotten.
That's the sort of man I am! What do I care?
I can live without sheep-skins.
I don't need them. My wife will fret, to be sure.
And, true enough, it is a shame — one works all day long, and then does not get paid. Hang on a minute!

If you don't bring that money along, sure enough I'll skin you, not a sheep.

How's that? He pays twenty kopeks at a time!

What can I do with twenty kopeks?

Drink it-that's all one can do!

Hard up, he says he is! So he may be, but what about me? You have a house, and cattle, and everything. I've only got these clothes I wear! You have corn of your own growing. I have to buy every grain.

And I must spend three roubles every week for bread alone. I come home and find the bread all used up, and I have to fork out another rouble and a half. So just pay up what you owe, and no nonsense about it!"

By this time he had nearly reached the chapel at the bend of the road. Looking up, he saw something whitish behind the chapel. The daylight was fading, and the shoemaker peered at the thing without being able to make out what it was. "There was no white stone here before. Can it be an ox? It's not like an ox. It has a head like a man, but it's too white. And what could a man be doing there?"

He came closer, so that it was clearly visible.

To his surprise it really was a man, alive or dead, sitting naked, leaning motionless against the chapel.

Terror seized the shoemaker, and he thought, "Some one has killed him, stripped him, and left him there. If I meddle I shall surely get into trouble."

So the shoemaker went on. He passed in front of the chapel so that he could not see the man. When he had gone some way, he looked back, and saw that the man was no longer leaning against the chapel, but was moving as if looking towards him. The shoemaker felt more frightened than before, and thought, "Shall I go back to him, or shall I go on?

If I go near him something dreadful may happen.

Who knows who the fellow is?

He has not come here for any good.

If I go near him he may jump up and throttle me, and there will be no getting away. Or if not, he'd still be a burden on one's hands.

What could I do with a naked man?

I couldn't give him my last clothes.

That would be absurd."

So the shoemaker hurried on, leaving the chapel behind him, when suddenly his conscience began to prick him, and he stopped in the road.

"What are you doing, Simon?" said he to himself.

"The man may be perishing of cold, and you slip past afraid.

Have you grown so rich as to be afraid of robbers?

Ah, Simon, shame on you!"

So he turned back and went up to the man.

Chapter 3

Simon approached the stranger, looked at him, and saw that he was a young man, fit, with no bruises on his body, only evidently freezing and frightened, and he sat there leaning back without looking up at Simon, as if too faint to lift his eyes. Simon went close to him, and then the man seemed to wake up. Turning his head, he opened his eyes and looked into Simon's face. That one look was enough to make Simon fond of the man. He threw the felt boots on the ground, took off his belt, laid it on the boots, and took off his cloth coat.

"It's not a time for talking," said he.

"Come, put this coat on at once!"

And Simon took the man by the elbows and helped him to rise. As he got up, Simon saw that his body was clean and in good condition, his hands and feet shapely, and his face good and kind. He threw his coat over the man's shoulders, but the latter could not find the sleeves. Simon guided his arms into them, and pull the coat up, wrapped it closely about him, and fastened the belt.

Simon even took off his tattered cap to put it on the man's head, but then his own head felt cold, and he thought: "I'm quite bald, while he has long curly hair." So he put his cap on his own head again. "It will be better to give him something for his feet," thought he. And he made the man sit down, and helped him to put on the felt boots, saying, "There, friend, now move about and will get warmed up. Other matters can be settled later on. Can you walk?"

The man stood up and looked kindly at Simon, but could not say a word.

"Why don't you speak?" said Simon. "It's too cold to stay

here, we must get to shelter. There now, take my stick, and if you're feeling weak, lean on that. Now step out!"

The man started walking, and moved easily, not lagging behind. As they went along, Simon asked him, "And where do you belong to?"

"I'm not from these parts."

"I thought as much. I know the folks hereabouts.

But, how did you come to be there by the chapel?"

"I cannot tell."

"Has some one been ill-treating you?"

"No one has ill-treated me. God has punished me."

"Of course God rules all.

Still, you'll have to find food and shelter somewhere.

Where do you want to go to?"

"It is all the same to me."

Simon was amazed.

The man did not look like a rogue, and he spoke gently, but yet he gave no account of himself.

Still Simon thought, "Who knows what may have happened?" And he said to the stranger: "Well then, come to my house, and at least warm yourself for a while."

So Simon walked towards his home, and the stranger kept up with him, walking at his side. The wind had risen and Simon felt it cold under his shirt.

The effect of the wine had now passed away, and he began to feel the frost. He went along sniffling and wrapping his wife's coat round him, and he thought to himself: "There now —talk about sheep-skins! I went out for sheep-skins and come home without even a coat to my back, and what is more, I'm bringing a naked man along with me. Matryona won't be pleased!" And when he thought of his wife he felt depressed. But when he looked at the stranger and remembered how he had looked up at him at the chapel, his heart was glad.

Chapter 4

Simon's wife had everything ready early that day. She had chopped wood, brought water, fed the children, eaten her own meal, and now she sat thinking. She wondered when she ought to make bread: now or tomorrow? There was still a large piece left.

"If Simon has had some dinner in town," thought she, "and does not eat much for supper, the bread will last out another day." She weighed the piece of bread in her hand again and again, and thought: "I won't make any more today. There's just enough flour to make one more loaf. We can manage to get along till Friday."

So Matryona put away the bread, and sat down at the table to patch her husband's shirt. While she worked she thought how her husband was buying skins for a winter coat. "If only the fur dealer does not cheat him. My good man is much too simple. He cheats nobody, but any child can take him in. Eight roubles is a lot of money. He should get a fine sheepskin at that price.

Not tanned skins, but still a proper one. How difficult it was last winter to get on without a warm coat. I could neither get down to the river, nor go out anywhere. Whenever he went outdoors, he put on all the clothes we had, and there was nothing left for me. He did not start very early today, but still it's time he was back. I only hope he has not gone on the spree!"

Just as Matryona had thought this, steps were heard on the threshold, and some one entered. Matryona stuck her needle into her work and went out into the entry. There she saw two men: Simon, and with him a man without a hat and in felt boots.

Matryona noticed at once that her husband smelt of spirits. "There now, he has been drinking," thought she. And when she saw that he had not his coat on, had only her jacket on, brought no parcel, stood there silent, but only simpered, her heart was ready to break with disappointment. "He has drunk the money," thought she, "and has been on the spree with some good-for-nothing fellow whom he has brought home with him."

Matryona let them pass into the hut, followed them in, and saw that the stranger was a young, slight man, wearing her husband's coat. There was no shirt to be seen under it, and he had no hat. Having entered, he stood, neither moving, nor raising his eyes, and Matryona thought: "He must be a bad man —he's afraid." Matryona frowned, and stood beside the oven looking to see what they would do.

Simon took off his cap and sat down on the bench as if things were all right. "Come, Matryona. If supper is ready, let us have some." Matryona muttered something to herself and did not move, but stayed where she was, by the oven. She looked first at the one and then at the other of them, and only shook her head. Simon saw that his wife was out of temper, but tried to pass it off. Pretending not to notice anything, he took the stranger by the arm.

"Sit down, friend," said he, "and let us have some supper." The stranger sat down on the bench.

"Haven't you cooked anything?" said Simon.

Matryona's anger boiled over. "I've cooked, but not for you. It seems to me you have drunk your wits away. You went to buy a sheep-skin, but come home without the coat you had on, and bring a naked vagabond home with you. I have no supper for drunkards like you." "That's enough, Matryona. What is the use of waging your tongue without reason? You had better ask what sort of man — And you tell me what you've done with the money?"

Simon found the pocket of the jacket, drew out the three-rouble note, and unfolded it. "Here is the money. Trifonov did not pay me, but promises to pay soon." Matryona grew still more angry. He had bought no sheep-skins, but had put his only coat on some naked fellow and had even brought him to their house. She snatched up the note from the table, took it to put away in safety, and said: "I have no supper for you. We can't feed all the naked drunkards in the world." "There now, Matryona, hold your tongue a bit. First hear what a man has to say..." "Much wisdom I shall hear from a drunken fool. Good reason I had for not wanting to marry you-a drunkard. My mother gave me linen and you have wasted it in drink. And now you've been to buy a sheepskin, and have drunk it, too!"

Simon tried to explain to his wife that he had only spent twenty kopeks. He tried to tell how he had found the man, but Matryona would not give him a chance to speak a word. She managed to speak two words at once, and brought up things that had happened ten years before. Matryona talked and talked, and at last she flew at Simon and seized him by the sleeve.

"Give me my jacket. It is the only one I have, and you took it from me and put it on yourself. Give it here, you mangy dog, and may the devil take you."

Simon began to pull off the jacket, and turned a sleeve of it inside out. Matryona seized the jacket and it burst its seams, She snatched it up, threw it over her head and started for the door. She intended to go out, but stopped undecided. She wanted to work off her anger, but she also wanted to learn what sort of a man the stranger was.

Chapter 5

Matryona paused and said: "If he were a good man he would not be naked.

Why, he hasn't even a shirt on him. If he were all right, you would say where you came across the fellow."

"That's just what I am trying to tell you," said Simon.

"As I came to the chapel I saw him sitting all naked and frozen.

It isn't quite the weather to sit about naked!

God sent me to him, or he would have perished.

What should I do? How do we know what may have happened to him?

So I clothed him, and brought him along.

Don't be so angry, Matryona. It is a sin.

Remember, we all must die one day."

Angry words rose to Matryona's lips, but she looked at the stranger and was silent. He sat on the edge of the bench, motionless. His hands were folded on his knees, his head was drooping on his chest, his eyes were closed, and his brows were knit as if in pain. Matryona was silent. And Simon said: "Matryona, have you no love of God?"

Matryona heard these words, and as she looked at the stranger, suddenly her heart softened towards him. She came back from the door, went to the oven and she got out the supper. Setting a cup on the table, she poured out some kvass.

Then she brought out the last piece of bread, and set out a knife and spoons.

"Have some food," said she.

Simon drew the stranger to the table.

"Take your place, young man," said he.

Simon cut the bread, crumbled it into the broth, and they began to eat.

Matryona sat at the corner of the table resting her head on her hand and looking at the stranger.

And Matryona was touched with pity for the stranger, and began to feel fond of him. And at once the stranger's face lit up. He ceased to frown, raised his eyes, and smiled at Matryona. When they had finished supper, the woman cleared away the things and began questioning the stranger.

"Where are you from?" said she.

"I am not from these parts."

"But how did you come to be on the road?"

"I may not tell."

"Did some one rob you?"

"God punished me."

"And you were lying there naked?"

"Yes, naked and freezing."

Simon saw me and had pity on me.

He took off his coat, put it on me and brought me here.

And you have fed me, given me drink, and shown pity on me.

"God will reward you!"

Matryona rose, took from the window Simon's old shirt which she had been patching, and gave it to the stranger. She also brought out a pair of trousers for him. "There," said she, "I see you have no shirt. Put this on, and lie down where you please, in the loft or by the oven ."

The stranger took off the coat, put on the shirt, and lay down in the loft. Matryona put out the candle, took the coat, and lay down beside her husband. Matryona drew the skirts of the coat over her and lay down, but could not sleep. She could not get the stranger out of her mind. When she remembered that he had eaten their last piece of bread and that there was none for tomorrow, and thought of the shirt and trousers she had given away, she felt grieved. But when she remembered how he had smiled, her heart was glad.

Long did Matryona lie awake, and she noticed that Simon also was awake.

"Simon!", said she.

"Well?"

"You have had the last of the bread, and there is no flour left to make bread.

I don't know what we shall do tomorrow.

Perhaps I can borrow some of neighbor Martha."

"If we're alive we shall find something to eat."

The woman lay still awhile, and then said, "He seems a good man, but why does he not tell us who he is?"

"I suppose he has his reasons."

"Simon!"

"Well?"

"We give. But why does nobody give us anything?"

Simon did not know what to say. So he only said, "Let us stop talking," and he turned over and went to sleep.

Chapter 6

In the morning Simon awoke. The children were still asleep. His wife had gone to the neighbor's to borrow some bread. The stranger alone was sitting on the bench, dressed in the old shirt and trousers, and looking upwards. His face was brighter than it had been the day before.

Simon said to him, "Well, friend, the belly wants bread, and the naked body clothes. One has to work for a living. What work do you know?"

"I do not know any."

Simon was amazed, but he said, "Men who want to learn can learn anything." "Men work, and I will work also."

"What is your name?"

"Michael."

"Well, Michael, if you don't wish to talk about yourself, that is your own affair. But you'll have to earn a living for yourself.

If you will work as I tell you, I will give you food and shelter."

"May God reward you! I will learn. Show me what to do."

Simon took yarn, put it round his thumb and began to twist it. "It is easy enough —see!"

Michael watched him, put some yarn round his own thumb in the same way, got the knack, and twisted the yarn also.

Then Simon showed him how to wax the thread.

This also Michael immediately learned to do.

Next Simon showed him how to twist the bristle in, and how to sew, and this, too, Michael learned at once.

Whatever Simon showed him he understood at once, and after three days he worked as if he had sewn boots all his life. He worked without stopping, and ate little. When work was over he sat silently, looking upwards. He hardly went into the street, spoke only when necessary, and neither joked nor laughed. They never saw him smile, except that first evening when Matryona gave them supper.

Chapter 7

Day by day and week by week the year went round. Michael lived and worked with Simon. His fame spread till people said that no one sewed boots so neatly and strongly as Simon's apprentice, Michael. And people from all around the area came to Simon for their boots, and he began to be well off. One winter day, as Simon and Michael sat working, a carriage with three horses and with bells drove up to the hut. They looked out of the window. The carriage stopped at their door, a fine servant jumped down from the box and opened the door. A gentleman in a fur coat got out and walked up to Simon's hut. Matryona hurried to the door, and opened it wide. The gentleman stooped to enter the hut, and when he drew himself up again his head nearly reached the ceiling, and he seemed quite to fill his end of the room.

Simon rose, bowed, and looked at the gentleman with astonishment. He had never seen any one like him. Simon himself was lean, Michael was thin, and Matryona was dry as a bone, but this man seemed to be from a different world. His face was red-faced and full, and his neck was like a bull's. It seemed as if he were cast in iron. The gentleman puffed, threw off his fur coat, sat down on the bench, and said, "Which of you is the master bootmaker?"

"I am, your honor," said Simon, coming forward.

Then the gentleman shouted to his lad, "Hey, Fedka, bring me the leather!"

The servant ran out and brought back a parcel.

The gentleman took the parcel and put it on the table.

"Untie it," said he. The lad untied it.

The gentleman pointed to the leather.

"Look here, shoemaker," said he, "do you see this leather?"

"Yes, your honor."

"But do you know what sort of leather it is?"

Simon felt the leather and said, "It is good leather."

"Good, indeed! Why, you fool, you never saw such leather before in your life.

It's German, and cost twenty roubles."

Simon was startled, and said, "Where should I ever see leather like that?"

"Well, that's all right. Can you make it into boots for me?"

"Yes, your honor, I can."

Then the gentleman shouted at him: "You can, can you? Well, remember whom you are to make them for, and what the leather is. You must make me boots that will wear for a year, neither losing shape nor coming unstitched. If you can do it, take the leather and cut it up. But if you can't, say so. I warn you now if your boots become unsewn or lose shape within a year, I will have you put in prison. If they don't burst or lose shape for a year I will pay you ten roubles for your work."

Simon was frightened, and did not know what to say.

He glanced at Michael and nudging him with his elbow, whispered: "Shall I take the work?"

Michael nodded his head as if to say, "Yes, take it."

Simon did as Michael advised, and undertook to make boots that would not lose shape or split for a whole year.

Calling his servant, the gentleman told him to pull the boot off his left leg, which he stretched out.

"Take the measure!" said he.

Simon cut off a piece of paper seventeen inches long, smoothed it out, knelt down, wiped his hand well on his apron so as not to soil the gentleman's sock, and began to measure. He measured the sole, and round the instep, and began to measure the calf of the leg, but the paper was too short. The calf of the leg was as thick as a beam.

"Take care. Don't make it too tight round the calf."

Simon was going to cut another piece of paper.

The gentleman sat there, rubbing his toes together in his stocking, and looking at the residents of the hut. And he caught sight of Michael.

"Whom have you there?" asked he.

"That is my workman. He will sew the boots."

"Look here," said the gentleman to Michael, "remember that they are to be made so as to last a whole year." Simon also looked at Michael, and saw that Michael was not looking at the gentleman, but was gazing into the corner behind the gentleman, as if he saw some one there. Michael looked and looked, and suddenly he smiled, and his face became brighter.

"What are you grinning at, you fool?" thundered the gentleman.

"You had better look to it that the boots are ready in time."

"They shall be ready in good time," said Michael.

"Mind it is so," said the gentleman, and he put on his boots and his fur coat, wrapped the latter round him, and went to the door.

But he forgot to stoop, and struck his head against the door frame.

He swore and rubbed his head.

Then he took his seat in the carriage and drove away.

When he had gone, Simon said, "that's a man of high station!

You could not kill him with a mallet.
He almost knocked out the door frame, but little harm it did him."
And Matryona said: "Living as he does, it is natural that he should be strong.
Death itself can't touch such a rock as that."

Chapter 8

Then Simon said to Michael: "Well, we have taken the work, but we must see we don't get into trouble over it. The leather is expensive, and the gentleman is hot-tempered. We must make no mistakes. Come, your eye is truer and your hands have become nimbler than mine. So you take this measure and cut out the boots. I will finish off the sewing of the vamps."

Michael did as he was told. He took the leather, spread it out on the table, folded it in two, took a knife and began to cut out. Matryona came and watched him cutting, and was surprised to see how he was doing it. Matryona was accustomed to seeing boots made, and she looked and saw that Michael was not cutting the leather for boots, but was cutting it round. She wished to say something, but she thought to herself: "Perhaps I do not understand how gentleman's boots should be made. I suppose Michael knows more about it — and I won't interfere."

When Michael had cut up the leather, he took a thread and began to sew not with two ends, as boots are sewn, but with a single end, as for soft slippers.

Again Matryona wondered, but again she did not interrupt. Michael sewed on steadily till noon. Then Simon rose for dinner, looked around, and saw that Michael had made slippers out of the gentleman's leather.

"Ah," groaned Simon, and he thought, "How is it that Michael, who has been with me a whole year and never made a mistake before, should do such a dreadful thing?

The gentleman ordered thick-soled boots, but Michael has made soft single-soled slippers, and has wasted the leather. What am I to say to the gentleman?

I can never replace leather such as this."

And he said to Michael, "What are you doing, friend? You have ruined me!

You know the gentleman ordered boots, but see what you have made!"

He was right in the midst of his talk with Michael when a knock came at the door. Someone was at the entrance.

They looked out of the window. A man had come on horseback, and was fastening his horse.

They opened the door, and the servant who had been with the gentleman came in.

"Good day," said he.

"Good day to you," replied Simon. "What can we do for you?"

"My mistress has sent me about the boots."

"What about the boots?"

"It is this. My master no longer needs them. He is dead."

"Is it possible?"

"He did not live to get home after leaving you, but died in the carriage. When we reached home and the servants came to help him alight from the carriage, he rolled over like a sack. He was dead already, and so stiff that they could hardly get him out of the carriage. My mistress sent me here, saying: 'Tell the bootmaker that the gentleman who ordered boots of him and left the leather for them no longer needs the boots, but that he must quickly make soft slippers for the corpse. Wait till they are ready, and bring them back with you.' That is why I have come."

Michael gathered up the remnants of the leather, rolled them up, took the soft slippers he had made, slapped them together, wiped them down with his apron, and handed them and the roll of leather to the servant, who took them and said: "Good-bye, masters, and good day to you!"

Chapter 9

Another year passed, and another, and Michael was now living his sixth year with Simon. He lived as before. He went nowhere, only spoke when necessary, and had only smiled twice in all those years —once when Matryona gave him food, and a second time when the gentleman was in their hut. Simon was more than pleased with his apprentice. He never now asked him where he came from, and only feared lest Michael should go away. They were all at home one day. Matryona was putting iron pots on the oven. The children were running along the benches and looking out of the window. Simon was sewing at one window, and Michael was fastening on a heel at the other. One of the boys ran along the bench to Michael, leaned on his shoulder, and looked out of the window.

"Look, Uncle Michael!

There is a lady with little girls!

She seems to be coming here. And one of the girls is lame."

When the boy said that, Michael dropped his work, turned to the window, and looked out into the street. Simon was surprised. Michael never used to look out into the street, but now he pressed against the window, staring at something. Simon also looked out, and saw that a well-dressed woman was really coming to his hut, leading by the hand two little girls in fur coats. The little girls looked so much alike that it was hard to tell them apart, except that one of them was crippled in her left leg and walked with a limp. The woman stepped into the porch and entered the entry. Feeling about for the entrance, she found the latch, which she lifted, and opened the door. She let the two girls go in first, and followed them into the hut.

"How do you do, friends!"

"Please come in," said Simon. "What can we do for you?"

The woman sat down by the table. The two little girls pressed close to her knees, afraid of the people in the hut.

"I want leather shoes made for these two little girls for spring."

"We can do that. We don't generally make such small shoes, but we can make them. My man, Michael, is a master at the work."

Simon glanced at Michael and saw that he had left his work and was sitting with his eyes fixed on the little girls. Simon was surprised. To be sure they were pretty and plump girls. They had dark eyes and rosy cheeks. And they wore nice kerchiefs and fur coats, but still Simon could not understand why Michael should look at them like that, just as if he had known them before. He was puzzled, but went on talking with the woman, and arranging the price. Having fixed it, he began to take the measures. The woman lifted the lame girl on to her lap and said: "Take two measures from this little girl. Make one shoe for the lame foot and three for the sound one. They both have the same size feet. They are twins."

Simon took the measure and, speaking of the lame girl, said: "How did it happen to her? She is such a pretty girl. Was she born so?"

"No, her mother crushed her leg."

Then Matryona joined in.

She wondered who this woman was, and whose the children were, so she said: "Are not you their mother then?"

"No, my good woman. I am neither their mother nor related to them.

They were quite strangers to me, but I adopted them."

"Even if they are not your children, you take good care of them."

"Why shouldn't I take good care of them?

I fed them both at my own breasts.

I had a child of my own, but God took him.

I was not so fond of him as I now am of them."

"Then whose children are they?"

Chapter 10

The woman became confidential and told them the whole story. "It is about six years since their parents died, both in one week. Their father was buried on the Tuesday, and their mother died on the Friday. These orphans were born three days after their father's death, and their mother did not live another day. My husband and I were then living as peasants in the village. We were neighbors of theirs, our yard being next to theirs. Their father was a lonely man, a wood-cutter in the forest. One day a tree fell on him. It fell across his body and crushed his bowels out. As soon as they got him home, his soul went to God. And that same week his wife gave birth to twins — these little girls. They were poor and alone, no one to take care of them, either grandmother or sister. Alone she gave them birth, and alone she met her death."

"The next morning I went to see her, but when I entered the

hut, she, poor thing, was already dead and cold. In dying she had rolled on to this child and crushed her leg. The village folk came to the hut, washed the body, laid her out, made a coffin, and buried her. They were good folk. The babies were left alone. What was to be done with them? I was the only woman there who had a baby at the time. I was nursing my first-born, eight weeks old. So I took them for a time. The peasants came together, and thought and thought what to do with them. And at last they said to me: 'For the present, Mary, you had better keep the girls, and later on we will arrange what to do for them.' So I nursed the sound one at my breast, but at first I did not feed this crippled one. I did not suppose she would live. But then I thought to myself, why should the poor innocent suffer? I pitied her, and began to feed her. And so I fed my own boy and these two — the three of them — at my own breast. I was young and strong, and had good food, and God gave me so much milk that at times it even overflowed. I used sometimes to feed two at a time, while the third was waiting. When one had enough I nursed the third. And God so ordered it that these grew up, while my own was buried before he was two years old. And I had no more children, though we prospered. Now my husband is working for the corn merchant at the mill. The pay is good, and we are well off. But I have no children of my own, and how lonely I should be without these little girls! I can't help loving them! They are the joy of my life!"

She pressed the lame little girl to her with one hand, while with the other she wiped the tears from her cheeks.

And Matryona sighed, and said: "The proverb is true that says, 'One may live without father or mother, but one cannot live without God.'"

So they talked together, when suddenly the whole hut was lighted up as though by summer lightning from the corner where Michael sat.

They all looked towards him and saw him sitting, his hands folded on his knees, gazing upwards and smiling.

Chapter 11

The woman went away with the girls.

Michael rose from the bench, put down his work, and took off his apron.

Then, bowing low to Simon and his wife, he said: "Farewell, masters. God has forgiven me. I ask your forgiveness, too, for anything done wrong."

And they saw that a light shone from Michael.

And Simon rose, bowed down to Michael, and said, "I see, Michael, that you are no common man. And I can neither keep you nor question you.

Only tell me this: how is it that when I found you and brought you home, you were gloomy, and when my wife gave you food you smiled at her and became brighter?

Then when the gentleman came to order the boots, you smiled again and became brighter still?

And now, when this woman brought the little girls, you smiled a third time, and have become as bright as day?"

Tell me, Michael, "why does your face shine so, and why did you smile those three times?"

And Michael answered, "Light shines from me because I have been punished, but now God has pardoned me.

And I smiled three times, because God sent me to learn three truths, and I have learned them.

One I learned when your wife pitied me, and that is why I smiled the first time. The second I learned when the rich man ordered the boots, and then I smiled again. And now, when I saw those little girls, I learn the third and last truth, and I smiled the third time."

And Simon said, "Tell me, Michael, what did God punish you for?

and what were the three truths?"

And Michael answered, "God punished me for disobeying Him. I was an angel in heaven and disobeyed God. God sent me to fetch a woman's soul. I flew to earth, and saw a sick woman lying alone, who had just given birth to twin girls. They moved feebly at their mother's side, but she could not lift them to her breast.

When she saw me, she understood that God had sent me for her soul, and she wept and said, 'Angel of God! My husband has just been buried, killed by a falling tree. I have neither sister, nor aunt, nor mother: no one to care for my orphans. Do not take my soul! Let me nurse my babes, feed them, and set them on their feet before I die. Children cannot live without father or mother.'

And I listened to the mother's request. I placed one child at her breast and laid the other in her arms, and returned to the Lord in heaven.

I flew to the Lord, and said, 'I could not take the soul of the mother.

Her husband was killed by a tree. The woman has twins, and prays that her soul may not be taken.

She says to me: 'Let me nurse and feed my children, and set them on their feet. Children cannot live without father or mother.'

I have not taken her soul."

And God said: 'Go and take the mother's soul, and learn three truths. Learn What dwells in man, What is not given to man, and What men live by.

When you has learned these things, you shall return to heaven.'

So I flew again to earth and took the mother's soul. The babes dropped from her breasts. Her body rolled over on the bed and crushed one babe, twisting its leg. I rose above the village, wishing to take her soul to God. But a wind seized me, and my wings drooped and dropped off. Her soul rose alone to God, while I fell back to earth."

Chapter 12

And Simon and Matryona understood who it was that had lived with them, and whom they had clothed and fed. And they wept with awe and with joy. And the angel said: "I was alone in the field, naked. I had never known human poverty, cold and hunger, till I became a man. I was famished, frozen, and did not know what to do. I saw, near the field I was in, a chapel built for God, and I went to it hoping to find shelter. But the chapel was locked, and I could not enter. So I sat down behind the chapel to shelter myself at least from the wind. Evening drew on. I was hungry, frozen, and in pain. Suddenly I heard a man coming along the road. He carried a pair of boots, and was talking to himself. For the first time since I became a man I saw the mortal face of a man, and his face seemed terrible to me and I turned from it. And I heard the man talking to himself of how to cover his body from the cold in winter, and how to feed wife and children."

And I thought: 'I am perishing of cold and hunger, and here is a man thinking only of how to clothe himself and his wife, and how to get bread for themselves. He cannot help me. When the man saw me he scowled and became still more terrible, and passed me by on the other side. I despaired. Suddenly I heard him coming back. I looked up, and did not recognize the same man. Before, I had seen death in his face, but now he was alive, and I recognized in him the presence of God. He came up to me, clothed me, and took me to his home.

I entered the house. A woman came to meet us and began to speak. The woman was still more terrible than the man had been. The spirit of death came from her mouth. I could not breathe for the stench of death that spread around her. She wished to drive me out into the cold, and I knew that if she did so she would die. Suddenly her husband spoke to her of God, and the woman changed at once. And when she brought me food and looked at me, I glanced at her and saw that death no longer dwelt in her. She had become alive, and in her, too, I saw God.

Then I remembered God's first lesson: 'Learn what dwells in man.' And I understood that in man dwells Love! I was glad that God had already begun to show me what He had promised, and I smiled for the first time. But I had not yet learned all. I did not yet know What is not given to man, and What men live by.

I lived with you, and a year passed. A man came to order boots that should wear for a year without losing shape or cracking. I looked at him, and suddenly, behind his shoulder, I saw my comrade — the angel of death. None but me saw that angel. But I knew him, and knew that before the sun set he would take that rich man's soul. And I thought to myself, 'The man is making preparations for a year, not knowing that he will die before evening.' And I remembered God's second saying, 'Learn what is not given to man.'

What dwells in man I already knew. Now I learned what is not given him. It is not given to man to know what is needed for their bodies. And I smiled for the second time. I was glad to have seen my comrade angel — glad also that God had revealed to me the second saying.

But I still did not know all. I did not know What men live by. And I lived on, waiting till God should reveal to me the last lesson. In the sixth year came the girl — twins with the woman. And I recognized the girls, and heard how they had been kept alive. Having heard the story, I thought: 'Their mother begged me for the children's sake, because she thought that it would be impossible for children to live without father or mother, but a stranger has nursed them, and has brought them up.' And when the woman showed her love for the children that were not her own, and wept over them, I saw in her the living God and understood What men live by. And I knew that God had revealed to me the last lesson, and had forgiven my sin. And then I smiled for the third time."

Chapter 13

And the angel's body became manifest, and he was clothed in light so bright that the eyes could not look on him. And his voice grew louder, as though it came not from him but from heaven above.

And the angel said: "I have learned that all men live not by care for themselves but by love. It was not given to the mother to know what her children needed for their life. Nor was it given to the rich man to know what he himself needed. Nor is it given to any man to know whether, when evening comes, he will need boots for his body or slippers for his corpse.

I remained alive when I was a man, not by care of myself, but because love was present in a passer-by, and because he and his wife pitied and loved me. The orphans remained alive not because of their mother's care, but because there was love in the heart of a woman, a stranger to them, who pitied and loved them. And all men live not by the thought they spend on their own welfare, but because love exists in man. I knew before that God gave life to men and desires that they should live. Now I understood more than that. I understood that God does not wish men to live apart, and therefore He does not reveal to them what each one needs for himself. But He wishes them to live united, and therefore reveals to each of them what is necessary for all. I have now understood that though it seems to men that they live by care for themselves, in truth it is love alone by which they live. He who has love, is in God, and God is in him, for God is love."

And the angel sang a hymn of praise to God, so that the hut trembled at his voice. The roof opened, and a column of fire rose from earth to heaven. Simon and his wife and children lay prostrate to the ground. Wings appeared upon the angel's shoulders, and he rose into the heavens.

And when Simon came to himself the hut stood as before, and there was no one in it but his own family.

Ivan the Fool

Chapter 1

In a certain kingdom there lived a rich peasant, who had three sons — Simeon (a soldier), Tarras (fat man), and Ivan (a fool). He also had one daughter, Milania, born dumb. Simeon went to war to serve the Czar. Tarras went to a city and became a merchant. And Ivan, with his sister, remained at home to work on the farm.

For his valiant service in the army, Simeon received an estate with high rank, and married a noble's daughter. Besides his large pay, he was in receipt of a handsome income from his estate, but he was unable to make ends meet. What the husband saved, the wife wasted in extravagance.

One day Simeon went to the estate to collect his money, when the steward informed him that there was no income, saying: "We have neither horses, cows, fishing-nets, nor implements. It is necessary to buy everything first, and then to look for profits."

So Simeon went to his father and said: "You are rich, father, but you have given nothing to me. Give me one-third of what you possess as my share, and I will transfer it to my estate." The old man replied: "You did not help to bring prosperity to our household.

For what reason, then, should you now demand a third of everything? It would be unjust to Ivan and his sister."

"Yes," said Simeon, "but he is a fool, and she was born dumb. They don't need much."

"See what Ivan will say."

Ivan's reply was: "Well, let him take his share."

Simeon took the portion allotted to him, and went again to serve in the army.

Tarras the Fat also became successful. He became rich and married a merchant's daughter, but even this failed to satisfy his desires, and he also went to his father and said, "Give me my share."

The old man, however, refused to comply with his request, saying: "You didn't give me a hand accumulating our property, and everything our household contains is the result of Ivan's hard work. It would be unjust," he repeated, "to Ivan and his sister."

Tarras replied: "But he does not need it. He is a fool, and cannot marry, for no one will have him. And sister does not require anything, for she was born dumb."

Tarras Turned to Ivan and continued: "Give me half the grain you have, and I will not touch the implements or fishing-nets. And from the cattle I will take only the dark mare, as she is not fit to plow."

Ivan laughed and said: "Well, I will go and arrange everything so that Tarras may have his share," whereupon Tarras took the brown mare with the grain to town, leaving Ivan with one old horse to work on as before and support his father, mother, and sister.

Chapter 2

It was disappointing to the Old Devil that the brothers did not quarrel over the division of the property, and that they separated peacefully. And he cried out, calling his three small devils.

"See here," said he, "there are three brothers — Simeon the soldier, Tarras the merchant, and Ivan the Fool. It is necessary that they should quarrel. Now they live peacefully, and enjoy each other's hospitality. The Fool spoiled all my plans. Now you three go and work with one brother each until they will be ready to tear each other's eyes out. Can you do this?"

"We can," they replied.

"How will you accomplish it?"

"In this way: We will first ruin them to such an extent that they will have nothing to eat, and we will then gather them together in one place and they will fight."

"Very well. I see you understand your business. Go, and do not return to me until you have created a feud between the three brothers or I will skin you alive."

The three small devils went to a swamp to consult as to the best means of accomplishing their mission. They disputed for a long time each one wanting the easiest part of the work and not being able to agree, concluded to draw lots. And it was decided that the one who was first finished had to come and help the others. This agreement being entered into, they appointed a time when they were again to meet in the swamp to find out who was through and who needed assistance.

The time having arrived, the young devils met in the swamp as agreed, when each related his experience. The first, who went to Simeon, said: "I have succeeded in my undertaking, and tomorrow Simeon returns to his father." His comrades, eager for particulars, inquired how he had done it.
"Well," he began, "the first thing I did was to blow some courage into his veins, and, on the strength of it, Simeon went to the Czar and offered to conquer the whole world for him. The Emperor made him commander-in-chief of the forces, and sent him with an army to fight the Viceroy of India. Having started on their mission of conquest, they were unaware that I, following in their wake, had wet all their powder. I also went to the Indian ruler and showed him how I could create numberless soldiers from straw.
Simeon's army, seeing that they were surrounded by such a vast number of Indian warriors of my creation, became frightened, and Simeon commanded to fire from cannons and rifles, which of course they were unable to do. The soldiers, discouraged, retreated in great disorder. Thus Simeon brought upon himself the terrible disgrace of defeat. His estate was confiscated, and tomorrow he is to be executed. All that I have to do," concluded the young devil, "is to release him tomorrow morning. Now, then, who wants my assistance?"

The second small devil (from Tarras) then related his story."I do not need any help," he began. "My business is also all right. My work with Tarras will be finished in one week. In the first place I made him grow greedy and fat. He afterward became so covetous that he wanted to possess everything he saw, and he spent all the money he had in the purchase of immense quantities of goods. When his capital was gone he still continued to buy with borrowed money, and has become involved in such difficulties that he cannot free himself. At the end of one week the date for the payment of his notes will have expired, and, his goods being seized upon, he will become a bankrupt. and he also will return to his father."

At the conclusion of this narrative they inquired of the third devil how things had fared between him and Ivan. "Well," said he, "my report is not so encouraging. The first thing I did was to spit into his jug of quass[a sour drink made from rye], which made him sick at his stomach. He afterward went to plow his summer-fallow, but I made the soil so hard that the plow could scarcely penetrate it. I thought the Fool would not succeed, but he started to work nevertheless. Moaning with pain, he still continued to labor. I broke one plow, but he replaced it with another, fixing it securely, and resumed work. Going under the ground I took hold of the plowshares, but did not succeed in stopping Ivan. He pressed so hard, and the plow was so sharp, that my hands were cut. And despite my utmost efforts, he went over all but a small portion of the field."

He concluded with: "Come, brothers, and help me, for if we do not conquer him our whole enterprise will be a failure. If the Fool is permitted successfully to conduct his farming, his brothers will not be hungry, for he will support them."

Chapter 3

Ivan having succeeded in plowing all but a small portion of his land, he returned the next day to finish it. The pain in his stomach continued, but he felt that he must go on with his work. He tried to start his plow, but it would not move. But it seemed to have struck a hard root. It was the small devil in the ground who had wound his feet around the plowshares and held them.

"This is strange," thought Ivan.

"There were never any roots here before, and this is surely one."

Ivan put his hand in the ground, and, feeling something soft, grasped and pulled it out. It was like a root in appearance, but seemed to possess life. Holding it up he saw that it was a little devil. Disgusted, he exclaimed, "See the nasty thing," and he proceeded to strike it a blow, intending to kill it, when the young devil cried out: "Do not kill me, and I will give you anything you wish."

"What can you do for me?"

"Tell me what it is you most wish for," the little devil replied.

Ivan scratched the back of his head as he thought, and finally he said: "I am dreadfully sick at my stomach. Can you cure me?"

"I can," the little devil said.

"Then do so."

The devil bent toward the earth and began searching for roots, and when he found them he gave them to Ivan, saying: "If you will swallow some of these you will be immediately cured of any disease you are afflicted with."

Ivan did as he was told, and obtained instant relief.

"I beg of you to let me go now," the little devil pleaded.

"I will pass into the earth, never to return."

"Very well, you may go, and God bless you."

And as Ivan pronounced the name of God, the small devil disappeared into the earth like a flash, and only a slight opening in the ground remained. Ivan placed in his hat what roots he had left, and proceeded to plow. Soon finishing his work, he turned his plow over and returned home.

When he reached the house he found his brother Simeon and his wife seated at the supper-table. His estate had been confiscated, and he himself had barely escaped execution by making his way out of prison. Now he had nothing to live on and had come back to his father for support. Turning to Ivan he said: "I came to ask you to take care of us until I can find something to do."

"Very well," Ivan replied, "you may remain with us."

Just as Ivan was about to sit down at the table Simeon's wife made a wry face, indicating that she did not like the smell of Ivan's sheep-skin coat.

She turned to her husband and said, "I shall not sit at the table with a peasant who smells like that."

Simeon the soldier turned to his brother and said:

"My lady objects to the smell of your clothes. You may eat in the porch."

Ivan said: "Very well, it is all the same to me. I will soon have to go and feed my horse any way."

Ivan took some bread in one hand, and his coat in the other, and left the room.

Chapter 4

The small devil finished with Simeon that night, and according to agreement went to the assistance of his comrade who took charge of Ivan, that he might help to conquer the Fool. He went to the field and searched everywhere, but could find nothing but the hole through which the small devil had disappeared.

"Well, this is strange," he said, "something bad must have happened to my companion, and I will have to take his place and continue the work he began. The Fool is through with his plowing, so I must look for some other means of destroying him. I must overflow his meadow and prevent him from cutting the grass." So the little devil overflowed the meadow with muddy water, and, when Ivan went at dawn next morning with his scythe and sharpened and tried to cut the grass, he found that it resisted all his efforts and would not yield to the implement as usual. Many times Ivan tried to cut the grass, but always without success.

At last becoming weary of the effort, he decided to return home and have his scythe again sharpened, and also to eat a lot of bread, saying: "I will come back here and will not leave until I have mown all the meadow, even if it should take a whole week."

Hearing this, the little devil became thoughtful, saying: "That Ivan is a hard case, and I must think of some other way of conquering him."

Ivan soon returned with his sharpened scythe and started to mow.

The small devil hid himself in the grass, and as the point of the scythe came down he buried it in the earth and made it almost impossible for Ivan to move the implement. He, however, succeeded in mowing all but one small spot in the swamp, where again the small devil hid himself, saying: "Even if he should cut my hands I will prevent him from accomplishing his work."

When Ivan came to the swamp he found that the grass was not very thick. Still, the scythe would not work, which made him so angry that he worked with all his might, and one powerful blow cut off a portion of the small devil's tail, who had hidden himself there. Despite the little devil's efforts he succeeded in finishing his work. He returned home and ordered his sister to gather up the grass while he went to another field to cut rye.

But the devil preceded him there, and fixed the rye in such a manner that it was almost impossible for Ivan to cut it. However, after continuous hard labor he succeeded, and when he was through with the rye he said to himself: "Now I will start to mow oats." On hearing this, the little devil thought to himself: "I could not prevent him from mowing the rye, but I will surely stop him from mowing the oats when the morning comes." Early next day, when the devil came to the field, he found that the oats had been already mowed. Ivan did it during the night, so as to avoid the loss that might have resulted from the grain being too ripe and dry. Seeing that Ivan again had escaped him, the little devil became greatly enraged, saying: "He cut me all over and made me tired, that fool. I did not meet such misfortune even on the battle-field. He does not even sleep," and the devil began to swear. "I cannot beat him," he continued. "I will go now to the heaps and make everything rotten."

So he went to a heap of the new-mown grain and began his fiendish work. After wetting it he built a fire and warmed himself, and soon was fast asleep. Ivan harnessed his horse, and, with his sister, went to bring the rye home from the field. After lifting a couple of sheaves from the first heap his pitchfork came into contact with the little devil's back, which caused him to howl with pain and to jump around in every direction.

Ivan exclaimed: "See here! What nasty thing! You again here?"

"I am another one!" said the little devil.

"That was my brother. I am the one who was sent to your brother Simeon."

"Well," said Ivan, "it doesn't matter who you are. I will fix you all the same."

As Ivan was about to strike the first blow the devil pleaded: "Let me go and I will do you no more harm. I will do whatever you wish."

"What can you do for me?" asked Ivan.

"I can make soldiers from almost anything."

"And what will they be good for?"

"Oh, they will do everything for you!"

"Can they sing?"

"They can."

"Well, make them."

"Take a bunch of straw and scatter it on the ground, and see if each straw will not turn into a soldier."

Ivan shook the straws on the ground, and, as he expected, each straw turned into a soldier, and they began marching with a band at their head.

"That was well done! How it will delight the village maidens!" he exclaimed.

The small devil now said: "Let me go. You do not need me

any longer."

But Ivan said: "No, I will not let you go just yet. You have converted the straw into soldiers, and now I want you to turn them again into straw, as I cannot afford to lose it, but I want it with the grain on."

The devil replied: "Say: 'So many soldiers, so much straw.'"

Ivan did as he was told, and got back his rye with the straw. The small devil again begged for his release.

Ivan, taking him from the pitchfork, said: "With God's blessing you may depart." And, as before at the mention of God's name, the little devil disappeared into the earth like a flash, and nothing was left but the hole to show where he had gone.

Soon afterward Ivan returned home, to find his brother Tarras and his wife there. Tarras could not pay his debts, and was forced to flee from his creditors and seek refuge under his father's roof. Seeing Ivan, he said: "Well, Ivan, may we stay here until I start in some new business?"

Ivan replied as he had before to Simeon: "Yes, you are perfectly welcome to stay here as long as it suits you."

With that announcement he removed his coat and seated himself at the supper-table with the others.

But Tarras's wife objected to the smell of his clothes, saying: "I cannot eat with a fool, neither can I stand the smell."

Then Tarras said: "Ivan, from your clothes there comes a bad smell. Go and eat by yourself in the porch."

"Very well," said Ivan, and he took some bread and went out as ordered saying, "It is time for me to feed my mare."

Chapter 5

The small devil who had charge of Tarras finished with him that night, and according to agreement proceeded to the assistance of the other two to help them conquer Ivan. Arriving at the plowed field he looked around for his comrades, but found only the hole through which one had disappeared. In the meadow he discovered the severed tail of the other, and in the rye-field found yet another hole.

"Well," he thought, "it is quite clear that my comrades have met with some great misfortune, and that I will have to take their places and arrange the feud between the brothers."

The small devil then went in search of Ivan. But he, having finished with the field, was nowhere to be found. He had gone to the forest to cut logs to build homes for his brothers, as they found it inconvenient for so many to live under the same roof.

The small devil at last discovered Ivan's whereabouts. Going to the forest, he climbed into the branches of the trees and began to interfere with Ivan's work. Ivan cut down a tree, but it failed to fall to the ground, becoming entangled in the branches of other trees. Finally he succeeded in getting it down after a hard struggle. In chopping down the next tree he met with the same difficulties, and also with the third.

Ivan had thought he could cut down fifty trees in a day, but he succeeded in chopping only ten before darkness. He put an end to his labors for a time. He was now exhausted, and, perspiring profusely, he sat down alone in the woods to rest. But he soon resumed his work, cutting down one more tree. However, the effort gave him a pain in his back, and he was obliged to rest again. Seeing this, the small devil was full of joy. "Well," he thought, "now he is exhausted and will stop work, and I will rest also." He then seated himself on some branches and congratulated himself. However, Ivan again arose, took his axe, and gave the tree a terrific blow from the opposite side, which felled it instantly to the ground, carrying the little devil with it.

And Ivan, proceeding to cut the branches, found the devil alive. Very much astonished, Ivan exclaimed: "Look you! Such nasty thing! Are you again here?"

"I am another one," replied the devil.

"I was with your brother Tarras."

"Well," said Ivan, "that makes no difference. I will fix you." And he was about to strike him a blow with the axe when the devil pleaded: "Do not kill me, and whatever you wish you shall have."

Ivan asked, "What can you do?"

"I can make for you all the money you wish."

Ivan then told the devil to go ahead.

So the devil began to explain to him how he might become rich.

"Take," said he to Ivan, "the leaves of his oak tree and rub them in your hands, and the gold will fall to the ground."

Ivan did as he was told, and immediately the gold began to drop about his feet.

He remarked: "This will be a fine trick to amuse the village boys with."

"Can I leave?" asked the devil, to which Ivan replied, "With God's blessing you may go."

At the mention of the name of God the devil disappeared into the earth.

Chapter 6

The brothers, having finished their houses, moved into their new houses and lived apart from their father and brother.

Ivan, when he had completed his plowing, made a great feast, to which he invited his brothers, telling them that he had plenty of beer for them to drink.

The brothers, however, declined Ivan's invitation, saying, "We have seen the beer that peasants drink, and want none of it."

Ivan then gathered around him all the peasants in the village and with them drank beer until he became intoxicated. He went to a street gathering of the village boys and girls, and told them they must sing his praises, saying that in return he would show them such sights as they had never before seen in their lives. The little girls laughed and began to sing songs praising Ivan, and when they had finished they said: "Very well, now give us what you said you would."

Ivan replied, "I will soon show you," and, taking an empty bag in his hand, he started for the woods.

The little girls laughed as they said, "What a fool he is!" and they forgot all about him. Some time after Ivan suddenly appeared among them carrying in his hand the bag, which was now filled.

"Shall I divide this with you?" he said.

"Yes, divide!" they sang in chorus.

So Ivan put his hand into the bag and drew out some gold coins, which he scattered among them.

"It's magic!" they cried as they ran to gather up the precious pieces. The peasants then appeared on the scene and began to fight among themselves for the possession of the yellow objects. In the fight one old woman was nearly crushed to death. Ivan laughed and was greatly amused at the sight of so many persons quarrelling over a few pieces of gold.

"Oh! You little fools," he said, "why did you almost crush the life out of the old grandmother? Be more gentle. I have plenty more, and I will give them to you."

He began throwing about more of the coins. The people gathered around him, and Ivan continued throwing until he emptied his bag. They clamored for more, but Ivan replied:

"The gold is all gone. Another time I will give you more. Now we will resume our singing and dancing."

The little children sang, but Ivan said to them, "Your songs are no good."

The children said, "Then show us how to sing better."
To this Ivan replied, "I will show you people who can sing better than you." With this remark Ivan went to the barn and found a bundle of straw. He did as the little devil had directed him, and presently a regiment of soldiers appeared in the village street, and he ordered them to sing and dance. The people were astonished and could not understand how Ivan had produced the soldiers. They sang for some time, to the great delight of the villagers. When Ivan commanded them to stop they instantly ceased. Ivan then ordered them off to the barn, telling the astonished and mystified peasants that they must not follow him. Reaching the barn, he turned the soldiers again into straw and went home to sleep off the effects of the alcohol.

Chapter 7

The next morning Ivan's exploits were the talk of the village, and news of the wonderful things he had done reached the ears of his brother Simeon, who immediately went to Ivan to learn all about it.

"Explain to me," he said.

"Where did you bring the soldiers, and where did you take them?"

"Why do you wish to know?" asked Ivan.

"Why, with soldiers we can do almost anything we wish — whole kingdoms can be conquered," replied Simeon.

This information greatly surprised Ivan, who said: "Well, why did you not tell me about this before? I can make as many as you want."

Ivan then took his brother to the barn, as he said: "I am willing to create the soldiers, but you must take them away from here. It will be necessary to feed them, and all the food in the village would last them only one day." Simeon promised to do as Ivan wished.

So Ivan proceeded to convert the straw into soldiers. Out of one bundle of straw he made an entire regiment.

In fact, so many soldiers appeared as if there was not a vacant spot in the field. Turning to Simeon Ivan said, "Well, is that enough?"

Beaming with joy, Simeon replied: "Enough! enough! Thank you, Ivan!"

"Glad you are satisfied," said Ivan, "and if you wish more I will make them for you. I have plenty of straw now."

Simeon divided his soldiers into battalions and regiments, and after having drilled them he went away to fight and conquer.

Simeon had just left the village with his soldiers when Tarras, the other brother appeared before Ivan. He had also heard of the previous day's performance and wanted to learn the secret of his power.

He sought Ivan, saying: "Tell me where you got that much gold, for if I had plenty of money I could with its assistance gather in all the wealth in the world."

Ivan was greatly surprised on hearing this statement, and said: "You should have told me this before, for I can make for you as much money as you wish."

Tarras was delighted, and he said, "You might get me about three barrels full of money."

"Well," said Ivan, "we will go to the woods, or, better still, we will harness the horse, as we could not possibly carry so much money ourselves."

The brothers went to the woods and Ivan proceeded to gather the oak leaves, which he rubbed between his hands, the dust falling to the ground and turning into gold pieces as quickly as it fell. When quite a pile had accumulated Ivan turned to Tarras and asked if he had rubbed enough leaves into money. Tarras replied: "Thank you, Ivan. That will be sufficient for this time."

Ivan then said: "If you wish more, come to me and I will rub as much as you want, for there are plenty of leaves."

Tarras, with his wagon filled with gold, rode away to the city to engage in trade and increase his wealth. Both brothers went their way, Simeon to fight and Tarras to trade. Simeon's soldiers conquered a kingdom for him and Tarras made plenty of money.

Some time afterward the two brothers met and confessed to each other from where sprang their prosperity, but they were not yet satisfied.

Simeon said: "I have conquered a kingdom and enjoy a very

pleasant life, but I have not sufficient money to procure food for my soldiers."

Tarras confessed that he was the possessor of enormous wealth, but the care of it caused him much uneasiness.

"Let us go again to our brother," said Simeon.

"I will order him to make more soldiers and will give them to you, and you may then tell him that he must make more money so that we can buy food for them." They went again to Ivan, and Simeon said: "I have not sufficient soldiers. I want you to make me at least two divisions more."

But Ivan shook his head as he said: "I will not create soldiers for nothing. You must pay me for doing it."

"Well, but you promised," said Simeon.

"I know I did," replied Ivan, "but I have changed my mind since that time."

"But, fool, why will you not do as you promised?"

"For the reason that your soldiers kill men, and I will not make any more for such a cruel purpose." With this reply Ivan remained stubborn and would not create any more soldiers.

Tarras next approached Ivan and ordered him to make more money, but, as in the case of Simeon, Ivan only shook his head, as he said: "I will not make you any money unless you pay me for doing it. I cannot work without pay."

Tarras then reminded him of his promise.

"I know I promised," replied Ivan, "but still I must refuse to do as you wish."

"But why, fool, will you not fulfill your promise?" asked

Tarras.

"For the reason that your gold was the means of depriving Mikhailovna of her cow."

"But how did that happen?" inquired Tarras.

"It happened in this way," said Ivan. "Mikhailovna always kept a cow, and her children had plenty of milk to drink. But some time ago one of her boys came to me to beg for some milk. And I asked him, 'Where is your cow?' He replied, 'A clerk of Tarras came to our home and offered three gold pieces for our mother. She could not resist the temptation, and now we have no milk to drink.' I gave you the gold pieces for your pleasure, and you put them to such poor use hat I will not give you any more."

The brothers, on hearing this, took their departure to discuss as to the best plan to settle their troubles. Simeon said: "Let us arrange it in this way. I will give you the half of my kingdom, and soldiers to keep guard over your wealth. And you give me money to feed the soldiers in my half of the kingdom." To this arrangement Tarras agreed, and both the brothers became rulers and very happy.

Chapter 8

Ivan stayed on the farm and worked to support his father, mother, and dumb sister. One day it happened that the old dog, which had grown up on the farm, was taken sick, when Ivan thought he was dying, and, taking pity on the animal, placed some bread in his hat and carried it to him. As he fed the bread to his dog, the root which the little devil had given him fell out of his pocket. The old dog swallowed it with the bread and was almost instantly cured. He jumped up and began to wag his tail as an expression of joy. Ivan's father and mother, seeing the dog cured so quickly, asked by what means he had performed such a miracle.

Ivan replied: "I have some roots which would cure any disease, and the dog swallowed one of them."

At about that time the Czar's daughter became ill, and her father had it announced in every city, town, and village that whosoever would cure her would be richly rewarded. And if the lucky person was a single man he would give her in marriage to him. This announcement, of course, appeared in Ivan's village. Ivan's father and mother called him and said: "If you have any of those wonderful roots, go and cure the Czar's daughter. You will be much happier for having performed such a kind act indeed, you will be made happy for all your after life."

"Very well," said Ivan. And he immediately made ready for the journey.

As he reached the porch on his way out he saw a poor woman standing directly in front of his house and holding a broken arm. The woman approached him, saying: "I was told that you could cure me, and will you please do so, as I am powerless to do anything for myself?"

Ivan replied: "Very well, my poor woman. I will help you if I can."

He took out a root which he handed to the poor woman and told her to swallow it. She did as Ivan told her and was instantly cured, and went away rejoicing that her arm had been healed. Ivan's father and mother came out to wish him good luck on his journey, and to them he told the story of the poor woman, saying that he had given her his last root.

On hearing this his parents were much distressed, as they now believed him to be without the means of curing the Czar's daughter, and began to scold him. "You had pity for a beggar and gave no thought to the Czar's daughter," they said.

"I have pity for the Czar's daughter also," replied Ivan, after which he harnessed his horse to his wagon and got ready for his departure. Just then his parents said: "Where are you going, you fool — to cure the Czar's daughter, and without anything to do it with?"

"Very well," replied Ivan, as he drove away.

In due time he arrived at the palace, and the moment he appeared on the balcony the Czar's daughter was cured. The Czar was overjoyed and ordered Ivan to be brought into his presence. He dressed him in the richest robes and addressed him as his son-in-law. Ivan was married to the Czar's daughter, and, the Czar dying soon after, Ivan became ruler. Thus the three brothers became rulers in different kingdoms.

Chapter 9

The brothers lived and reigned. Simeon, the eldest brother, with his straw soldiers took the genuine soldiers prisoner and trained all alike. He was feared by every one. Tarras, the other brother, did not squander the gold he obtained from Ivan, but instead greatly increased his wealth, and at the same time lived well. He kept his money in large trunks, and, while having more than he knew what to do with, still continued to collect money from his subjects. The people had to work for the money to pay the taxes

which Tarras levied on them, and life was made burdensome to them. Ivan the Fool did not enjoy his wealth and power to the same extent as did his brothers. As soon as his father-in-law, the late Czar, was buried, he discarded the Imperial robes which had fallen to him and told his wife to put them away, as he had no further use for them. Having cast aside the insignia of his rank, he once more donned his peasant garb and went back to his old work.

"I felt lonesome," he said, "and began to grow enormously stout, and yet I had no appetite, and neither could I sleep." Ivan sent for his father, mother, and dumb sister, and brought them to live with him, and they worked with him at whatever he chose to do. The people soon learned that Ivan was a fool. His wife one day said to him, "The people say you are a fool, Ivan."

"Well, let them think so if they wish," he replied.

His wife pondered this reply for some time, and at last decided that if Ivan was a fool she also was one, and that it would be useless to go contrary to her husband, thinking affectionately of the old proverb that "where the needle goes there goes the thread also." She therefore cast aside her magnificent robes, and, putting them into the trunk with Ivan's, dressed herself in cheap clothing and joined her dumb sister-in-law, with the intention of learning to work. She succeeded so well that she soon became a great help to Ivan. Seeing that Ivan was a fool, all the wise men left the kingdom and only the fools remained. They had no money, their wealth consisting only of the products of their labor. But they lived peacefully together, supported themselves in comfort, and had plenty to spare for the needy and afflicted.

Chapter 10

The old devil grew tired of waiting for the good news which he expected the little devils to bring him. He waited in vain to hear of the ruin of the brothers, so he went in search of the emissaries which he had sent to perform that work for him. After looking around for some time, and seeing nothing but the three holes in the ground, he decided that they had not succeeded in their work and that he would have to do it himself. The old devil next went in search of the brothers, but he could learn nothing of their whereabouts. After some time he found them in their different kingdoms, contented and happy. This greatly incensed the old devil, and he said, "I will now have to accomplish their mission myself."

He first visited Simeon the soldier, and appeared before him as a general, saying: "You, Simeon, are a great warrior, and I also have had considerable experience in warfare, and am desirous of serving you." Simeon questioned the disguised devil, and seeing that he was an intelligent man took him into his service. The new General taught Simeon how to strengthen his army until it became very powerful. New implements of warfare were introduced. Cannons capable of throwing one hundred balls a minute were also constructed, and these, it was expected, would be of deadly effect in battle. Simeon, on the advice of his new General, ordered all young men above a certain age to report for drill. On the same advice Simeon established gun-shops, where immense numbers of cannons and rifles were made.

The next move of the new General was to have Simeon declare war against the neighboring kingdom. This he did, and with his immense army marched into the adjoining territory, which he pillaged and burned, destroying more than half the enemy's soldiers. This so frightened the ruler of that country that he willingly gave up half of his kingdom to save the other half. Simeon, overjoyed at his success, declared his intention of marching into Indian territory and subduing the Viceroy of that country. But Simeon's intentions reached the ears of the Indian ruler, who prepared to do battle with him. In addition to having secured all the latest implements of warfare, he added still others of his own invention. He ordered all boys over fourteen and all single women to be drafted into the army, until it became much larger than Simeon's. His cannons and rifles were of the same pattern as Simeon's, and he invented a flying-machine from which bombs could be thrown into the enemy's camp. Simeon went forth to conquer the Viceroy with full confidence in his own powers to succeed. This time luck forsook him, and instead of being the conqueror he was himself conquered. The Indian ruler had so arranged his army that Simeon could not even get within shooting distance, while the bombs from the flying-machine carried destruction and terror in their path, completely routing his army, so that Simeon was left alone. The Viceroy took possession of his kingdom and Simeon had to run for his life.

Having finished with Simeon, the old devil next approached Tarras. He appeared before him disguised as one of the merchants of his kingdom, and established factories and began to make money. The "merchant" paid the highest price for everything he purchased, and the people ran after him to sell their goods. Through this "merchant" they were enabled to make plenty of money, paying up all their arrears of taxes as well as the others when they came due. Tarras was overjoyed at this condition of affairs and said: "Thanks to this merchant, now I will have more money than before, and life will be much more pleasant for me."

He wished to erect new buildings, and advertised for workmen, offering the highest prices for all kinds of labor. Tarras thought the people would be as anxious to work as formerly, but instead he was much surprised to learn that they were working for the "merchant." To make them to leave the "merchant," he increased his offers, but the merchant, equal to the emergency, also raised the wages of his workmen. Tarras, having plenty of money, increased the offers still more, but the "merchant" raised them still higher and got the better of him. Thus, defeated at every point, Tarras was compelled to abandon the idea of building. Tarras next announced that he intended laying out gardens and erecting fountains, and the work was to be commenced in the fall, but no one came to offer his services, and again he was obliged to forgo his intentions.

Winter set in, and Tarras wanted some sable fur with which to line his great-coat, and he sent his man to procure it for him. But the servant returned without it, saying: "There are no sables to be had. The 'merchant' has bought them all, paying a very high price for them."

Tarras needed horses and sent a messenger to purchase them, but he returned with the same story as on former occasions that none were to be found, the "merchant" having bought them all to carry water for an artificial pond he was constructing. Tarras was at last compelled to suspend any business, as he could not find any one willing to work for him. They had all gone over to the "merchant's" side. The only dealings the people had with Tarras were when they went to pay their taxes. His money accumulated so fast that he could not find a place to put it, and his life became miserable. He abandoned all ideas of entering upon the new venture, and only thought of how to exist peaceably.

He found it difficult to form plans and live in peace, for his plans always hit an fresh obstacles. Even his cooks, coachmen, and all his other servants forsook him and joined the "merchant." With all his wealth he had nothing to eat, and when he went to market he found the "merchant" had been there before him and had bought up all the provisions. Still, the people continued to bring him money. Tarras at last became so indignant that he ordered the "merchant" out of his kingdom. He left, but settled just outside the boundary line, and continued his business with the same result as before, and Tarras was frequently forced to go without food for days. It was rumored that the "merchant" wanted to buy even Tarras himself. On hearing this Tarras became very much alarmed and could not decide what to do. About this time his brother Simeon arrived in the kingdom, and said: "Help me, for I have been defeated and ruined by the Indian Viceroy."

Tarras replied: "How can I help you, when I have had no food myself for two days?"

Chapter 11

The old devil, having finished with the second brother, went to Ivan the Fool. This time he disguised himself as a General, the same as in the case of Simeon, and, appearing before Ivan, said: "Get an army together. It is disgraceful for the ruler of a kingdom to be without an army. You call your people to assemble, and I will form them into a fine large army." Ivan took the supposed General's advice, and said: "Well, you may form my people into an army, but you must also teach them to sing the songs I like."

The old devil then went through Ivan's kingdom to find recruits for the army, saying: "Come, shave your heads, join the army, and I will give each of you a red hat and plenty of vodka."

At this the fools only laughed, and said: "We can have all the vodka we want, for we distill it ourselves. And our little girls make all the hats we want, of any color we please.

Thus was the devil foiled in securing recruits for his army. So he returned to Ivan and said: "Your fools will not volunteer to be soldiers. It will therefore be necessary to force them."

"Very well," replied Ivan, "you may use force if you want to." The old devil then announced that all the fools must become soldiers, and those who refused, Ivan would punish with death.

The fools went to the General and said: "You tell us that Ivan will punish with death all those who refuse to become soldiers, but have omitted to state what will be done with us soldiers. We have been told that we are only to be killed."

"Yes, that is true," was the reply.

The fools on hearing this became stubborn and refused to go.

"Better kill us now if we cannot avoid death, but we will not become soldiers," they declared.

"Oh! you fools," said the old devil, "soldiers may and may not be

killed. But if you disobey Ivan's orders you will certainly die."

The fools remained absorbed in thought for some time and finally went to Ivan to question him in regard to the matter. On arriving at his house they said: "A General came to us with an order from you that we were all to become soldiers, and if we refused you were to punish us with death. Is it true?"

Ivan began to laugh heartily on hearing this, and said: "Well, how I alone can punish you with death is something I cannot understand. If I was not a fool myself I would be able to explain it to you, but as I am a fool I cannot."

"Well, then, we will not go," they said.

"Very well," replied Ivan, "you need not become soldiers unless you wish

to."

The old devil, seeing his schemes about to prove failures, went to the ruler of a neighboring kingdom and became his friend, saying: "Let us go and conquer Ivan's kingdom. He has no money, but he has plenty of cattle, provisions, and various other things that would be useful to us."

The neighboring kingdom's ruler gathered his large army together, and equipping it with cannons and rifles, crossed the boundary line into Ivan's kingdom. The people went to Ivan and said: "The ruler of our neighboring kingdom is here with a large army to fight us."

"Let them come," replied Ivan.

The neighboring kingdom's ruler, after crossing the line into Ivan's kingdom, could not find any soldiers to fight against. After waiting some time and none appearing, he sent his own warriors to attack the villages. They soon reached the first village, which they began to plunder. The fools looked calmly on, offering not the least resistance when their cattle and provisions were being taken from them. On the contrary, they invited the soldiers to come and live with them, saying: "If you, dear friends, find it is difficult to earn a living in your own land, come and live with us. We have plenty of food."

The soldiers decided to remain with the people, finding them happy and prosperous, with enough surplus food to supply many of their neighbors. They were much surprised at the cordial greetings which they everywhere received, and, returning to their ruler, they said: "We cannot fight with these people. Take us to another place. We would much prefer the dangers of actual warfare to this unsoldierly method of subduing the village."

The neighboring kingdom's ruler, becoming enraged, ordered the soldiers to destroy the whole kingdom, plunder the villages, burn the houses and provisions, and slaughter the cattle. "Should you disobey my orders," said he, "I will have every one of you executed."

The soldiers, becoming frightened, started to do as they were ordered, but the fools wept bitterly, offering no resistance, men, women, and children all joining in the general lamentation.

"Why do you treat us so cruelly?" they cried to the invading soldiers.

"Why do you wish to destroy everything we have? If you have more need of these things than we have, why not take them with you and leave us in peace?" The soldiers, becoming saddened with remorse, refused further to pursue their path of destruction, and the entire army scattered in many directions.

Chapter 12

The old devil, failing to ruin Ivan's kingdom with soldiers, transformed himself into a nobleman, dressed exquisitely, and became one of Ivan's subjects, with the intention of ruining his kingdom as he had done with that of Tarras. The "nobleman" said to Ivan: "I desire to teach you wisdom and to serve you. I will build you a palace and factories."

"Very well," said Ivan, "you may live with us."

The next day the "nobleman" appeared on the Square with

a sack of gold in his hand and a plan for building a palace, saying to the people: "You are living like pigs, and I am going to teach you how to live decently. You are to build a palace for me according to this plan. I will superintend the work myself, and will pay you for your services in gold," showing them at the same time the contents of his sack.

The fools were amused. They had never before seen any money. Their business was conducted entirely by exchange of farm products or by hiring themselves out to work by the day in return for whatever they most needed. They therefore glanced at the gold pieces with amazement, and said, "What nice toys they would be to play with!"
In return for the gold they gave their services and brought the "nobleman" the produce of their farms. The old devil was overjoyed as he thought, "Now my plan is going well and I will be able to ruin the Fool as I did his brothers."
The fools obtained sufficient gold to distribute among the entire community,
the women and young girls of the village wearing much of it as ornaments, while to the children they gave some pieces to play with on the streets.

When they had secured all they wanted, they stopped working and the "noblemen" did not get his palace more than half finished. He had neither provisions nor cattle, and ordered the people to bring him both. He directed them also to go on with the building of the palace and factories. He promised to pay them liberally in gold for everything they did. No one responded to his call. Only once in awhile a little boy or girl would call to exchange eggs for his gold. Thus was the "nobleman" deserted, and, having nothing to eat, he went to the village to procure some provisions for his dinner. He went to one house and offered gold in return for a chicken, but was refused, the owner saying: "We have enough of that already and do not want any more." He next went to a fisherman to buy some herring, when he, too, refused to accept his gold in return for fish, saying: "I do not wish it, my dear man. I have no children to whom I can give it to play with. I have three pieces which I keep as curiosities only."

He then went to a peasant to buy bread, but he also refused to accept the gold. "I have no use for it," said he. "But if you are begging in the name of Christ, I will tell my wife to cut a piece of bread for you."

The old devil was so angry that he ran away from the peasant, spitting and cursing as he went. Not only did the offer to accept in the name of Christ anger him, but the very mention of the name was like the thrust of a knife in his throat. The old devil did not succeed in getting any bread, and in his efforts to secure other articles of food he met with the same failure.

The people had all the gold they wanted and what pieces they had they regarded as curiosities. They said to the old devil: "If

you bring us something else in exchange for food, or come to beg in the name of Christ, we will give you all you want."
But the old devil had nothing but gold, and was too lazy to work. He was unable to accept anything for Christ's sake, so he was greatly enraged.

"What else do you want?" he said. "I will give you gold with which you can buy everything you want, and you need labor no longer."

But the fools would not accept his gold, nor listen to him. Thus the old devil was obliged to go to sleep hungry.

Tidings of this condition of affairs soon reached the ears of Ivan. The people went to him and said: "What shell we do? This nobleman came to us. He is well dressed. He wishes to eat and drink well, but is unwilling to work, and does not beg for food for Christ's sake. He only offers every one gold pieces. At first we gave him everything he wanted, taking the gold pieces. But now we have enough of them and refuse to accept any more from him. What shall we do with him? He may die of hunger!"

Ivan heard all they had to say, and told them to employ him as a shepherd, taking turns in doing so. The old devil saw no other way out of the difficulty and was obliged to submit. It soon came the old devil's turn to go to Ivan's house to look after his sheep. He went there to dinner and found Ivan's dumb sister preparing the meal. She was often cheated by the lazy people, who while they did not work, yet ate up all the food. But she learned to know the lazy people from the condition of their hands.

Those with great calluses on their hands she invited first to the table, and those having smooth white hands had to take what was left. The old devil took a seat at the table, but the dumb girl, taking his hands, looked at them, and seeing them white and clean, and with long nails, swore at him and told him to leave the table.

Ivan's wife said to the old devil: "You must excuse my sister-in-law. She will not allow any one to sit at the table whose hands have not been hardened by toil, so you will have to wait until the dinner is over and then you can have leftovers. With it you must be satisfied."

The old devil was very much offended that he was made to eat what is left, and complained to Ivan, saying: "The foolish law you have in your kingdom, that all persons must work, is surely the invention of fools. People who work for a living are not always forced to labor with their hands. Do you think wise men labor so?"

Ivan replied: "Well, what do fools know about it? We all work with our hands."

"And for that reason you are fools," replied the old devil. "I can teach you how to use your brains, and you will find such labor more beneficial."

Ivan was surprised at hearing this, and said: "Well, it is perhaps not without good reason that we are called fools."

"It is not so easy to work with the brain," the old devil said.

"You will not give me anything to eat because my hands have not the appearance of being toil-hardened, but you must understand that it is much harder to do brain-work, and sometimes the head feels like bursting with the effort of thinking."

"Then why do you not select some light work that you can perform with your hands?" Ivan asked.

The devil said: "I torment myself with brain-work because I have pity for you fools. If I did not torture myself, people like you would remain fools for all eternity. I have exercised my brain a great deal during my life, and now I am able to teach you."

Ivan was greatly surprised and said: "Very well, teach us. Then when our hands are tired we can use our heads to replace them."

The old devil promised to instruct the people, and Ivan announced the fact throughout his kingdom. The devil was willing to teach all those who came to him how to use the head instead of the hands, so as to produce more with the former than with the latter.

In Ivan's kingdom there was a high tower, which was reached by a long, narrow ladder leading up to the balcony. Ivan told the old devil that every one could see him from the top of the tower. So the old devil went up to the balcony and addressed the people. The fools came in great crowds to hear what the old devil had to say, thinking that he really meant to tell them

how to work with the head. But the old devil only told them in words what to do, and did not give them any practical instruction. He said that men working only with their hands could not make a living. The fools did not understand what he said to them and looked at him in amazement, and then departed for their daily work. The old devil addressed them for two days from the balcony, Then feeling hungry, he asked the people to bring him some bread. But they only laughed at him and said: "if you could work better with your head than with your hands, you could also find bread for yourself."
He addressed the people for yet another day, and they went to hear him from curiosity, but soon left him to return to their work.
Ivan asked, "Well, did the nobleman work with his head?"
"Not yet," they said, "so far he has only talked."

One day, while the old devil was standing on the balcony, he became weak, and, falling down, hurt his head against a pole. Seeing this, one of the fools ran to Ivan's wife and said, "The gentleman has at last commenced to work with his head."
She ran to the field to tell Ivan, who was much surprised, and said, "Let us go and see him."
He turned his horses' heads in the direction of the tower, where the old devil remained weak from hunger and was still suspended from the pole, with his body swaying back and forth and his head striking the lower part of the pole each time it came in contact with it.

While Ivan was looking, the old devil started to slide down the steps head-first.

"Well," said Ivan, "he told the truth after all — that sometimes from this kind of work the head bursts. This is far worse than calluses on the hands."

The old devil fell to the ground head-first. Ivan approached him, but at that instant the ground opened and the devil disappeared, leaving only a hole to show where he had gone. Ivan scratched his head and said: "See here. What a nasty thing! This is yet another devil. He looks like the father of the little ones."

Ivan still lives, and people flock to his kingdom. His brothers come to him and he feeds them. To every one who comes to him and says, "Give us food," he replies: "Very well, you are welcome. We have plenty of everything."

There is only one unchangeable custom observed in Ivan's kingdom. The man with toil-hardened hands is always given a seat at the table, while the possessor of soft white hands must be contented with leftovers.